Knowing God

Knowing God:
Jewish Journeys
to the
Unknowable

Elliot N. Dorff

JASON ARONSON INC.
Northvale, New Jersey
London

This book is set in 12 point Bem by Lind Graphics of Upper Saddle River, New Jersey, and printed at Haddon Craftsmen of Scranton, Pennsylvania.

10 9 8 7 6 5 4 3 2 1

Library of Congress Cataloging-in-Publication Data

Dorff, Elliot N.
  Knowing God : Jewish journeys to the unknowable / Elliot N. Dorff.
    p. cm.
  Includes bibliographical references and index.
  ISBN 0-87668-599-8
  1. God (Judaism)—Knowableness. 2. God (Judaism)—Worship and love. 3. Jewish way of life. 4. Judaism—20th century. I. Title.
  BM610.D65 1993
  296.3'11—dc20   92-23253

Manufactured in the United States of America. Jason Aronson Inc. offers books and cassettes. For information and catalog write to Jason Aronson Inc., 230 Livingston Street, Northvale, New Jersey 07647.

In cherished and honored memory of my parents
Sol Ervin Dorff
Anne Nelson Dorff

After dealing with the seventh day [the Fourth of the Ten Commandments], He gives the Fifth Commandment on the honor due to parents. This commandment He placed on the borderline between the two sets of five: it is the last of the first set, in which the most sacred injunctions, those relating to God, are given, and it adjoins the second set, which contain the duties of human beings to each other. The reason, I think, is this: we see that parents by their nature stand on the borderline between the mortal and the immortal sides of existence—the mortal, because of their kinship with people and other animals through the perishableness of the body; the immortal, because the act of generation assimilates them to God, the progenitor of everything. . . .

Some bolder spirits, glorifying the name of parenthood, say that a father and mother are in fact gods revealed to sight, who copy the Uncreated in His work as the Framer of life. He, they say, is the God or Maker of the world; they [the parents] only of those whom they have begotten. How can reverence be rendered to the invisible God by those who show irreverence to the gods who are near at hand and seen by the eye?

—Philo, *Treatise on the Decalogue*

CONTENTS

The Functions of Images in Worship
How Images Mean
The Truth of Images
The Authority of Images
A Sample Case: Feminine Images for God
Good and Bad Images

Preface

I have been eager to write this book from the time I was fifteen. It was then that I first became seriously interested in Judaism, and it was then that the problem of faith in God became a burning issue for me. After undergraduate and doctoral degrees in philosophy, after rabbinical school, and after many subsequent years of conversations, reading, and teaching, I have finally been able to address squarely the problem that has accompanied me since my youth. I sincerely hope that my philosophical and religious explorations will help others who, like me, find a life without religion narrow and vapid, but a life with religion intellectually problematic.

There are a number of people who have aided me in this journey. The many rabbis and laypeople who have made Camp Ramah possible are certainly first on my list, for it was there that both my interest in Judaism and my intellectual problems with it began. Rabbi David Mogilner, whose memory is certainly a blessing, led the discussions that launched me on this track during the summer of 1958 at Camp Ramah in the north woods of Wisconsin, and it has continued through the help of friends, teachers, and students there, at Camp Ramah in the Poconos, and at Camp Ramah in California ever since. I owe my philosophical training to the faculty of Columbia University, with special thanks to my longtime teacher, dissertation advisor, and friend, Professor David Sidorsky. I am deeply appreciative of my teachers, friends, and colleagues at the Jewish Theological Seminary of America in New York and at the University of Judaism in Los Angeles, who have made sure that the buds of religious knowledge, practice, and sensitivity planted at Camp Ramah would continue to grow.

My good friends from Seminary days, Rabbis Barry Cytron and Moshe Rothblum, stimulated me to finally write this book, and so its readers who do not like it have them to blame! Rabbi Neil Gillman, Rabbi Moshe Tutnauer, and Mr. Robert Geskin did me the special favor of reading an earlier version of this book, and Rabbis Michael Goldberg and Gordon Tucker read sections of it. The revisions they suggested have improved it immensely. The same is certainly true of my beloved and long-suffering wife, Marlynn, who suggested the title, showed me where points needed to be clarified or rethought, and who tolerated hours upon hours spent at the computer, time that by right belonged to her. Mr. Sam Mitnick afforded me a professional perspective on the manuscript, encouraged me to publish it, and found the wonderful people at Jason Aronson to do so. My heartfelt thanks to all of the above. None of the faults of this book, of course, can be legitimately attributed to any of these people—especially since, at least in part, they all disagree with me! I am, though, deeply grateful for their stimulation, encouragement, insight, and friendship.

Finally, I would like to thank my parents, to whose blessed memory this book is dedicated. The warmth, the sensitivity, the good humor, the emphasis on education, the Jewish commitment, and the sense of mission to improve the world that permeated the home they created have been real models for me of what it means to live in the presence of God.

ACKNOWLEDGMENT

As Chapter 1 makes clear, this book is the result of my own personal search for knowledge of God during a period of over thirty years. It therefore should not be surprising that some of the sections of this book have previously appeared in print as I was thinking through and testing specific ideas. The constructive criticism I received over the years has modified much of this earlier work, and writing this book has enabled me to revise and synthesize it further; but some of it appears in literal or paraphrased form in the chapters of this book. I would, then, like to thank the publishers listed below, first for publishing my work so that I could learn from the reactions to it, and then for allowing me to use it in the present volume.

CHAPTERS 1, 2, AND 3

Sections of these chapters appeared in my article, " 'This is my God': One Jew's Faith," in *Three Faiths—One God,* John Hick and Edmund S. Meltzer, eds. (Albany, NY: State University of New York Press, 1989), pp. 7–29; copyright held by The Claremont Graduate School.

CHAPTERS 3 AND 4

The material on the Sabbath and on the role of law in effectuating principles in Chapter 3, and the material on creation-revelation-redemption in Chapter 4, are based on work that first appeared in my article, "A Certain Spice: Sabbath Spirit and Sabbath Law," in *Slow Down and Live: A Guide to Shabbat Observance and Enjoyment,* Stephen Garfinkel, ed. (New York: United Synagogue of America, Department of Youth Activities, 1982), pp. 23–48.

CHAPTER 4

I first distinguished the three Conservative positions on revelation from the Orthodox and Reform approaches in my *Conservative Judaism: Our Ancestors to Our Descendants* (New York: United Synagogue of America, Department of Youth Activities, 1977), pp. 110–157. The first statement of my own understanding of revelation, on which the present formulation is based, appeared in my article, "Revelation," *Conservative Judaism* 31:1–2 (Fall-Winter 1976), pp. 58–69. My analysis of the process of reading the Torah first appeared in my *Mitzvah Means Commandment* (New York: United Synagogue of America, Department of Youth Activities, 1989), p. 93.

CHAPTER 5

Sections of this chapter are based on my article, "God and the Holocaust," *Judaism* 26:1 (Winter 1977), pp. 27–34.

CHAPTER 6

Parts of this chapter, especially in the first section, are based on my article, "Prayer for the Perplexed," *University Papers* (Los Angeles: University of Judaism, 1982). Some of the second section is based on my article, "Two Ways to Approach God," *Conservative Judaism* 30:2 (Winter 1976), pp. 58–67.

CHAPTER 7

This chapter is based on my article, "In Defense of Images," *Proceedings of the Academy for Jewish Philosophy,* David Novak and Norbert Samuelson, eds. (Lanham, MD: University Press of America, 1992), pp. 129–154.

Know God in *all* your ways.
—Proverbs 3:5

And you shall love the Lord your God
with all your heart,
and with all your soul,
and with all your might.
—Deuteronomy 6:5

1

A PERSONAL QUEST

SEEKING AN HONEST, INTEGRATED FAITH

For a long time, the Jewish belief in God, as I understood it, was an embarrassment to me. Because I was lucky enough during my teenage years to be shown the wisdom and meaning of the Jewish way of life and thought, I have been a religious Jew—but not an Orthodox one—in intellect, conscience, feeling, and action since then. For approximately twenty years, though, from the age of fifteen to my mid-thirties, I lived my life suffused with most aspects of the Jewish tradition without being able to make sense of its assertions about God.

This, of course, is an inherently unstable condition. It required me to obey what the tradition understands as God's commandments without a clear conviction that there is a God behind them. It also necessitated praying to God several times a day without knowing whether I believed in the One who is supposed to be listening.

I nevertheless did these things, and I derived much meaning from them. Indeed, I recall feeling quite often that I was in touch with God when I consciously obeyed a commandment as a commandment or prayed with intention and feeling. But that only made matters worse—how could I have these feelings when I was unconvinced of the basic tenet on which they rested? Moreover, how could I, who valued the life of the intellect sufficiently to earn a doctorate in philosophy, engage in traditional practices and even feel that I was in touch with God in the process when intellectually I could not explain to myself why I should believe in the God on whom they were based?

Since I believe strongly in the values of honesty and integrity, this situation was not only philosophically problematic, but personally disconcerting. I could explain many of the Jewish practices I had adopted on the grounds of the specific values they expressed and promoted, but I knew all the while that that was not the primary way in which Judaism presented them. Judaism connected them to God. How, then, could I engage in them in this skewed way? It seemed to me to be dishonest both to the tradition and to myself.

Moreover, I deeply feel that one's faith should integrate one's intellect, emotions, body, and will. In light of that, how could I devote so much of my life to Jewish commitments that I could not make sense of intellectually? Emotions are certainly an important part of life, but I knew that forms of religion based primarily on them are often not only blind, but dangerous. I needed integrity as well as honesty in my faith.

This book is the record of how I have come to terms with God. It is not a personal biography—although I shall engage in a little of that later in this chapter—but rather a philosophical odyssey. In all fairness, I must warn the reader at the outset that I have not answered all the questions; indeed, I doubt that any human being, whether a believer or not, honestly could. I offer my thoughts, however, in the hope that they may aid anyone who, like me, finds meaning in religion but is too philosophically skeptical to accept its assertions without seeing evidence for them and without knowing how they fit into the other things that one believes, feels, and does. I have concentrated on the Jewish experience because it is my own, but I suspect that much of what I have to say will apply, with some differences, to Christians and Muslims as well.

THE TRADITIONAL STANCE

It will be helpful first to articulate the traditional Jewish position on God. That will not only clarify the conception of God that Judaism, and later Christianity and Islam, fostered; it will also alert us to some crucial features of traditional belief that religious philosophers through the ages have neglected, to their peril.

Judah Halevi is probably the most important exception. He has been called "the most Jewish of Jewish philosophers"[1] because he rejected the attempts of the other philosophers of his time to arrive at an understanding of God through reason. Instead, like that of the Bible and the Talmud, his approach to God is empirical and experiential. Writing in the twelfth century, he created an imaginary dialogue between a rabbi and the king of the Khazars, whose historical counterpart and other leaders of the realm had converted to Judaism in the eighth century.[2] In convincing the king of the truth of Judaism, Halevi's rabbi argues that rational speculation is subject to mistakes and often leads to doctrinal errors. Even at its best, reason may inform us of an abstract, philosophic God but not the living, commanding Lord with whom the religious Jew interacts. Only revelation and God's actions in the history of Israel can provide an accurate (even if only a partial) description of God, an explanation of the real grounds of the believer's creed, and an understanding of why believers are prepared to sacrifice so much for their beliefs. Anticipating Blaise Pascal by 500 years, Halevi carefully and consistently distinguishes between the God of Abraham and the God of the philosophers (which, for him, meant primarily the Aristotelians) in their differing depictions of God, the reasons for believing in God, and the conduct that grows out of that belief.

In insisting on the primacy of revelation and the interaction with God in history, Halevi represents both the position and the epistemology of the tradition against which all modern Jewish philosophies must be measured. Consequently, I shall quote him at some length to set the context for our exploration of a Jewish philosophy designed for the modern age.

THE RABBI: I believe in the God of Abraham, Isaac, and Israel, who led the Israelites out of Egypt with signs and miracles; who fed them in the desert and gave them the Holy Land after having made them traverse the sea and the Jordan in a miraculous way; who sent Moses with His Law, and subsequently thousands of prophets; who confirmed His law by promises to those who observed, and threats to the disobedient. We believe in what is contained in the Torah—a very large domain.

THE KING OF THE KHAZARS: I had intended from the very beginning not to ask any Jew, because I am aware of the destruction of their books and of their narrow-minded views, their misfortunes having deprived them of all commendable qualities. Should you, O Jew, not have said that you believe in the Creator of the world, its Governor and Guide, who created and keeps you, and such attributes which serve as evidence for every believer, and for the sake of which he pursues justice in order to resemble the Creator in His wisdom and justice?

THE RABBI: That which you express is speculative and political religion, to which inquiry leads, but this is open to many doubts. Now ask the philosophers, and you will find that they do not agree on one action or on one principle, since they rely on theories; some of these can be established by arguments, some of them are only plausible, some even less capable of being proved.

THE KING OF THE KHAZARS: What you say now, O Jew, seems to me better than the beginning, and I should like to hear more.

THE RABBI: But the beginning of my speech was the very proof, yea, the evidence which makes every argument superfluous. . . . The way of inference is misleading and may produce heresy and error. . . . True, there are differences in the ways of demonstration; some of them are exact, others insufficient; but the most exact of all are the ways of the philosophers, and even they are led by their inferences to say that God neither benefits nor injures, nor knows anything of our prayers or offerings, our obedience or disobedience, and that the world is as eternal as He Himself! . . . There is a broad difference, indeed, between the believer in a religion and the philosopher. The believer seeks God for the sake of various benefits, apart from the benefit of knowing Him; the philosopher seeks Him only that he may be able to describe Him accurately, as he would describe the earth . . . ignorance of God would therefore be no more injurious than ignorance concerning the earth. . . .

The meaning of "God" [elohim] can be grasped by way of speculation, a Guide and Manager of the world being inferred by Reason; opinions about Him differ among men according to their faculty of thought; the most evident of them is that of the philosophers. The meaning of "The Lord" [yhwh], however, cannot be grasped by analogic thought, but only by that prophetic intuition by which man ascends, so to say, from his kind and joins the angels. . . . Then there vanish all previous doubts of man concerning God, and he despises all these analogic proofs by means of which men endeavor to attain knowledge of His dominion and unity. Then he becomes a servant who loves his master, and is ready to perish for the sake of his love, finding the greatest sweetness in his connection with Him, the greatest sorrow in separation from Him. Otherwise the philosophers; they consider Divine worship only as refinement of conduct and confession of truth, so that they extol Him above all other beings, just as the sun is to be extolled above all other visible things, and the denial of God only as a mark of a low standard of the soul which acquiesces in untruth.

THE KING OF THE KHAZARS: Now I understand the difference between "God" and the "Lord," and I see how great is the difference between the God of Abraham and the God of Aristotle. To the Lord we yearn, tasting and viewing Him; to God we draw near through speculation. And this feeling invites its votaries to give their life for the love of Him and to suffer death for Him. Speculation, however, tends to veneration only as long as it entails no harm, nor causes pain for its own sake. We must not take it amiss that Aristotle thinks lightly of the observance of religious laws since he doubts whether God has any cognizance of them.

THE RABBI: Abraham, on the other hand, bore his burden honestly, in Ur Kasdim, in emigration, circumcision, removal of Ishmael, in the painful resolution to sacrifice Isaac; for he conceived the Divine power by tasting, not by speculating; he had observed that no detail of his life escaped God, that He rewarded him instantly for his piety and guided him along the best path, so that he moved forwards or backwards only according to God's will. How should he not despise his former speculations? The Sages [*Shabbat* 156a] explain the verse, "He took Abraham outside" [Genesis 15:5] as meaning, "give up your astrology." That is to say: He commanded him to leave off his speculative researches into the stars and other matters, and to devote himself to the service of Him whom he had tasted, as it is written: "Taste and see that the Lord is good" [Psalm 34:9]. The Lord is therefore rightly called "God of Israel" because this seeing is not found elsewhere, and "God of the land" because the peculiarity of its air, soil, and heaven aids this vision, together with actions such as the cultivating and tilling of the soil for the higher prosperity of the species. All followers of the Divine law follow these "seeing" men; they find satisfaction in the authority of their tradition, in spite of the simplicity of their speech and the clumsiness of their similes, not in the authority of philosophers, with their graphic elegance, their excellent dispositions, and their brilliant demonstrations. For all that, the masses do not follow them, as if the soul had a presentiment for truth, as it is said, "The words of truth are recognizable" [*Sotah* 9b].[3]

THE MODERN REALITY OF JEWISH BELIEF

Halevi's epistemological trust in divine revelation and God's actions in history is difficult for contemporary Jews to accept. Their problem is not that of their medieval ancestors, who needed to explain why Judaism is to be preferred to other religions and other revelations. It is rather the question of why religion is necessary in the first place. More than contemporary Christians, and certainly more than contemporary Muslims, Jews in large numbers profess little or no belief in God and even less in revelation. Their doubts about God are not so much the philosophic ones; in the spirit of Halevi, even the reasons for Jews' disbelief are not primarily philosophical! For some, the unspeakable evil of the Holocaust is the chief factor in their disbelief, but, for most, God is simply not part of reality as they know it. In other words, many Jews have become thoroughly secularized. They do not actively deny God; they simply ignore the whole issue, for, like Voltaire, they feel that they have no need of such a hypothesis.

Revelation is even more problematic. In addition to the competition among revelations that troubled the medievals so much, contemporary Jews sometimes know about questions raised by the modern, historical approach to the texts of revelation. Even if verbal revelation took place, we do not have one, undisputed, verbatim record of it.[4] Instead, the Torah is composed of several different documents written centuries after Sinai. This raises major questions about the theological authority of the text: if we do not definitely have God's word in the Torah, why obey it? For most modern Jews, the problem goes even deeper: knowledge as they know it derives from scientific method and experimentation, not revelation. No text or tradition commands their adherence without question.

Nevertheless Jews are not generally interested in denying their Jewishness; they just identify as Jews for reasons not grounded in God or religion. Historical rootedness, family ties, communal feelings and activities (aided by occasional flare-ups of anti-Semitism), identification with the State of Israel or with Jewish causes such as the rescue of Soviet and Ethiopian Jewry, and, especially, a commitment to social equality and other liberal causes motivate their identification as Jews.[5]

That is not enough to prevent intermarriage or check assimilation, but it is enough to set Jews off in a variety of areas as being different from non-Jews. Thus the traditional Jewish emphasis on education still permeates many secularized Jewish homes so that 47 percent of Jews complete bachelor's or higher degrees, compared to only 18 percent of the American popula-

tion as a whole, and Jews become professionals (especially in
education, medicine, law, and social work) in much greater
proportions than do Americans generally. Until very recently,
traditional family values made the Jewish home a bastion of
stability. The divorce rate among Jews is now much higher than
in times past, but it is still lower than that of other Americans,
and divorced Jews tend to remarry, making the percentage of
divorced or separated Jews significantly lower than that of the
general population (6 percent versus 10 percent). Jewish social
activism, rooted in the strong emphasis in Judaism on improving
this world, is still highly evident in the Jewish community. Fully
41 percent of Jews describe their political orientation as liberal,
in comparison to 18 percent of Americans as a whole.[6] This aptly
describes the Jewish commitment to equality and to communal
action to redress economic woes. Jewish social activism makes
itself felt not only on a political level, but individually as well.
So, for example, Jewish lawyers are both numerous and prominent in areas of public interest law *pro bono publico,* and Jews give
heavily to philanthropic causes.[7]

Christians and Muslims rarely understand how Jews can fail to
be religious in their outlook and still carry on traditional values
and patterns of living. The key is the strong sense of peoplehood
that Jews inherit, a sense that is made all the stronger by its in-
dependence of land and governmental structure. Even so, the real
question is how long such an ethnic Jewishness can last. Rabbi
Robert Gordis has claimed that secular Jews are only living off the
capital of their religious parents and grandparents and that will
cease to be possible once a generation no longer even has memories of religious forebears.[8] Recent studies of young American
Jews seem to support his thesis. In any case, the vast majority of
Jews are a far cry from Halevi's brand of Jewish identity.

And yet there are signs of a religious revival among Jews.
Since my own case is typical in many respects, perhaps it will be

best to begin with me, remembering the admonition of Professor James McClendon, Jr., that theology makes no sense detached from biography.[9] Protestants will call what I am about to do "giving my witness," but I once told my story to a Protestant seminary class that asked me to do that, and they told me that it was a very strange form of giving witness. Its very strangeness to Protestants, though, will help to identify what is characteristically Jewish in theology.

MY OWN GROWTH INTO RELIGIOUS BELIEF

I grew up in a typical, "second-generation" home. Although there have been Jews in the United States since 1654, the vast majority of Jews came here from Eastern Europe in the last decades of the nineteenth century and the first decades of the twentieth. The immigrants, the "first generation," had all they could do to eke out a living, and they made sure that their children learned English and the skills necessary to get by in America. Their Judaism was largely that which they brought with them from Europe.

When their children, "the second generation" of American Jews, became adults, they carried out their parents' interest in making it in America, but in their understanding that often meant giving up many of their traditions in order to become as much like white, Anglo-Saxon Protestants as possible. Consequently, third-generation youngsters learned quickly that their parents' real interest in their Jewish education was that they fulfill whatever remaining obligation their parents felt was necessary to make sure that their children identified as Jews. The socially accepted and, indeed, expected manifestation of that was the Bar Mitzvah or Bat Mitzvah ceremonies for, respectively, boys and girls of age thirteen. Beyond that, no further learning

was expected ("After all, do you want him to be a rabbi?"), and
Jewish practice beyond that which the parents were doing (or
even at that same level) was considered to be unusually religious,
bordering on the fanatic.

I grew up in just such an atmosphere. The vast majority of my
contemporaries dropped out of Jewish education after their Bar
or Bat Mitzvah, and they generally remember the experience of
religious school as meaningless and boring. Those who have
found meaning in Judaism as adults commonly talk about their
childhood religious education in anger, questioning how the
adults of that time could ever have distorted the richness of Judaism and failed to communicate its meaning so completely. Many
Jews have assimilated or intermarried, raising real questions
about the survival of a viable Jewish community two or three
generations hence. One of the real ironies of history is that Jews
may find it more difficult to survive under conditions of freedom
than they did during centuries of ghettoization and persecution.

My own case was very different because my parents sent me
to Camp Ramah, a chain of seven camps of the Conservative
Movement in the United States and Canada, with more camps in
Argentina, Chile, and Israel. I was twelve years old during my
first summer at Camp Ramah in Wisconsin, and I am convinced
that had I not been there then, I would have dropped out of
Jewish religious life after my Bar Mitzvah ceremony the following June, following the example of virtually all of my
friends. It was not that I had some kind of religious revelation at
Ramah; at the beginning it was simply a nice camping experience. Even at age twelve, however, I was impressed by the fact
that Judaism was truly a way of life for the people at camp. It was
not restricted to prayer and study, although we did more of
those than I had ever done before; Judaism affected every aspect
of life at camp, from discussions with friends to the evening
activities to the sports field. I loved the singing and the dancing,
the Hebrew that I was learning to speak in classes and at the

waterfront and on the baseball diamond, and the beauty of the traditional Sabbath observances. It was all so natural and unself-conscious. For the first time in my life, Judaism was a source of guidance and joy and not simply a burden that I carried as a member of a minority in a Christian culture.

Through my summers at Ramah as a camper and counselor, and through my Jewish studies during the academic years that intervened, I came to recognize the factors that were involving me more and more in religious life. I liked the depth of the relationships the Jewish environment created. We were certainly not saints in any sense of the term, but at Ramah we had a heightened awareness of moral norms and of the need to be sensitive to other people's needs. We were not embarrassed by talking about behavior and helping people with their problems; it was simply part of what was expected of every one of us.

The intellectual stimulation grew by leaps and bounds as I became older. Indeed, the most exciting and mind-stretching conversations I had anywhere took place at camp. Ironically, in this religious environment, rather than anywhere else, I felt much more able to raise any questions that occurred to me. The leaders of the camp, in fact, prodded us to confront our problems with religious commitment. We were encouraged to ask questions we had never dared to discuss publicly, and the leaders themselves raised issues none of us had ever thought of. This exciting intellectual ferment was coupled with a sense of structure, of rootedness, and of purpose to life that was missing in the lives of all of my nonreligious friends. Consequently, when I decided to become a rabbi, my chief aim was to reproduce the experiences Ramah had given me—to share the spoils, as it were.

While my commitment to Judaism was multifaceted and deeply rooted, it was not based upon a settled view of, and belief in, God. That was not because I was tormented by the evils that beset human beings; I was living a comfortable life within a warm, loving family, largely unexposed to the personal traumas of others. This was the 1950s, when social consciousness was not predominant and few even spoke about the Holocaust.

My problems with God were more abstract and philosophical, for by nature I am a skeptic—indeed, an intellectual rebel. Professor Arthur Danto, a teacher of mine at Columbia University, once characterized a philosopher as a five-year-old child who never stops asking "Why?"—and that accurately describes me.

I could sense the beauty and order in nature and the moral dimension of life, but it was not clear to me why I needed God for those. Moreover, the usual empirical evidence supporting my other beliefs was not as readily available for God; on the contrary, there seemed to be some cogent grounds for doubt. I was not even completely sure what would constitute evidence for believing in God in the first place. And since my moral, ritual, and ethnic commitments seemed to fit together on their own, I set the whole issue aside. Amazingly, even prayer worked for me at that time: I just invoked the "Man on the Mountain" image during prayer and returned to my skepticism in times of intellectual contemplation. This, however, was not a good resolution of the problem; avoidance rarely is. My commitment to Judaism was based on the inherent wisdom and value that I sensed in the tradition and not on its own structure of authority rooted in God. At some point, I knew, I would have to think through the underlying theology of Judaism with all of the inherent risks involved. If God proved to be an untenable belief, would I be left with just an ethnic tie to the tradition? Would that be sufficient? Given the strong theological basis of classical Judaism and the patent dangers of chauvinism, immorality, and prejudice inherent in pure ethnicity and nationalism, I doubted that. The tradition includes a lengthy literature of rationales for the commandments based on considerations of morality, psychology, and aesthetics, but until the Enlightenment they were always conceived of as secondary to the primary theological motive for being an observant Jew, namely, that God commanded us to be so.[10]

I therefore deeply wanted to have a belief in God that would explain and motivate all of the Jewish patterns of action and association that I had found so meaningful, but I also knew that it would have to be one which I could embrace wholeheartedly and without significant intellectual reservations. Paraphrasing the Shema, a central prayer of Judaism, I needed a theology that would enable me to love God "with all my heart, with all my soul, and with all my might."[11]

EPISTEMOLOGICAL MOORINGS

I have become increasingly convinced that theology makes sense only in the context of the person believing it. I know that my own beliefs and experiences have deeply colored my way of thinking and acting, and I have every reason to believe that the same is true for others. That is certainly not to say that interpersonal, rational analysis is useless; on the contrary, an unexamined and unenlightened faith is greatly lacking. But I do think that there is a limit to which people can be convinced of things, not only because of their varying abilities to comprehend and feel, but because people begin with their own unique sets of conceptual eyeglasses through which they see the world. I am, in the terminology used by some epistemologists, a "soft perspectivist": I believe neither that people are all the same and see the world through transparent lenses (the "nonperspectivist" position), nor that they are so bound to their views that no new thinking or experience can change them (the "hard perspectivist" position), but rather that people's beliefs and actions are malleable, although only to an extent.[12] It is therefore important to get a sense of the person talking to you as you hear what he or she has to say, especially in matters as broad in scope and deep in significance as one's conception of God.

In my own case, one belief and one set of experiences undergird everything I think and feel about God. The belief concerns the human ability to know. I am deeply convinced of both the value and the limitations of human knowledge. I honor and pursue knowledge, pushing reason as far as it will take me in understanding my experience; in that sense I am a rationalist. At the same time, I assume from the beginning that ultimately there will be features of my experience that will not fit into a neat intellectual system, sometimes because of my own individual failings to understand, and sometimes because no human being can know and integrate all there is.

I therefore do what the rabbis, in contrast to the Greeks, did— that is, I entertain and pursue any explanation that sheds light on an issue; I expect that conflicting analyses may each be true and helpful to some degree, discordant though they be; and I prefer to live with inconsistency rather than distort or ignore features of my experience that do not fit into a given theory, however helpful that theory may be in explaining other facets of my experience. Keeping the limitations of human knowledge in mind does not lead me to abandon the effort to know, but it does afford me a healthy sense of epistemological humility and humor; I must let go of the human quest for certainty and adopt instead a mellow, almost playful, posture vis-à-vis earnest human attempts to understand everything.[13]

This means that in theology I am a "constructivist"; that is, I think that we human beings have no unmediated knowledge of God but that we rather have to construct our conceptions of God on the basis of the experiences we have. We do this for all of our knowledge of reality, but we are most conscious of this process when dealing with the more elusive dimensions of it. Like our other conceptions, except perhaps more so, our understanding of God will be built on a combination of those experiences that we all share and those that are unique to each one of us—hence the benefit of discussing God with each other and the concurrent necessity of recognizing the limits that each person's perspective will impose on that discussion.

GOD IN CONTEMPLATION VERSUS GOD IN ACTION AND PRAYER

If that is my fundamental methodological belief in these matters, my root experience is that "God" is a term that means one thing to me in moments of thought and another in moments of prayer and action. When thinking about God, "God" signifies, among other things, the superhuman (and maybe supernatural) powers of the universe, the moral thrust in human beings, the sense of beauty in life, and the ultimate context of experience. Although these phenomena do not offer proof of God's existence, and although they do not point unambiguously to one clear-cut, consistent conception of the Eternal, they persuade me that theological language is appropriate in describing experience and ultimately more adequate than a totally secular conceptual framework.[14]

The depictions of God produced by reason, however, are very abstract. This, I have come to recognize, is more a result of the character of reason than it is a reflection of God.[15] Reason by its very nature seeks to generalize over specific phenomena and draw analogies among them. We prize reason because it introduces order and clarity into our experience and gives us a secure sense of understanding and sometimes even mastery.

We do, however, have to be careful that the generalizing nature of reason does not blind us to the reality and uniqueness of individual occurrences, whether they concern inanimate objects, animals, people, or God. Our knowledge of each other, after all, is not exclusively (or perhaps even primarily) an awareness of the species homo sapiens with definite, general characteristics; they are of Mark or Sarah, who differ from each other in almost as many ways as they are alike. Similarly, when I experience God in prayer or action, the God I encounter is a unique personality who interacts with the world, most especially in requiring everyone to obey the laws of morality and in commanding the People Israel to observe additionally the stipulations of His Covenant with them. If anything, the fact that Judaism perceives of God as One makes generalizing all the more suspect as an avenue to find the God of the tradition, and it makes God's unique personal characteristics all the more significant. I am not surprised, then, that in moments of prayer and in carrying out other commandments I interact with a highly personal God not all that different from the Man on the Mountain but very different from the God to which reason leads.[16]

This is similar to Halevi's distinction, mentioned earlier, between the God of the philosophers and the God of Abraham, Isaac, and Jacob;[17] but, unlike Halevi, I am not convinced by the evidence of personal experience that philosophy is hopelessly useless in explicating religious experience. On the contrary, the more we are able not only to report a given experience, but to integrate it into our knowledge of other areas of life, the stronger and clearer our claim to knowledge of that experience will be, for then we not only know the experience firsthand but we also know its relationship to our other experiences.

The goal, then, is to articulate a strong epistemological basis for traditional belief. Ideally, I want a theology that commands intellectual respect, that preserves the strong personal element of traditional Jewish theology and our own individual experience with God and other human beings, and that explains and motivates Jewish principles, values, and practice. I do not pretend that the thoughts that follow fully accomplish this goal, but they have made me more comfortable in thinking and speaking theologically and increasingly at home in the tradition's conceptual structure.

2

USING REASON TO KNOW GOD

KNOWING GOD AS ONE KNOWS AN OBJECT

How can we know about God? Medieval and modern philosophers have commonly treated this question as one branch of the
general epistemological search for grounds for our knowledge
of objects. We learn about God, they assume, in much the same
way as we learn about tables. Even Kant's objections to the
classical proofs for the existence of God were objections to
specific features of the arguments, not to the program of at-
tempting to learn about God as scientists learn about objects.

Logical Positivism

The impact of science in our own century has reenforced this
methodology, most evidently in the school of logical positivism.
Ludwig Wittgenstein and the Vienna Circle are historically the
founders of this philosophical school—although it has strong
roots in the positivism of Auguste Comte and other nineteenth-

century figures. It was A. J. Ayer's *Language, Truth, and Logic,* however, which caused the most comment in religious circles because he applied the method openly and straightforwardly to religion—some would say ruthlessly—and the results were downright startling.

According to Ayer, it is neither necessary nor possible to test the truth of religious, metaphysical, moral, or aesthetic sentences, since they do not make a proper truth claim in the first place. Only empirically verifiable or falsifiable sentences do that. Religious, metaphysical, moral, and aesthetic sentences express our approval or disapproval about aspects of life that we may consider important; as such they may be emotionally meaningful for us. We might have, for example, a meaningful relationship with someone. Sentences asserting such emotional significance are, however, cognitively meaningless in that they do not make an empirically verifiable or falsifiable truth claim. As such, they are not factually meaningful, and there is no point in testing for their truth. A sentence must be cognitively meaningful before it can be adjudged true or false; it must claim to be true before one can determine whether it is or not.[1]

Ayer made it clear that, for him, atheism is just as cognitively meaningless as theism, since an atheistic assertion, just like a theistic one, is not factual. The criterion for cognitive meaningfulness, after all, was not whether a statement was true or false, but whether it was factual, that is, *capable* of being empirically true or false. Some followers of Ayer, in fact, claimed that falsification, even more than verification, had to be possible for a statement to be meaningful.[2]

Nevertheless, the impact of Ayer's thought was felt most strongly in the camp of theism. It seemed as if Ayer had undercut religion in one fell swoop. All of the argumentation throughout centuries about the truth of the various religions was based on the logical mistake of looking for truth where none was claimed in the first place. One had to use the hardheaded methods of science to test whether a sentence was meaningful before one could logically make any claims whatsoever about its truth.

This result was greeted with joy by avowed secularists and atheists, as one might expect, but it also found support in some religious camps. Protestant conservatives thought that Ayer and his followers had demonstrated once and for all the folly of using reason or even normal human experience in religious matters. Religion, for them, is based on revelation and/or a mystic experience, and as such it is no wonder that the methods of science do not work in explaining it. The methods of inquiry that we use in analyzing and controlling the empirical world are simply the wrong tools to understand God, an afterlife, creation, prayer, and other religious phenomena. This does not mean that religious sentences are cognitively meaningless, as Ayer thought; it only means that the subject matter of religion requires completely different rules of meaning and justification.[3]

This response to logical positivism proved to be inadequate, both philosophically and religiously. The staunchest rationalist would agree that human reason is limited, and the most radical empiricist would admit that the same is true for human experience. This, however, does not justify the claim that reason, as applied to everyday human experience, is totally inapplicable to any particular area of life. On the contrary, our experience has been that, to varying degrees, we can use a combination of reason and normal human experience to stretch beyond that experience and make factual claims about it. Many of the theoretical statements of science are precisely of that nature. Moreover, our analyses of the various areas of life often impinge upon and support one another. Therefore isolating religion from rational analysis as applied to normal human experience is philosophically dangerous, potentially threatening the truth status of all of our knowledge.

There are also religious problems with such an approach. If religion is completely divorced from reason, it ceases to be vulnerable to rational attack, but it also ceases to be eligible for rational support. For religion to be truly a matter of "all your heart, all your soul, and all your might," as the Bible demands (Deuteronomy 6:5), it must involve a person's mind as well as his or her body, emotions, and will. Any "soft-headed" religion is neither genuine nor ultimately satisfying.

On the other end of the spectrum, Protestant liberals embraced these early positivistic results in a very different way. R. B. Braithwaite and Paul Van Buren were two of the chief protagonists for the position that Ayer was right about religion: religion is not about truth or falsity but rather about morality, historical associations, community involvement, and the like. Religious texts should therefore be analyzed for their practical import, not their cognitive truth.[4]

Just as divorcing religion from reason proved to be inadequate, so too was the attempt to separate religion from truth. Even those antipathetic to religion recognized that this was playing fast and loose with it. Religion certainly is concerned with morality, history, and so on, but it also makes factual claims. To deny that this is so is to win by pretending that the opponent is not there. Those sympathetic to religion were, of course, even more distressed; now even friends of religion like Braithwaite and Van Buren were denying its claims to truth. That was not only inaccurate; it was traitorous!

Linguistic Analysis and Religion

By the 1950s philosophers had discovered a number of problems with the verifiability criterion itself. In the confident, straightforward way in which Ayer originally formulated it, the criterion ruled out the meaningfulness of many theoretical assertions of science—a bitter result for a philosophy motivated by the desire to be scientific. Ayer and others attempted to modify the criterion to accommodate such statements, but they were not able to construct a formulation that would at once affirm the cognitive meaningfulness of theoretical propositions in science and yet deny the cognitive meaningfulness of all moral, aesthetic, metaphysical, and religious sentences. Each version of the verifiability test ruled out either too much or too little.[5]

That dilemma led to a change in the goal and name of this philosophic movement. Philosophers understood that we can know whether a sentence is capable of being true or false only if we first know what it means and how it acquires that meaning. Consequently, instead of trying to devise a uniform linguistic test to distinguish between sentences that have truth value and those that do not, they turned to the logically prior step of analyzing how language gains meaning in the first place. To mark this change in program, those investigating language as a key to truth no longer called their approach logical positivism, denoting the logical necessity for a sentence to have positive, empirical implications to be considered meaningful. Instead they used the term *linguistic* (or philosophic) *analysis,* indicating that the meaningfulness of language used in a wide range of contexts must be accepted and analyzed.

This shift significantly softened the power and acrimony of the initial positivist attack on religion, and religious thinkers could therefore be less defensive and more forthcoming in their analyses. The first attempts were developed in the late 1950s and early 1960s. Taking their cue from Wittgenstein's *Philosophical Investigations,* philosophers like Ian Ramsey suggested that religious language was a discreet "language game," with its own definitions of member entities and its own rules for their interaction. According to the theory, the fact that scientific analysis does not work in the realm of religion is not a reflection on religion but is rather the result of using the rules of one game to play another. It is like finding basketball meaningless because you cannot produce a checkmate in it.[6]

That approach served to alert people to the multifaceted nature of experience, but it ultimately foundered on issues similar to the ones we have discussed before. If religion is a language game on its own, how do we ever understand it? How can it be described using many of the same words that we use in other contexts (e.g., father, justice)? What is the relationship between religious language and other language games? At bottom the fact is, after all, that we are integrated human beings; we are not exclusively artists, thinkers, basketball players, or worshipers. Our language must reflect that integration if it is to be an adequate tool to describe our experience.

DISCERNING PATTERNS IN EXPERIENCE: KNOWLEDGE THROUGH NONHYPOTHETICAL DISCOVERY

While this exploration was going on, analytic philosophers developed another explanation of religious language. I will suggest that this approach indeed helps us to understand how religious statements gain meaning and truth but that it needs to be broadened along the lines of traditional Judaism's epistemology and modes of verification. In this area, as in so many others, Jewish civilization and the other elements of Western culture are mutually fructifying.

In 1945, John Wisdom published his celebrated paper, "Gods." In it he told the famous Invisible Gardener parable:

> Two people return to their long neglected garden and find among the weeds a few of the old plants surprisingly vigorous. One says to the other, "It must be that a gardener has been coming and doing something about these plants." Upon inquiry, they find that no neighbor has ever seen anyone at work in their garden. The first man says to the other, "He must have worked while people slept." The other says, "No, someone would have heard him, and besides, anybody who cared about the plants would have kept down these weeds." The first man says, "Look at the way these are

arranged. There is purpose and a feeling for beauty here. I believe that someone comes, someone invisible to mortal eyes. I believe that the more carefully we look, the more we shall find confirmation of this." They examine the garden ever so carefully and sometimes they come on new things suggesting that a gardener comes and sometimes they come on new things suggesting the contrary and even that a malicious person has been at work.[7]

Antony Flew later modified this parable to make a point similar to Ayer's—specifically that religious people begin by making cognitive claims but retreat from those claims as soon as they are scientifically challenged so that the claims "die the death of a thousand qualifications."[8] Wisdom, however, intended something completely different. For Wisdom, the evidence is genuinely ambiguous; there are points in favor of both the assertion and the denial of the existence of the gardener. Believers and nonbelievers do not differ in their knowledge of the evidence but rather in their evaluation of it. Their dispute in regard to the import of the various pieces of evidence leads them to see the garden in two vastly different contexts. We do not simply see a conglomeration of evidence; we see it as fitting into one pattern or another—if we have enough evidence and imagination to discern an appropriate pattern at all.

Are these patterns subject to rational argument? As mentioned earlier, there are three views on that question. Hard perspectivists—or absolute relativists—claim that differences on fundamental principles are intractable because there are no common elements that provide a framework for people with widely differing views to persuade each other, or sometimes even to talk with each other. Many of the discussions between the North Vietnamese and the Americans in the 1970s, and between the Israelis and the Arabs since 1948, could serve as supporting examples for hard perspectivists. The parties in such cases have such widely variant views of the situation that they interpret everything oppositely and sometimes actively ignore facts contrary to their political agenda.

Ayer, Flew, and other logical positivists are examples of non-perspectivists—that is, those who claim that viewpoints are wholly amenable to rational analysis, for there are really no differences among human communities about what it means to be rational or humane or reverent or scientific. All current disputes on these issues are the product of ignorance or perversity or both, but with enough time and effort, they will all be resolved.

Wisdom and his followers (Hare, Mitchell, and others) are soft perspectivists. They stress that disagreements about the existence or nonexistence of patterns within the facts are not simply a matter of adducing evidence; the disputants may know all the evidence and yet interpret and apply it differently. On the other hand, disagreements about perspectives are cognitive in that evidence *is* relevant to the reasonableness of asserting a particular pattern. People may differ about the proper interpretation of phenomena and about what constitutes evidence in the first place, but human beings have enough in common to make discourse on many issues possible. Perspectives are not the product of ignorance, lack of time or energy, or perversity, however. They remain a crucial part of our thinking no matter how much we learn because they represent differing evaluations of what is important. That is true for science as well as for other areas of life. As R. M. Hare said:

> Hume saw [that] without a *blik* [perspective] there can be no explanation, for it is by our *bliks* that we decide what is and what is not an explanation. Suppose we believed that everything that happened happened by pure chance. This would not of course be an assertion, for it is compatible with anything happening or not happening, and so, incidentally, is its contradictory. But if we had this belief, we should not be able to explain or predict or plan anything. Thus, although we should not be *asserting* anything different from those of a more normal belief, there would be a great difference between us; and this is the sort of difference that there is between those who really believe in God and those who really disbelieve in Him.[9]

Kellenberger: Hypothetical and Nonhypothetical Discovery

From the time that Wisdom and Hare first announced this position, there have been, in my view, two major advances in its defense. In 1972, James Kellenberger published his book *Religious Discovery, Truth, and Knowledge*. In it he distinguishes between hypothetical discovery and nonhypothetical discovery.

The model of learning that we most commonly have in mind is the scientific model, in which there is an hypothesis that is proved or disproved by the accumulation of evidence. Hypothetical discovery of this sort is certainly what Ayer and Flew had in mind, and due to the pervasive influence of science in our own day, it is probably the epistemological method that most of us have in mind too.

As Kellenberger points out, however, that is not the way we learn things in vast areas of our lives. Probably more often than we use the scientific model of hypothetical discovery, we learn about ourselves and our world through nonhypothetical discovery. The easiest way to describe the difference is to reproduce the chart through which Kellenberger summarizes his position.[10]

Hypothetical discovery	Nonhypothetical discovery
Example: A discovers that B is jealous of his (A's) son.	Example: A discovers that he is jealous of his own son.
1. A *suspects* that B is jealous of his son.	1. A dismisses the thought that he is jealous of his son (if it occurs to him).
2. He *investigates*.	2. No investigation.
3. He collects evidence.	3. No collection of evidence; it is already familiar, although not seen as evidence.
4. He knows what will establish his suspicion or hypothesis and investigates to see if there is evidence.	4. The discovery is made when what is familiar is seen in its significance as evidence.
5. The discovery is made when a clear hypothesis confirming condition is seen to be met.	

Kellenberger's model is designed to alert us to both the way we gain information and the way we verify it. We learn not only by creating an hypothesis and then seeking confirming evidence (hypothetical discovery), but also—and perhaps more often—by seeing patterns in data which are already familiar to us. Sometimes we come to see such patterns when others point them out to us, as, for example, when a literature teacher demonstrates a recurrent, but underlying theme in a novel. On other occasions we come to see a pattern on our own. When that happens, we are often not quite sure how we arrived at the perception; it just occurs to us. At other times, after long, hard work, we all of a sudden see it; we have a "eureka!" experience.

Nonhypothetical discovery, however, need not be so dramatic. We can perceive something after a certain amount of experience, as, for example, when Allan discerns that Barry is after his job even though Barry does not appear to be very aggressive. The apperception occurs to Allan at a particular time, but there are no rules that define the process by which Allan sees the pattern in Barry's behavior; it just occurs to him. And when it does, Allan has learned something new and significant about Barry, something which may well change his attitudes toward Barry and his interaction with him.

The fact that nonhypothetical knowledge comes upon us unexpectantly, without our pursuing a planned course of action, is probably what motivates those philosophers who base knowledge on intuition. Kellenberger's model shows why and how there is such knowledge, why the process of gaining it is so frustrating to delineate, and why the intuitionist position in epistemology is true but is not the whole truth: we do have nonhypothetical knowledge, but we have hypothetical knowledge too.

The Scope and Verification of Nonhypothetical Discoveries

Kellenberger's example of nonhypothetical discovery involves a strong emotional component, where the discovery is essentially the clarification and recognition of the man's feelings of jealousy toward his own son. Similar nonhypothetical discoveries can take place with regard to other emotions. So, for example, Carl and David may know the same facts about the way in which Ellen relates to Carl, but Carl may think that Ellen is in love with him and David may not think so.

Nonhypothetical discoveries, however, can also take place on a totally cognitive plane. Other, less emotional examples will demonstrate just how widespread and how cognitive nonhypothetical discovery often is.

Nonhypothetical discovery is used in legal contexts in several ways. A detective must do some footwork to discover the facts, but ultimately what distinguishes a good detective from a bad one is the ability to see pieces of evidence as clues to the identity of the crime and the criminals. The judge and/or jury must not only know the evidence presented; they must decide whether it constitutes sufficient grounds for a verdict of guilt. History is similarly not just the collection and recollection of facts, but the linking of those facts in patterns which put the facts into a context and thereby explain them.

The impact of logical positivism, though, was in large measure due to its claim to be scientific. It was going to substitute the hard, objective criteria for truth used in science for the soft-headed, confused thinking of people writing about morals, aesthetics, and religion. As we have seen, that philosophical program failed due to the inability to construct an adequate verifiability criterion, and people today are not as convinced as they were in the first half of this century that science can and will cure all ills and provide the answers to all our questions. Nevertheless, many people still have the impression that pure, objective truth exists in science and in science alone, such that every other sort of inquiry is inexact and shaky by comparison.

That is why it is especially important to note that nonhypothetical discovery is used in science as much as it is in other areas of life. In routine cases physicians can proceed in a totally hypothetical way: their training prompts them to suspect a particular disease, and they test for it. But the true mettle of a physician is proved in those cases which are difficult to diagnose. The good doctor is one who can discover a pattern in the test results and clinical data which points to a correct diagnosis of the disease. Similarly, the creative engineer or architect is the one who can see the potential within difficult circumstances to enable the building or bridge to be built.

And it is not only practical science that uses nonhypothetical reasoning; theoretical science uses it even more. Scientific theorizing, in fact, is crucially dependent upon the formation of paradigms. These frameworks link phenomena together so that the scientist can understand them better and decide upon fruitful avenues of research. They form a picture, as it were, in the scientist's mind. This picture, to be sure, must be tested for its truth, but scientists would not even know what to look for until and unless they had a map suggested by their research to date. Book learning and experimentation are certainly necessary to produce such models, but they are not enough. The known data must be seen from a new perspective, and once they are, the scientist can potentially gain an immense amount of new knowledge about the world. Indeed, except for the narrowest of experimental contexts, science regularly uses nonhypothetical reasoning in the search for appropriate paradigms. Some of the most revolutionary scientific discoveries, in fact, including those of Galileo and Einstein, are due precisely to this type of nonhypothetical reasoning.[11]

Since the process by which we discover things nonhypothetically does not conform to any clear rules, it is especially important that we be able to verify our nonhypothetical discoveries. First-person statements can, after all, be false: I can delude myself, and I can be mistaken in interpreting my sensations. We guard against such errors in the patterns we discern in our experience by checking them against the evidence. A pattern is confirmed when it pulls together many disparate phenomena; it is disconfirmed‑ when there are many related phenomena that conflict with it or that it must ignore or distort in order to keep the pattern intact.

Sometimes the process of testing a pattern reduces to the hypothetical, experimental model, and then it is relatively straightforward. A physician, for example, may be presented with data that would support several different diagnoses, but then he or she would normally test each possibility separately along the lines of the hypothetical mode.

Often, however, no conclusive tests are available, either because we do not know enough about the situation to devise one, or, more importantly, because the data alone will not decide the issue since evaluation is required. The legal, literary, and historical cases cited above are good examples. If there is no evidence at all for a legal finding, or overwhelming evidence for it, then there is no difficulty in arriving at a decision. But many cases— the vast majority of those which are actually tried—fall in between these two extremes. Perhaps there is some, but not much, evidence to support the legal finding (or literary interpretation or historical theory), or there is some evidence for it but also some evidence against it. Then judgment is required, and thoughtful people may legitimately dispute the existence of a pattern in the data. If a pattern is reasonably well demonstrated, however, then new knowledge is gained and new action and attitudes may be required or made possible.

The application of the nonhypothetical model to religion is clear: religious claims about God, a purpose in life, creation, the People Israel, and so on are all assertions based at least in part upon the recognition of patterns in human experience. Justification of such beliefs does not call for new evidence but rather requires sensitization to the *significance* of specific parts of the experiences which we have already had and continue to have. Religious education follows suit. Both philosophical justification of religious beliefs and religious education of the uninitiated or skeptical are not so much the learning of new facts about the world as they are the acquisition of a framework through which our experiences can be tied together and their significance appreciated. As John Wisdom says, this requires a process of connecting and disconnecting possible links in our experience, not serially in a chain of deductive reasoning, but rather more like locating the legs of a chair, exposing the factors which support a given interpretation of our experience over others.

> In such cases, we notice that the process of argument is not a *chain* of demonstrative reasoning. It is presenting and representing of those features of the case which *severally co-operate* in favour of the conclusion, in favour of saying what the reasoner wishes said, in favour of calling the situation by the name by which he wishes to call it. The reasons are like the legs of a chair, not the links of a chain.

In this effort, Wisdom points out, we encounter our unconscious predilections to connect things in certain ways and our resistance to linking them in others.[12] Indeed, this process involves a combination of our cognitive, emotional, and conative faculties, and it is for that reason that neither the wholly cognitive, hypothetical model nor the wholly noncognitive, positivist thesis has proved adequate as a description of religious knowledge. There *are* truth claims in religion, and they *can* be substantiated, but their justification follows the nonhypothetical, discovery model, and that involves our will and emotions as well as our intellect.

The Risks in Adopting Patterns—and in Not Adopting Them

When it comes to God, however, our experience does not unambiguously reveal a pattern demonstrating the existence and activity of God nor a pattern refuting such a God. Some features of our experience—the very fact of existence, its order, our consciousness, our ongoing struggle with the nature and substance of morality, the phenomenon of beauty, and so forth—support a theistic interpretation, and some factors—most especially the existence of evil—argue against such an interpretation.

Under these circumstances, one could take refuge in what appears to be the safe haven of agnosticism. One would, in other words, simply say that the evidence is not clear one way or the other and that one therefore cannot commit oneself to either possibility. This would presumably preserve one's sense of epistemological security, for one would affirm only that for which the evidence is conclusive.

This benefit, though, comes at a heavy price: one must consciously ignore the many aspects of our experience which we do not fully understand—or, at least, renounce any epistemological responsibility for them. As William James pointed out in his famous essay, *The Will to Believe,* this cost is not only epistemological, but existential; it affects the scope of not only our knowledge, but of our lives. There are surely dangers in affirming what one does not know with full certainty, and there are even more hazards in acting on such affirmations. If one chooses not to take such risks, however, one thereby loses opportunities for a much fuller cognitive appreciation of human experience and for living a much fuller life.[13]

An example will make this point clear. You never know for sure whether a given person is the right person to wed; the evidence is never all in—never, that is, until you or the potential partner dies, and then it is much too late. Moreover, with most couples, the evidence is mixed: there are some things you love about him or her, some things that you could take or leave, and some things that you frankly wish were different. Given this lack of full evidence and the ambiguous nature of what you do know, you could choose never to marry. That would preserve your epistemological purity, as it were, but it would come with the great cost of never learning about life from interacting with one's spouse and children, to say nothing of never experiencing the depth of positive and negative emotions that marriage brings.

This does not mean that one should plunge blindly into epistemological or existential commitments; that would not only be dangerous, but irresponsible. Philosophers, in fact, have attempted to articulate the ethic for belief which underlies our common practice, spelling out when we generally deem it proper to believe and to act, and when not.[14] To refuse to stretch one's knowledge and experience beyond the limits of absolute security, however, comes at great cost—and probably is not in keeping with our ethic of propriety in belief and action.

Atheism, from this perspective, assumes a new guise. Atheists generally claim that their position is required by a rational assessment of the preponderance of evidence. The problem of evil—that is, how can there be evil if there is an all-powerful, all-knowing, benevolent God—is usually the crux of their argument. The existence of unjustified evil is, without question, a trenchant objection to theism, one to which we shall return in a later chapter. However, to pretend that the evidence is fully available and that what we know is unambiguous is to misrepresent the situation: we do not know all the relevant facts, and what we do know suggests opposite conclusions. Ultimately the evidence does not force one conclusion or the other, and one must choose which pattern to believe in and act upon on the basis of other, personal factors. As John Hick said:

From the fact that there are particular considerations which count as *prima facie* evidence both for and against theism, it follows that if we attend only to selected items, we may well receive the impression that the evidence as a whole tends in one direction—which direction depending upon which items of evidence are in the forefront of our attention. However since theism and naturalism can each alike lay claim to *prima facie* evidences and must each admit the existence of *prima facie* difficulties, any fruitful comparison must treat the two alternative interpretations as comprehensive wholes, each with its own distinctive strengths and weaknesses. . . .

In what sense, however, or on what basis can it be claimed to be established that one such total interpretation is more probable than another? Can we, for example, simply count points for and against? . . . Clearly, no such mechanical procedure will do, for the conflicting considerations do not constitute units of equal weight. . . . There are no common scales in which to weigh, for example, human wickedness and folly against the fact of man's moral experience. . . . Judgments on such matters are intuitive and personal, and the category of probability, if it is applied, no longer has any objective meaning.[15]

Our choice, then, is either to see a theistic or an atheistic pattern in our experiences, even with its rough edges, or to affirm that no pattern exists until and unless every piece of evidence fits neatly into it. The latter option—i.e., agnosticism—is not, however, risk-free. It comes at the price of requiring us to ignore pieces of our experience because we cannot make them fit into a totally coherent pattern. It also robs us of the life experiences which follow upon adopting such a pattern—in this case, the actions and emotions of a religious life.

The central mistake of agnosticism is its lack of confidence in the human ability to know—to the point of assuming that human beings must either know fully, or they cannot know at all. As our examples above demonstrate, this is simply not true. Some elements of a given case may support a verdict of guilty, and some an acquittal; such cases are precisely the ones that usually go to court. The jury must then weigh the evidence, with all its imponderables, and it must try to see a pattern in the thicket of evidence, even if it is not an altogether clear one. Juries in fact do this every day and with conviction "beyond a reasonable doubt." In civil cases, they need only decide what conclusion "a preponderance of the evidence" supports; that is, even further doubt is permitted in reaching their conclusion. Despite the lack of as much evidence as we would like, then, and even in the presence of contradictory evidence, we make judgments with serious consequences, and we do so with reasonable assurance that we have discovered the truth about the matter and have therefore judged justly.

Atheism makes the opposite mistake. It asserts that if some evidence contradicts a pattern, the pattern must be denied, even if it is supported by much other evidence. We can and do see patterns in our experience, however, even when the evidence is not conclusive, and even when some elements of our experience contradict them. In scientific practice, in fact, a forty or fifty percent corroboration of a theory is considered to be very good evidence for it—even though that means that much of the evidence argues against it! Atheism's fallacy is, ironically, the exact opposite of that embedded in the ontological argument: while those who posit the ontological argument assume that whatever the human mind can contemplate must exist, atheists believe that whatever the human mind cannot integrate must not exist. Both are based on a false assessment of the power and scope of human knowledge.

These arguments do not, in and of themselves, prove theism. They merely point out that human knowledge is based upon seeing patterns in our experience; that, because of the limits of the human ability to know, the patterns are often not fully or unambiguously substantiated; but that refusing to see a pattern in experience bears a price just as much as seeing a pattern does. The choice of whether or not to see a given pattern depends, in part, on our detached, objective analysis of the evidence at hand—and on what we choose to consider as evidence in the first place. It also, however, depends crucially upon our will and our emotions—that is, on our choice to accept the costs of believing in the pattern or the risks of denying it.

Personal and Communal Factors in Forming and Testing Convictions

This choice also involves our communal and historical associations, and that brings us to the second major development in the understanding of religious claims by the method of philosophical analysis. In 1975 James McClendon, Jr., and James M. Smith published their book, *Understanding Religious Convictions*. In it they shift the focus of attention from assertions to convictions:

> A "conviction," as we shall use the term, is a persistent belief such that if X (a person or a community) has a conviction, it will not easily be relinquished without making X a significantly different person (or community) than before.[16]

This shift calls attention to a fact that has often been neglected in philosophical discussions of religious claims, specifically, the extent to which they are embedded in personal and communal stories and histories. The adoption and defense of a framework for seeing the world and acting in it is *not* a detached, intellectual exercise carried on by individuals devoid of personal and communal histories. It is rather an ongoing, living process in which the biographies and communal attachments of the people involved play a crucial role in determining what will count as evidence and the extent to which rational argumentation is possible or relevant in the first place. This, in fact, is the essence of a community: it connects and disconnects, not only people, but the ideas, emotions, and histories which bind them. McClendon and Smith aptly speak of "convictional communities" and discuss the process by which convictions are justified within communities and across communal lines.

As one might imagine, this process is much more complex than testing to find out whether the facts fit the hypothesis, but it is *not* an impossible task, even across communal lines, because of the contingent fact that human beings commonly do share some criteria for judgment, however differently they understand and apply them. A crucial one of these is truth, and that makes the justification of convictions more than a political or emotional process. It is a genuinely cognitive task:

> . . . there is no easy appeal "to the facts" in questions of convictional difference: our apprehension of facts, the very kinds of facts there are, will be determined in part by the convictions we hold. Yet this does not free us from the task of referring to the discoverable facts, in adjusting our convictions themselves to the way things really are. To seek to do so is to take truth seriously. And if truth or falsity is irrelevant to the most important commitments we make, it will be difficult indeed to insist on the importance of truth in less momentous questions.[17]

The process of discovering truth, however, takes place within the context of the researcher's personal and communal biography, and that is especially important to note when the truth to be discerned is not simply another fact but a whole metaphysical structure for linking phenomena, understanding them, and determining their implications for action. Such frameworks are not proved or refuted; they are made more or less acceptable on the basis of a series of criteria, such as truth, consistency, coherence, good practical effects, and beauty. Criteria such as these are chosen, rank-ordered, and applied by individuals and communities. Consequently, the acceptance and significance of an assertion is crucially dependent upon the place which the specific tenet occupies within the life of a person or a community— whether that community be a scientific one or a religious one.

Appropriate Methods to Know a Personal God

Why do the methods of hypothetical discovery, so common in science, fail us in trying to know God? Why do we have to pay attention to nonhypothetical discovery and the formation of convictions when we want to use reason to know God?

Part of the reason for this is a point noted earlier. Writing in widely different contexts, Judah Halevi in the twelfth century and Blaise Pascal in the seventeenth century each noted that the God of the philosophers is not the same as that of Abraham, Isaac, and Jacob.[18] The philosophers' arguments seek to demonstrate the existence of a God who creates and orders but not one who interacts personally with human beings, takes a direct and abiding interest in them, and evokes their loyalty unto death. The conception of God in the classical sources of the three Western religions certainly includes these latter characteristics; these traits may, in fact, be more prominent and common in the minds of the faithful than the ones on which the philosophical proofs are based. God's personal attributes are certainly at the heart of the thought and practice of Judaism, Christianity, and Islam; any theology which ignores them distorts the fundamentally theistic character of these religions. Consequently, while religious people in the West may seek philosophic reassurance that the God they worship does not offend their intellects, they find much philosophy of religion curiously off-point since the demonstrations proffered, even if valid, point to a God lacking some crucial qualities of the God they worship.

But the point is stronger. Religious people have not only been right in rejecting the abstract God which results from the philosophers' use of scientific methods; they have also been right in feeling that the philosophers' very methods were wrongheaded. The God of the Western religions is, after all, not like the many objects of science which can be categorized and studied as a group; God is instead both personal and unique. The methods of scientific experimentation and abstract, philosophic reasoning, based as they are on the ability to generalize over particulars, are therefore not suited to learning about God.

Indeed, adherents of all three Western religions have consistently felt that their knowledge of God comes primarily from sources other than those of observation and reasoning. This does not mean that observation and reason are to be excluded from an examined, deep faith; they certainly must play a role if one's faith is to be reasonable and whole. Analysis and testing of one's faith through reason and observation, however, must come chronologically, educationally, and logically *after* one gains faith in the first place, and that comes from interacting with God.

Again, Judah Halevi articulated the point most forcefully, with modern existentialists like Franz Rosenzweig and Martin Buber following suit.[19] All three emphasize that the primary Jewish experience of God does not come from detached observation, but rather from an involved, direct interaction with God. God first communicated with the People Israel at Sinai through revelation, and ever since then, committed Jews have responded through prayer and adherence to God's commands. God, in turn, has played a role in both nature and history, at times an active and easily recognizable one and at times less so. Over time these interactions have formed a long-term relationship between God and the People Israel, and it is through the elements of this relationship that Jews continue to know God. This approach to religious epistemology is at the heart of the Jewish experience of God—and of the Christian and Muslim experiences as well.[20]

The Model of Learning about Other People

In light of Western religions' insistence on the personal nature of God, it is logical to focus on the ways we learn about people in order to choose an appropriate method for learning about God. Human beings clearly differ from God, and we shall later consider the significance of the differences for our knowledge of God; but the personal nature of God suggests that we first look at how we come to know persons and then see whether we can know God in similar ways.

When we consider how we come to know people, we discover both that it is difficult to learn about individuals and that scientific methods are not very helpful. In part that is because personalities are not directly observable by others, as objects are. We use bodily clues and our own experiences to guess what other people think and feel, but we are never able to observe the mind, the emotions, or the will of another person directly.

To further complicate matters, each of us is the product of a unique combination of factors which make up human personality, and many would claim that we have a degree, at least, of free will. These facts make it virtually impossible to formulate accurate rules about a person's nature and conduct in the way that scientists construct laws describing the behavior of objects. We are not totally helpless, of course: we have learned some common features of human thought, feeling, and behavior through the work of psychologists, sociologists, and the like. We are even discovering some biological bases for human personality. But the fact remains that knowing another person is not amenable to fixed, general rules and that analogies to other people are often misleading.

Moreover, even when we know a person in one context, we find that he or she may think, feel, and act very differently in other contexts. We know this from studies that have been done of mob psychology and peer pressure, and we know this more pervasively on the basis of our own experience with other people. Objects sometimes behave differently when their environment is altered, but human behavior seems to vary with the context even more.

All these factors make it difficult to know another person, and they render the methods of science only moderately helpful in that task. Probably the most significant stumbling block in knowing another person, however, is the fact that such knowledge depends upon the willingness of both parties to engage in a relationship. I cannot force others to open themselves up to me; they must agree to do so. Initiating contact therefore involves a risk on my part, the risk of rejection. The other person may either ignore me or actually scorn me. And there is even a greater risk involved: to create a relationship, I must also be willing to open myself up to the other person. That requires self-confidence and trust in the other. Beyond that, I have to be willing to expend the physical and psychological energy needed to maintain and explore the relationship once it has been formed.

These personal investments on the part of both parties make forming a relationship a hard thing to do, and yet that is the only way we can escape our loneliness. It is also the only way we can truly get to know another person as the individual being that he or she is.

Nevertheless, we *do* manage to overcome all of these obstacles to form relationships, and in that way we *do* gain knowledge about others. However difficult the process, then, the model of forming human relationships is a promising program for learning about a personal God.

How do we begin? We learn most about people and we foster relationships with them through doing things together and through talking with each other. Observation and cogitation have limited value in such contexts. There are differences, of course, between what outside observers can learn from others' interactions with a given person and what the participants themselves come to know, and we shall need to keep this in mind as we explore the knowledge claims of those who profess to know God directly. Since God in the Jewish tradition is both personal and unique, however, human experience would suggest that we use common action and verbal communication in seeking knowledge about God, just as we do when we want to get to know another person. The Jewish tradition would confirm that suggestion, for historically Jews have experienced God not so much in cogitation, but rather in carrying out God's commandments, in revelation, and in prayer.

We shall explore the phenomenology and epistemological basis for these approaches to God in the chapters that follow. Halevi and recent theologians[21] appropriately warn us of the particular nature of each religious community's experience with God. Therefore, although I suspect that much of what I say is applicable in some form to Christianity and Islam, I shall leave it to devotees and scholars of those traditions to determine that, as I focus on Judaism.

The Proper Use of Reason to Know God

In light of the success we have had in modern times in using the methods of science to solve many kinds of problems, it is certainly understandable that logical positivists used science as their model for knowledge and measured all religious claims to know God by scientific criteria. Moreover, any claims to knowledge about God must be consistent with, and integrated into, our knowledge of other areas of life, and that too would argue for using scientific methods to obtain knowledge of God.

And yet those methods—observation, experimentation, and the reasoning based upon them—have been peculiarly unavailing in this endeavor. Even when philosophers thought they could prove the existence of God through observation and ratiocination, their work remained largely peripheral to the religious life of the masses and clergy—to say nothing of the theologically unconvinced.

This does not mean that experimental, scientific reason is irrelevant to the search for God; on the contrary, any theological quest which does not involve all of our reasoning powers as applied to all of our everyday experiences cannot possibly involve our whole beings and will most likely have difficulty making a justifiable claim for truth. What we have seen in this chapter, however, is that reason can be used in a variety of ways, and the mode of its use must be tailored to the subject matter to which it is being applied.

In religion, as in many aspects of science and other areas of life, it is nonhypothetical reasoning which is most often appropriate, and one must be aware of the communal and convictional nature of religious claims. Instead of straightforwardly applying the methods we use when we want to know objects, we must pay attention to the patterns in experience to which the religion attests, the grounds for asserting or denying such patterns, the meanings which they carry in the life of the person or community, and the degree of significance they have for the people who affirm them. We must also keep in mind that it is a personal God we are seeking to know, and so the methods we use to know God should be similar to those we use to know human persons. Since the actual religious life of Jews, Christians, and Muslims is centered on a personal God worshiped in a convictional community, the use of reason in this way holds the promise of producing a philosophy of religion more adequate than classical rational approaches to the phenomenon it seeks to explain.

3

KNOWING GOD THROUGH
HUMAN ACTION

Jews traditionally experienced God through divine words and actions and through their own. Their knowledge of God, then, derived from all four of these modes of interaction: God's words and deeds, and human utterances and actions. We shall examine each one of them to determine what contemporary Jews can and should learn from each mode.

We shall first consider what we can learn from human actions, then divine words, then divine actions, and finally human words. This order may seem strange at first. One might have expected, for example, to concentrate first on the human component of the relationship by considering what human words and deeds can tell us about God, followed by the parallel, divine elements. Such an order would keep our attention on the same agent in each of two sets of succeeding chapters. Alternatively, we might have kept the mode of interaction constant and switched the agent, looking first at the words with which human beings and God communicate and then at the acts they share (or vice versa). Although there is a clear logic behind any of these progressions, I have chosen to arrange the following chapters according to their educational, rather than their logical, order. Specifically, we shall go from the mode of divine-human interaction that moderns can most easily accept to that which is most problematic.

METHODOLOGY: HOW ACTION AFFORDS THEOLOGICAL KNOWLEDGE

Action as an Avenue to Knowledge

An oft-quoted rabbinic Midrash says the following:

> "They have deserted Me and have not kept My Law" (Jeremiah 16:11). God says, "Would that they had deserted Me and kept My Law, for if they had occupied themselves with the Law, the leaven [or, perhaps, the light] in it would have brought them back to Me."[1]

The boldness of God's willingness to be forgotten on condition that the People Israel observe His law accounts for the renown of this passage, but that unfortunately obscures the epistemological point that the last clause makes: practice of the law can be a method of coming into contact with God. The Jewish tradition makes that point emphatically through its insistence on observing Jewish law and on understanding it as God's commandments. The law is not only a set of decrees by an absolute monarch; it is a mode of revelation of God's will and, indirectly, of God's self. It is also the means by which we can imitate the Divine and join forces with God in acting in the world.

Contemporary Jews generally have not considered the epistemological basis for such claims, but many have intuitively adopted this approach. Secular Jews gingerly rediscovering their Judaism often begin the process by adopting some Jewish practices in their lives. This enables them to test the waters, so to speak, without making any further commitments, either in action or in belief. One can light candles on Friday night and have a Sabbath meal with family and friends, for example, simply because of the aesthetic beauty of these rituals. Even more demanding components of Jewish religious life like the dietary laws or fair business practices might be adopted for their inherent moral values without any theological commitments. What some Jews find, however, is what the rabbinic statement described—namely, that in carrying out these actions one may come, unexpectedly and perhaps even unwillingly, to know God.

How can action provide such knowledge? How, in fact, can action produce knowledge about anything? Since our early schooling makes a strong impression on all of us, we most often think of acquiring knowledge through a combination of verbal and mental processes, just as we did in school,[2] and not through what we do. How, then, can action serve in this capacity?

What We Learn through Action

Probably the clearest examples of how actions produce knowledge come from the area of technical skills. "Book learning" is often unnecessary and usually not sufficient to impart a skill. In athletics, for example, knowing all there is to know about the rules, the history, and the strategies of baseball will not make a good baseball player, but plenty of practice under the tutelage of an accomplished player or coach might. Similarly, one may know much about the history or philosophy of art, but one cannot learn to be an artist that way. One's own experience in

painting and the guidance one gains from the experience of
others are the tried and true ways of becoming an artist. Book
learning is more relevant to the training of automobile mechanics since the machinery is more complicated than bats and
balls or brushes and paints, but most mechanics only sharpen
their skills through formal courses. They learn their trade primarily by watching others more experienced than they and then
following their lead.

Our emotional maturity and sophistication are also dependent
upon experience. People often say, "You do not know what it
feels like until you have done it," and in many areas of life this is
true. One cannot understand or fully empathize with the joy of
having a child or the pain of a parent's death, for example, unless
one has experienced these events personally. Jewish law gives
poignant expression to this when it requires that all judges in a
capital case be people who have had children of their own;[3] only
then does one know fully the stakes involved, for the defendant
is, after all, somebody's child.

Similar considerations apply to morality. Children learn
about right and wrong through the reactions of their family and
friends to their behavior long before they are able to verbalize
anything about such standards, and that process carries on into
adulthood. Professional ethics, for instance, emerges primarily
from the actions and expectations of members of the profession.
Many professional groups, in fact, have only recently articulated
formal principles of ethics. Even when we are mature enough to
contemplate issues of moral conflict without being personally
involved in them, the most memorable and effective forms of
moral education ask us to imagine ourselves confronted with a
concrete case in which we have to act.

It is not only technical, emotional, and moral knowledge that
we acquire through action; we gain factual knowledge as well. I
learn, for example, what happens to skin if I sit in the sun too

long—however painful that lesson may be! I may learn this ahead of time (and without the pain) from books or discussions, but such detached learning is really only a substitute for my own, firsthand suffering. Moreover, that substitute is available to me only because somebody was sunburned before and warned me in writing about the consequences of too much exposure to the sun. In effect, much of our knowledge about ourselves, other people, and the world around us is gained either directly through our own experiences or vicariously through the actions and observations of others.

Confronting the Limits of Human Knowledge of God

It is considerably more complex epistemologically, though, to learn about the nature of God through obeying God's specific commandments. In contrast to the cases mentioned in the previous section, such learning through action cannot be easily confirmed by other modes of gleaning information, such as firsthand sensory experience or the reliable reports of others. I might be convinced that I am imitating and actually experiencing God when I help the downtrodden or do something to honor my parents, but atheists would say that I was simply acting on moral impulse or principal. In some situations, they might even claim that I was acting from self-interest while pretending to be motivated by more lofty concerns. In any case, they would deny that the theological language I use to describe my experience is either necessary or accurate.

If that is true for my own experiences, it is all the more so with regard to the allegedly theological experiences of others: why should I believe in *their* theological interpretation of their experiences? After all, to do so I would not only have to take their word that they had had the particular experiences in question, but I would also have to accept their understanding of their experiences. If I have had similar experiences of my own, and if I have no particular reason to distrust the people recounting their experiences to me, I might believe them. If I have not had such experiences, however, or if I have had them but hesitate myself to describe them in theological terms, or if I distrust the honesty or intelligence of those reporting their theological experiences, I would find them even less credible as evidence of God than my own potentially theological experiences.

All of these problems and more apply to the biblical account of Sinai. Modern scholarship concerning the recording and transmission of biblical texts has cast doubt on whether the biblical text we have in hand is an exact transcript of what went on at Sinai. Even if it is, in order to base one's belief in God on that account one must also accept the biblical author's interpretation of that event as indeed being a revelation of God. As Hume points out, however, there are very good reasons to distrust the Bible's story, and especially its interpretation of those events, since we are reading the reaction of slaves who most likely were easily overawed and deluded.[4] In sum, then, while I can justify my interpretations of my experiences with other human beings on the basis of relevant and clearly confirming evidence, I cannot readily do that for a theological interpretation of my own actions or those of others.

On the other hand, *all* of our modes of inquiry are the products of our human experiences, and all of them will have to be stretched if they are to enable us to deal with theological matters. One could, of course, refuse to do this; that is, one could choose not to make any rational commitments about matters which, by their very nature, do not lend themselves to full human understanding. As we have seen in the last chapter, however, this comes at a great cost: one cannot see the patterns which seem to inhere in the evidence, albeit with some rough edges, and one cannot therefore reap the benefits of acting on such patterns.

This, of course, does not excuse sloppy thinking in religion, but it does bespeak one of its central truths and foundations—specifically, that human knowledge is limited. This need not and should not lead religious people to abandon reason; on the contrary, that would not only be dangerous, but irreligious—an unappreciative squelching of the gift of reason given us by God.[5] What *is* needed is a conviction that our inability to understand fully need not and must not make us abandon the struggle to make sense out of what we can.

This epistemological stance makes good sense for all of our inquiries, but the subject matter of religion makes it especially important in that area. One of religion's central roles, after all, is to foster our thinking about ultimate issues, such as the meaning and goals of life, the import of our mortality for how we should think and live, the nature of human interaction and how to improve it, and the relationships among humanity, nature, and God. These are crucial matters for us all, affecting the very warp and woof of our being, but they do not lend themselves to full closure. We grapple with them throughout our lives. Religion provides a context to make us aware of the issues, encourage us to wrestle with them, and enhance our ability to do so through the perspective and the communal support it offers. In that way, we as individuals and as a community can better respond to the gamut of life's experiences, including those that we understand and those that we do not.

The Advantages of Using Action to Know God

One insight of the Jewish tradition is that learning through action is, in many ways, a better method to learn what we can about God than the usual observational and verbal alternatives. That is the message of the Midrash with which this chapter began, and it is the lesson that Judaism conveys through its focus on action. Of the 613 commandments in the Torah, virtually all require or prohibit specific actions. Obedience to these rules, of course, is logically based on, and rationalized by, certain beliefs; but the educational order is the opposite of the logical order.

> Rav Papa said: Scripture said: "That you may learn them and observe them faithfully" (Deuteronomy 5:1): [since observing the commandments is here presented as the ultimate goal, this verse teaches us that] whoever is engaged in observance is [also regarded as engaged] in study, but whoever is not engaged in observance is not [regarded as engaged] in study.
>
> [Rabban Gamliel's] son, Shimon, taught: . . . Not study, but doing mitzvot is the essence [of life].[6]

This is not to discourage study of the traditional texts; quite the contrary, the Rabbis much exalted it. In other places, in fact, they maintained that study is more important than action because study leads to action and, probably for that reason, study is to be counted as equivalent to performing all the other commandments.[7] The point is thus not that action can or should be our *only* road to God, but that its power to function as an independent road to God should be recognized, examined, and used. This is especially true for all Jews who have lived after the generation that stood at Sinai, for, lacking direct experience of that event, we generally come into contact with Jewish beliefs by first getting involved in Judaism's pattern of actions.

Action is central to knowing God for several reasons important to the objectives of religion. Actions are concrete and more easily learned than complex theological argumentation. Therefore, this type of learning is available to the young and uneducated as well as to the mature and learned.

Moreover, actions are repeatable, especially if they are short and specific, as many of the *mitzvot* (commandments) of Judaism are. It is difficult, if not impossible, to sustain any relationship on the basis of infrequent encounters, and that applies not only to our ties to other people but also to our links with God. The mind can be used for some of our learning about, and contacts with, God, but most of us do not spend much time cogitating about God. We therefore cannot depend exclusively upon an intellectual approach to God to sustain an ongoing relationship with the Eternal. That is why the system of commandments is so important: it reminds us about God and other elements of Judaism in numerous, brief spurts throughout each day. This insures that our knowledge of God does not become merely a piece of our intellectual storehouse, but rather influences how we think and live.

We want our knowledge of God to influence our whole being, not just a part of us. Cognitive knowledge all too often has little effect on our behavior. Rules for action, on the other hand, give specific instructions to the individual to act. If followed, they have an immediate impact on both the person acting and the animate and inanimate objects of the act. Moreover, actions enlist our bodies and often our mind, will, and emotions. A pattern of actions is thus a means of education especially appropriate to religion's goal of influencing not only one's mind, but one's whole being.

This last educational advantage in using actions to learn about God and to come in contact with the Holy One has a reciprocal disadvantage: rules for action directly influence our bodies, but they sometimes do not affect our minds or emotions. As creatures of habit, people often do things mechanically, not paying attention to the theological and/or social rationales for what they do. When that happens, many of the theological benefits that the Jewish system hopes to accomplish through its rules for action are lost. One can become, in Abraham Heschel's terms, a "religious behaviorist."[8]

Nevertheless, the Rabbis endorsed action as a means to know

God, for, as they said, "When one does something not for its own sake, one will ultimately come to do it for its own sake."[9] That is, an individual who abides by a rule will act with varying levels of awareness of the dimensions of its meaning. In the meantime, the pattern of actions will not only benefit others; it will also afford a constant invitation to the person acting and to the others affected to think about God. That opportunity will not always be realized, even for those most committed to religious thought and action; but the system of rules always holds out the promise of providing the means and motivation for future interactions with God. A pattern of repeated actions has the potential of making us much more frequently aware of God, such that religion has a constant and significant effect on our lives.

Even if we restrict our attention to the cognitive claims of religion, learning through action is no more problematic as a way to God than is learning through observation and thought. We do, after all, learn about the existence and nature of other people by doing things with and for them—more, probably, than we learn through observing them or thinking about them. Applying that mode of learning to God clearly involves an extension of our normal experience, but it is an extension of the method by which we gain the type of knowledge in human affairs closest to the type of knowledge that we seek in regard to God, i.e., knowledge of a personal being. As Halevi emphasized, the God of Abraham interacts with him, demands things, is open to persuasion, cares for people, and so forth; He has all of the traits, in other words, which we associate with a personality. Thus the way we learn about another entity with a personality, namely, human beings, seems like the most appropriate method to learn about God.

As explained in the previous chapters, all of our routes to knowledge—including observation, thinking, relationships, and action—make us aware of some aspects of reality which we then have to fit into our understanding of humanity, the world, and God. If we fail to use a method that can provide us with relevant information, or if we ignore what we can learn from any of our sources of knowledge, our conceptions will, to that extent, be a less adequate reflection of reality and in that fundamental sense, less true. Our actions, then, like our other paths to knowledge, should alert us to features of reality that should be part of our *construction* of experience, the way we sift through our experience and link parts of it with each other to make sense of it. Our actions should inform us of aspects of reality which we must build into our conception of ourselves, the world in which we live, and of God.

In this process, it is important to keep the active role of the knower in mind. It is, after all, *our* conception of God which we develop, in part, through attention to our actions. We each individually gain data from our actions to build into our concept of God, and we do that together as a convictional community as well.

Recognizing the limits of human knowledge, we must remember that no human conception can be totally adequate to reality, that, indeed, the differing conceptions of individuals and human communities may each have ingredients of truth. At the same time, we must also acknowledge that religious beliefs may make legitimate claims to truth and wisdom to the extent that they reflect the world as it is and ought to be. My Jewish affiliation, then, is only partly a matter of family history; it is also—perhaps centrally—an affirmation that the Jewish conception of God is convincing in its perception of reality and in its recipe for human action—i.e., in its vision of truth and in its wisdom. Judah Halevi, who stressed the role of family ties to a given religion and questioned the power of rational argument, was only partly right.

CONTENT: TWO EXAMPLES OF WHAT WE LEARN OF GOD THROUGH ACTION—DUTIES TO PARENTS AND OBSERVANCE OF THE SABBATH

In the remainder of this chapter we shall consider some concrete examples of what and how a Jew learns about God from action. The examples chosen are by no means exhaustive; but since one, honor and reverence for parents, deals with interpersonal relations and the other, the Sabbath, more directly expresses our relationship to God, and since the former partakes more of what we call the moral aspect of life and the latter is more ritual in nature, they will together provide a good illustration of how and what we learn from the variety of actions mandated by the tradition. We certainly come to know and feel the tenor of these commandments through the performance of them; the purpose of spelling out these examples is to demonstrate how and what they tell us about God.

After we have plumbed at least some of the theological content of both examples, we shall, in the next section of this chapter, examine the reasons for embodying such theological tenets in law and, in the section after that, the ways in which we can evaluate the truth and wisdom of principles embedded in actions. We shall, in other words, explore why one needs law to find God through action, and how we test whether we have indeed found God.

God as Worthy of Honor and Respect

The command to honor parents, the fifth of the Ten Commandments, is, for the Rabbis, not simply a matter of attitude. It requires specific actions, including the provision of food, clothing, and companionship.[10] The Midrash teaches a poignant

lesson based upon the juxtaposition of this, the Fifth Commandment, with the prohibition against murder, the Sixth:

> "Honor your father and your mother. . . . You shall not murder." Why are
> these two cases juxtaposed [in Exodus 20:12, 13]? To teach you: If a man
> has food in his house and does not share it with his father and mother, even
> when they are young, and most certainly when they are old, then he is
> considered as if he were an habitual murderer.[11]

Philo, a first-century Jewish thinker, suggests another lesson
based on the placement of the Fifth Commandment within the
structure of the Ten. The Ten Commandments are commonly
divided into two groups, the first five referring to the relationships between human beings and God, and the second group of
five referring to strictly human relationships. That makes the
command to honor parents the last of the commandments governing our relationship with God, just before those relating to
the human community exclusively. Noting this, Philo suggests
that the command to honor one's parents is placed in that
position so that it acts as a bridge between God and human
beings, for it is our parents who teach us both how to behave in
human society and how we are to think and act toward God.
That is, in the process of growing up, we learn to honor God by
first honoring our parents; as we grow older, we continue to
experience and honor God each time we do something to honor
our parents.

> After dealing with the seventh day [the Fourth of the Ten Command-
> ments], He gives the Fifth Commandment on the honor due to parents.
> This commandment He placed on the borderline between the two sets of
> five: it is the last of the first set, in which the most sacred injunctions
> [relating to God] are given, and it adjoins the second set, which contain the
> duties of human beings to each other. The reason, I think, is this: we see
> that parents by their nature stand on the borderline between the mortal and
> the immortal sides of existence—the mortal, because of their kinship with

people and other animals through the perishableness of the body; the
immortal, because the act of generation assimilates them to God, the
progenitor of everything. . . .

Some bolder spirits, glorifying the name of parenthood, say that a father
and mother are in fact gods revealed to sight, who copy the Uncreated in
His work as the Framer of life. He, they say, is the God or Maker of the
world; they [the parents] only of those whom they have begotten. How
can reverence be rendered to the invisible God by those who show
irreverence to the gods who are near at hand and seen by the eye?[12]

Parents prepare the psyche of the child for the experience of
honoring God, and by acting to honor parents, one honors God.
Rabbinic literature expresses the same theme:

Rabbi [Judah the President] says: the honoring of one's father and mother
is very dear in the sight of Him by whose word the world came into being,
for He declared honoring them to be equal to honoring Him, revering
them to revering Him, and cursing them to cursing Him. [This is followed
by biblical proof texts to demonstrate exactly how one can learn that God
has equated these.][13]

There is another commandment in the Torah shaping relationships to parents: "You shall each *revere* his mother and his
father and keep my Sabbaths: I the Lord am your God" (Leviticus 19:3). In analyzing this text, the Rabbis ask two important
questions: how is it related to the command to *honor* one's
parents, and what are we to learn from its juxtaposition of
reverence for parents and keeping the Sabbath? To the first
question, they answer thus:

Our Rabbis taught: What is reverence *(mora)* and what is honor *(kavod)?*
Reverence means that he [the son] must neither stand in his [the father's]
place nor sit in his place, nor contradict his words, nor tip the scales against
him [in an argument with others]. Honor means that he must give him
food and drink, clothe and cover him, lead him in and out.[14]

Another rabbinic passage on the same page of Talmud requires that, as an act of reverence, one not address one's parents by their first names but rather call them, "My father (mother), my teacher."

In these talmudic specifications of the biblical commands, reverence involves *refraining* from certain activities; honor consists in positive obligations to *act*. Both apply throughout one's life. One gets the impression, however, that the duties of reverence primarily fit one's childhood while those of honor apply most often when one is already an adult. Both reverence and honor are demanded of daughters as well as sons, and apply to mothers as well as fathers.[15]

What do these commands teach us about God? In almost Freudian terms, God serves, in part, as an extension of our parents. According to the Rabbis, in fact, God is one of our parents:

> There are three partners in the creation of every human being: the Holy One, blessed be He, the father, and the mother. The father provides the white matter [probably because semen is white], from which are formed the bones, sinews, nails, brain, and the white part of the eye. The mother provides the red matter [probably because menstrual blood is red], from which are formed the skin, flesh, hair, and pupil of the eye. The Holy One, blessed be He, infuses into each person breath, soul, features, vision, hearing, speech, power of motion, understanding, and intelligence.[16]

Through showing honor and respect for parents, then, one learns, as Philo noted, how to relate to God.

Honor and respect are appropriate in both cases because both God and parents have a role in bringing us into being, in nurturing us physically and psychologically, and in teaching us how to live. Both also have physical power over us—at least, in the case of parents, in our early years—and both influence us psychologically throughout our lives. One must learn these attitudes and the justifications for them intellectually, incorporating awareness of them into one's perspective of oneself and one's relations to others; indeed, a portion of this one must apply even to the inanimate world, recognizing our dependence on it and the aptness of our gratitude for it. Beyond our intellects, however, this knowledge must penetrate our being, shaping our personalities. Humility, care and concern for others, piety, and gratitude are the virtues one learns from honoring and respecting one's parents.

These lessons are so important, that, according to the Rabbis, God puts honor and reverence for parents on a par with the honor and reverence due God; according to one rabbinic text, God makes it even more obligatory:

> Great is the precept to honor parents since the Holy One, blessed be He, attached to it still greater importance than the honoring of Himself. It is written, "Honor your father and mother" (Exodus 20:12), and also "Honor the Lord with your substance" (Proverbs 3:9). With what do you honor God? With that which He has bestowed upon you, as when you carry out such laws as the forgotten sheaf, the corner of the field, tithes, charity to the poor, etc. If you possess the means of fulfilling these commandments, do so; but if you are destitute, you are not under the obligation. With the honoring of parents, however, no such condition is made. Whether you have means or not, you must fulfill the commandment, even if you have to go begging from door to door.[17]

There are two exceptions to this ranking. The Torah includes an explicit, positive command to "love the Lord your God with all your heart, with all your soul, and with all your might" (Deuteronomy 6:5), a verse which is included in a central prayer, the *Shema*, recited twice daily. Although one must honor and revere one's parents, one important strain in the tradition asserts that a child is not obligated to love them. Rabbi Shelomo Yizhaki ("Rashi," 1035–1104), the most popular Jewish medieval commentator on the Bible, and other medieval and modern rabbis claim that one must, reasoning that love of parents is included in the command to honor them or to love one's neighbor as oneself (Leviticus 19:18).[18] Maimonides, however, draws a distinction:

> Know that the Torah has placed us under a heavy obligation in regard to the proselyte. For we were commanded to honor and revere our parents, and to obey the prophets. . . . Now it is possible for a man to honor and revere and obey those whom he does not love. But with the proselyte there is a command to love him with a great, heartfelt love . . . much as we are commanded to love God Himself.[19]

Clearly, it is best to honor one's parents out of love and to love them while fulfilling the duties of honoring them, but that is not always how we feel. The law demands honor and respect of parents, but, at least according to Maimonides, it does not demand love of them. It does, however, require not only honor and reverence for God, but also love of God, even when, as in the case of the biblical Job, one feels anything but love.

There is another way in which honor and respect for God supersedes that for parents, and that is derived from the juxtaposition of the commands to revere one's parents and keep My Sabbaths in Leviticus 19:3. The Rabbis read the "and" of this verse such that the second clause is a condition for the first: "You shall each revere his mother and his father and [that is, *on condition that,* or, *as long as*] you keep My Sabbaths." They therefore say:

> It is possible to think that even if the father ordered his son to defile himself or not to return a lost article which he had found, he is to obey him; consequently there is a verse to teach, "You shall each revere his mother and his father, and keep My Sabbaths." All of you are alike bound to honor Me.[20]

Thus the honor of God required of us exceeds that of parents when the latter would entail disobedience of a divine command. We *are* children of our human parents, but our divine parentage takes precedence. Even parents are not to be treated as gods; the fitting object for unlimited piety and gratitude is God, upon whom one depends for everything during all of one's life.

Three Themes of the Sabbath

This sets the stage for the second part of Leviticus 19:3, the command to observe the Sabbath. The laws of the Jewish Sabbath, as the Rabbis said, "are like mountains hanging on a hair, for they consist of little Bible and many laws."[21] Nevertheless, in obeying them, the Jew is powerfully reminded of the two themes that the Bible attaches to the Sabbath in no less prominent a position than the Ten Commandments. In the first version of the Fourth Commandment, the Sabbath is to remind us of God's creation, while the second version has it remind us of the Exodus from Egypt:

Exodus 20:8–11:
  Remember the Sabbath day and keep it holy. Six days you shall labor and do all your work, but the seventh day is a sabbath of the Lord your God: you shall not do any work—you, your son or daughter, your male or female slave, or your cattle, or the stranger who is within your settlements. For in six days the Lord made heaven and earth and sea, and all that is in them, and He rested on the seventh day; therefore the Lord blessed the Sabbath day and hallowed it.

Deuteronomy 5:12–15:
  Observe the Sabbath day and keep it holy, as the Lord your God has commanded you. Six days you shall labor and do all your work, but the seventh day is a sabbath of the Lord your God: you shall not do any work—you, your son or your daughter, your male or female slave, your ox or your ass, or any of your cattle, or the stranger in your settlements, so that your male and female slave may rest as you do. Remember that you were a slave in the land of Egypt and the Lord your God freed you from

there with a mighty hand and an out-stretched arm; therefore the Lord your God has commanded you to observe the Sabbath day.

In addition to these biblical themes, the Rabbis added faith in redemption to the ideational structure of the Sabbath. To convey these theological messages to each and every Jew, the Rabbis made these three topics—creation, exodus/revelation, and redemption—the major themes of Sabbath worship.

Specifically, aside from the *Shema* and its accompanying blessings, the central prayer of all Jewish daily services is the *Amidah* (literally, "standing," since it is recited while standing). Each *Amidah* throughout the year begins with the same three blessings (together with the paragraphs which precede those blessings and develop their themes) and ends with the same three blessings; it is the middle section of the *Amidah* which varies according to the occasion. On the Sabbath the middle section concludes with one blessing thanking God for sanctifying the Sabbath day, but the paragraphs which precede that blessing vary. On Friday evening they speak primarily of God's creation, on Saturday morning of God's revelation, and on Saturday afternoon of God's redemption.[22] In other words, the holiness of the Sabbath, the special character of the day, is a product of at least these three interlocked motifs which constitute its message.

How does obeying the Sabbath rules teach and remind the Jew of these three theological themes? In this chapter, we shall briefly indicate how Sabbath observance conveys the import of God's creation and redemption, the two themes most directly connected to knowing God through action, leaving revelation to the next chapter.

God as Creator

"You have hallowed the seventh day for Your name's sake, the goal of the creation of heaven and earth, and You have blessed it above all days and sanctified it above all seasons." These are the words with which the middle section of Friday evening's *Amidah* begins. They spell out clearly that the reason for observing the day is to celebrate God's creative act. Part of the meaning of this is that we should imitate God *(imitatio dei)*, that since God rested on the seventh day, we should also—an implication of the creation theme which was recognized as early as the writings of Philo (first century) and the *Mekhilta of Rabbi Simeon bar Yohai* (second century).[23]

It is moreover that the Sabbath is a day that God set aside, and we rest in obedience of God's commandment and in gratitude for God's creative act. This is undoubtedly the root meaning of the Bible's linking of the Sabbath to creation, for, as Moshe Greenberg, Professor of Bible at Hebrew University, has pointed out, when the Sabbath is understood this way its theme is precisely the same as that of the first three and the fifth of the Ten Commandments, that is, honor of God. As we have noted, the Jewish tradition has long understood the first five of the Ten Commandments as a set dealing with the relationship between God and humanity, while the second five concern the relationships of people with each other. Greenberg points out that the first five not only have a common subject, but also a common theme, specifically, that we should honor God. From this perspective, the inclusion of the Sabbath in the Ten Commandments and its placement among the first five make very good sense: we are to rest on the Sabbath as a mark of respect for God.[24]

Rabbi Samson Raphael Hirsch (1815–1889), founder of the Neo-Orthodox approach to Judaism, has spelled out in detail how Sabbath observance expresses honor of God. While we are allowed—actually, commanded—to shape the world for human purpose during six days of the week, Jews must desist from that every seventh day in recognition of the fact that God owns the world and human beings enjoy only delegated and limited authority to manipulate it.[25] Consequently the association of the Sabbath with Creation articulates nothing less than the proper relationship between God and humanity: the Sabbath is a graphic expression and reminder of the fact that God owns the world, not we.

Those who have been in New York City may know of an interesting parallel that will illustrate this. There is a street in Rockefeller Center that is open to the public every day of the year except December 25th. It must be closed at least one day a year in order to reassert the owner's authority over that piece of property; otherwise ownership would pass to the public. Similarly, we lose the right to use the world for our purposes each Sabbath so that God's ownership may be reasserted and recognized.

But it is not only our own desires to work that must be set aside on the Sabbath; it is also those of any other human being. Rest thus clearly proclaims that God, rather than any person, is our master, since we must obey God's command to rest in preference to the command of any human authority. Judah Halevi (1075–1141), in his philosophical dialogue between a rabbi and the king of the Khazars, emphasizes this theme by putting most of the following remarks in the mouth of the king. He thus indicates that even the king, the highest ranking human master, recognizes that one implication of Sabbath rest is that human authorities take second place to God. He also points out that Sabbath rest adds dignity to our lives because we reaffirm our connection to God, and it simultaneously preserves our identity as Jews:

> The King of the Khazars: I have often reflected about you, and I have come to the conclusion that God has some secret design in preserving you, and that He appointed the Sabbath and holy days among the strongest means of preserving your strength and lustre. The nations broke you up

and made you their servants. . . . They would even have made you their warriors were it not for those festive seasons observed by you with so much conscientiousness. . . . Had these not been, not one of you would put on a clean garment; you would hold no congregation to remember the law, on account of your everlasting affliction and degradation. Had these not been, you would not enjoy a single day in your lives. Now, however, you are allowed to spend the sixth part of your life in rest of body and soul. Even kings are unable to do likewise, as their souls have no respite on their days of rest. If the smallest business calls them on that day to work and stir, they must move and stir, complete rest being denied to them. Had these laws not been, your toil would benefit others, because it would become their prey. Whatever you spend on these days is your profit for this life and the next, because it is spent for the glory of God.[26]

Rabbi Abraham Joshua Heschel (1907–1972) elucidated another theological meaning inherent in the creation theme of the Sabbath. He points out that "reality to us is thinghood, consisting of substances that occupy space; even God is conceived by most of us as a thing." Judaism does not negate the reality or value of the concrete; on the contrary, none other than God created the world and declared it good. Moreover, "time and space are interrelated, [and] to overlook either of them is to be partially blind." However, "it is not a thing that lends significance to a moment; it is the moment that lends significance to things."

In order to release people from their enslavement to things and simultaneously to impart significance to the world of space, Judaism sanctifies moments. Indeed, "Jewish ritual may be characterized as the art of significant forms in time, as *architecture of time*," for most of its observances are initiated by a specific time. Thus, in addition to the Sabbath, the festivals, the High Holy Days, the New Moons, and the Sabbatical and Jubilee years all must be marked at their appointed seasons. Similarly, the daily services become mandatory at given times of the day, not at particular places. Furthermore, "the main themes of the faith lie in the realm of time. We remember the day of the exodus from Egypt, the day when Israel stood at Sinai; and our messianic hope is the expectation of a day, of the end of days . . ."

Why this emphasis on time? Because, says Heschel, time is "a dimension in which the human is at home with the divine; a dimension in which man aspires to approach the likeness of the divine." No mountain or sea can approach the essence or grandeur of God, "yet the likeness of God can be found in time, which is eternity in disguise." Heschel is at pains to avoid any denigration of space or denial of its reality—a popular position among the Orientals, the Greeks, the Gnostics, and segments of Christianity—but in this era, when we overemphasize the importance of things and neglect the significance of time, he underscores the necessity to shed our insensitivity to that dimension. We must not only measure time and calculate salaries by it; we must set aside and appreciate moments, not only for our own greater enjoyment of life, but so that we can learn and remind ourselves of, and partake in, an attribute of God.

> The meaning of the Sabbath is to celebrate time rather than space. Six days a week we live under the tyranny of things of space; on the Sabbath we try to become attuned to *holiness in time*. It is a day on which we are called upon to share in what is eternal in time, to turn from the results of creation to the mystery of creation, from the world of creation to the creation of the world.[27]

Rabbi Mordecai Kaplan (1881–1983) derives other theological lessons from the Sabbath's creation theme. "The Sabbath," according to Kaplan, "implies an affirmation that the world is so constituted as to afford man the opportunity for salvation." It does that through three of its themes: creation, holiness, and covenantship. The first, creation, proclaims that the world is not frozen in its present state; it can be molded. Just as God "renews each day the works of creation," in the language of the daily liturgy, so too human beings can create. Human efforts to improve ourselves and the world about us are not inevitably futile; when we plan and execute things well, we can succeed, for God has made the world so that it can be shaped and reshaped.

> *The moral implication of the traditional teaching that God created the world is that creativity, or the continuous emergence of aspects of life not prepared for or determined by the past, constitutes the most divine phase of reality.* . . . The Sabbath is regarded in Jewish tradition as celebrating the creation of the world. . . . The belief in God as a creator, or its modern equivalent, the conception of the creative urge as the element of godhood in the world, is needed to fortify the yearning for spiritual self-regeneration. That yearning dies down unless it is backed by the conviction that there is something which answers to it in the very character of life as a whole. *There can hardly be any more important function for religion than to keep alive this yearning for self-renewal and to press it into the service of human progress.*[28]

These three implications of the Creation theme—that God owns the world, that we share a piece of eternity with God when we sanctify moments, and that our own creative efforts are, given the structure of the world God created, reasonable, worthy, and indeed divine—convey important elements of Judaism's perspective of God as well as its view of humanity. God neither creates as a random act, nor abandons the world after creation. Instead, God continues to assert ownership over the world and expects us to recognize that claim. God is eternal and we are not, but we are aware of the domain of time and can even share a piece of God's eternity by devoting one day in seven to an appreciation of time and eternal values. On that day, among other things, we reinforce our understanding of ourselves as potentially creative beings whose efforts can make a difference, for God continues to create and bids us do likewise. This gives us a sense of the divine worth that God has imparted to each one of us.

God as Redeemer

"What was created on the Sabbath day after God rested? Peace of mind, rest, contentment, and quiet."[29] The Jewish Sabbath lasts from shortly before sunset on Friday to approximately 45 minutes after sunset on Saturday. Jews who observe the Sabbath commonly sleep longer on Friday nights than on other nights of the week, and the Sabbath afternoon nap is an honored institution. This additional rest on the Sabbath day is one of the many joys of the Sabbath.

It has, however, deeper meanings—some of which are misunderstood. Sabbath rest is certainly not for lack of other things to do, and it is not a pragmatic measure to give one energy for the tasks of the week to come.[30] It is rather an integral part of the mood and messages of the day.

The middle section of the *Amidah* on Saturday afternoon speaks of the Sabbath rest as "a true and genuine rest that yields peace and tranquility, serenity and confidence, a perfect rest." The text is based in part on Chapter 14 of the Book of Zekhariah, which looks forward to an ideal future in which everyone recognizes God as Lord. Moreover, the special melody *(nusah)* designated for that service is slow and relaxing, communicating the mood of the afternoon of the Sabbath and the hopes for messianic times in which people live in harmony with each other and with nature.[31] The meaning of the root of the Hebrew word for Sabbath, *Shabbat,* is *shavat,* "desist." On the Sabbath we desist from interfering with nature and the social order, and live with the world as it is.

There is nothing wrong with the work that we do during the week; on the contrary, we must work for pragmatic, psychological, and theological reasons. Pragmatically, we do not live in an ideal world, in which everything is provided; we must labor to satisfy our needs. Adam is put into the Garden of Eden "to work it and safeguard it" (Genesis 2:15), and when he is expelled from the garden, it is only with the sweat of his brow that he can eat bread (Genesis 3:19). The Rabbis similarly insisted that only when a person toils with both hands will the Holy One grant blessing.[32]

Psychologically, too, we need to work. As the Rabbis noted:

> If one is unemployed, what should he do? If he has a courtyard or a field in a state of decay, let him busy himself with it. For Scripture says, "Six days shall you labor and do all your work" (Exodus 20:9). For what purpose were the words "and do all your work" added [it being assumed that the Torah would not say anything superfluous and would not use two different words for the exact same activity]? It is to include an [unemployed] person who has a courtyard or a field in a state of decay, that he should go and busy himself with them. . . . A man only dies through idleness.[33]

Similarly, even a wife with a hundred servants must do some work, for idleness, according to the Mishnah, leads to lewdness and the mental anguish of boredom.[34] Put positively, the Rabbis said: "Great is work, for it honors the laborers."[35]

For the Jewish tradition, work also has several theological dimensions. God's commandment is, "Six days shall you labor and do all your work" as well as "the seventh day is a Sabbath of the Lord your God: you shall not do any work" (Exodus 20:9–10).[36] We thus follow God's command when we work. Moreover, God specifically created the world unfinished so that we can and must work to complete it, thereby becoming God's partners in creation.[37] We must, in other words, engage in work not only for our livelihood, but also for *tikkun olam,* for "fixing the world." God, in fact, respects work to such an extent that He refused to dwell among the Israelites until they had done the work of constructing a proper sanctuary for Him.[38]

The point of desisting from work on the Sabbath is therefore not that Judaism disdains work, but rather that in doing our work we not forget the goal for which we strive. Work must not become an idol which we worship with all our time and effort. Instead, it is to be done to enable us to live, to study, to have and educate children, and to contribute to others. Ultimately, we work to do our part in creating the messianic era, a time in which there is no need for changes in nature or the social order brought about by our labor because everything is provided and all creatures live in perfect harmony. Rest on the Sabbath thus simultaneously conveys two messages that are two sides of the same coin: work is necessary, dignified, and indeed commanded; but it is not the ultimate goal in life, and, thus, should not occupy all our time and energy.

As a graphic reminder of these lessons, the Sabbath is, as the Saturday afternoon liturgy describes it, God's gift of splendor, salvation, rest, and holiness. Through it we taste redemption. As the Rabbis put it, the Sabbath is "a foretaste of the World to Come."[39]

God as Holy

Chapter 19 of Leviticus is a collection of laws dealing with varied aspects of life, including our two examples—revering parents and observing the Sabbath—as well as agricultural rules and commands to provide for the poor, to maintain honest weights and measures, and to love one's neighbor as oneself. All of these are specific instances of the general principle with which the chapter begins, "You shall be holy, for I, the Lord your God, am holy."

Since English is a language created and spoken mostly by Christians, the English word "holiness" may connote holy ghosts and other nonterrestrial entities or characteristics. The Hebrew term for which "holiness" is a translation, though, means "separate." One is to be special in one's behavior—

separated from most human beings—in the ways specified in
Chapter 19 of Leviticus in order to be Godlike. As the Rabbis
later put it:

> "Follow the Lord your God" (Deuteronomy 13:5). What does this mean?
> Is it possible for a mortal to follow God's Presence? The verse means to
> teach us that we should follow the attributes of the Holy One, praised be
> He. As He clothes the naked, you should clothe the naked. The Bible
> teaches that the Holy One visited the sick; you should visit the sick. The
> Holy One comforted those who mourned; you should comfort those who
> mourn. The Holy One buried the dead; you should bury the dead.[40]

Notice that, for the Rabbis, acting in these ways is not just to
imitate God *(imitatio dei);* it is the human way of following God's
Presence, of becoming as close as we can to being one with God.

Thus, one comes in contact with God not only in actions such
as honoring and revering parents, where we are reminded of our
subordinate status; but we link ourselves to God each time we
do any of the myriad of actions mandated by the Commandments. Rabbi Shelomo Yizhaki ("Rashi") notes that only some
of the verses of Chapter 19 of Leviticus end with the words,
"And you shall revere (fear) the Lord." Since all of the laws
derive their authority from God's command, why, he asks, do
the others lack that closing phrase? He suggests that those that
have it are the rules that we would be most tempted to violate
since other human beings cannot know that we have trans-
gressed; hence the need to be reminded that God stands behind
them. In reality, though, all of the commandments should be
done from an awareness of God's command, for then the commandments are most effective in linking us with God.[41] If one
obeys the laws indicated with the intent of fulfilling God's
directive, one acts not only in response to God; one acts as the
Jewish tradition holds that God acts. One responds to the world
as God does. One becomes, in a word, holy.

The Role of Law in Effectuating Principles

Even if one accepts all or most of the principles discussed above, why must they be encased in law? Christianity historically has objected to Judaism's insistence on using law as one of religion's forms, and many contemporary Jews, influenced by the Western emphasis on individualism and autonomy, share this view.[42] For that matter, the Jewish tradition itself was painfully aware of one of the chief dangers in using law—namely, that acting in accordance with the law will become for some people an end rather than a means. In performing the required actions out of habit rather than out of conviction, people become "religious behaviorists," doing what they are required to do, but blind to the phenomena and meanings the law was intended to reveal. The Rabbis therefore repeatedly raise the question, in a variety of contexts, of whether fulfillment of the commandments requires appropriate intention, and if so, what the nature of that intention must be.[43] Why, then, does Judaism link these matters of the conscience and the spirit to law? Put more broadly, how is law supposed to help us find God?

Law gives principles concrete application and reality. Values and ideas are at the heart of what it means to be a person and a Jew, and yet we live in a world of objects and forces. Thoughts and values can only become part of our lives if they are somehow translated into the world of concrete objects. Law does that. It coordinates ideas and values with specific patterns of action that express them. In so doing, law enables us to make them an active part of our lives.

Let us see how this works in the examples we have used in this chapter. Honor and reverence for parents, when delineated and demanded in law, are no longer exclusively matters of emotion or pious, but ephemeral ideals; they are instead the values that require us to provide food and clothing for parents, call parents

"Mother" and "Father" or the affectionate "Mom" and "Dad" but not by their first names, refrain from contradicting one's parents in public, and so forth. Obeying these commands can be a reminder of our obligations to God and of the ways in which parents symbolize the divine for us. Similarly, God's creation of the world is not restricted to the world of metaphysical principles when the Sabbath laws transform it into a special day to experience the import of that principle in what we say and do. The laws requiring Jews to perform specific acts on the Sabbath and refrain from others make the principle part of our consciousness and behavior. We not only think about God's continuing ownership of everything and everyone, but we experience the ramifications of it. With that principle embedded in our minds, throughout the week we are less likely to take the world for granted and more likely "to use it and safeguard it."

In providing specific details and demands, *law defines principles.* Honoring one's parents, for example, *could* be interpreted to require merely a specific attitude. Alternatively, it *could* prescribe total obedience to parents' demands, or love, or actions other than the ones specified in Jewish law. Similarly, the Jewish Sabbath *could* be like the Christian or the Muslim one. By requiring certain activities and prohibiting others, Jewish law defines (literally, "sets limits to") the Sabbath by establishing what behavior is inside and what behavior is outside its boundaries. Without that kind of definition both the ideas of the Jewish Sabbath and the experience of it would become vague and amorphous. The distinctively Jewish character and message of the Jewish Sabbath are thus largely the products of Jewish law.

Law is a teaching device. Logically, principles precede the actions which express them, but what comes first logically is not necessarily what comes first educationally or practically. We discover, for example, that we may not steal Johnny's marbles long before we learn the general theories of ethics that explain why.

At first we may refrain from stealing the marbles simply because we do not want to make Mommy or Daddy—or Johnny—angry; it is only later that we acquire general notions of property, divine and social expectations, and action on principle. When that time comes, the experience we have had in interacting with people and their property helps us considerably in mastering the abstract idea because we can relate it to situations and actions that we have already experienced. As we have seen, Judaism adopts this as a general principle: while it is clearly best to do the right thing for the right reasons, if one cannot do that, Judaism would have one do the right thing anyway, "for out of doing the right thing for the wrong reason one will come to do it for the right reason."[44]

Our two examples are no exception. We learn the meaning of reverence and honor for parents (and, as Philo reminds us, for God) when we discover that certain behaviors toward them are condemned and others are expected. We may not even be able to understand the meaning of the words "honor" and "reverence" until we have had such experiences. Similarly, when we begin to observe the Sabbath, we may not fully comprehend all of its ideas and values, but the law at least directs our actions to be in consonance with them. It does more: it establishes a framework of special actions that begs us to ask "Why?" It thereby encourages us to probe the meaning of the Sabbath legislation and to become more conscious of the Sabbath's themes. Ultimately, we can come to appreciate its messages of God's Creation, Revelation, and Redemption, with the Sabbath experiences a guide to their specific Jewish meaning. The law thus teaches us what to do, it stimulates us to ask questions so that we can more fully understand the meaning of life, and it provides a framework to understand some answers.

Finally, *the law creates a community*. On the most obvious of practical grounds, one cannot have a community unless people agree to abide by rules governing their behavior toward each other. The need for law goes beyond this, however. Communities need law not only to establish minimally acceptable behavior, but also to motivate their members to accomplish social ideals. Honor and respect for parents are good examples. A community can surely survive without effectuating those values, but its character would be quite different—from my perspective, much impoverished—from one that embodied them. The law specifies the behavior required of people to make honor and reverence of parents a living value in society, and it communicates the group's insistence that its members follow its rules to accomplish that end. This contributes mightily to both group identity and group spirit.

Communities also need rituals to express their social cohesion and character. The Sabbath certainly functions in that way for Jews. Those who abide by the laws of the Sabbath feel an immediate kinship with others who do so. Such people know the same enriching experiences, and their observance of the Sabbath indicates that they hold many of the same values and beliefs. This, of course, excludes others who do not obey the Sabbath laws, but not out of prejudice; any Jew who decides to "join the club" may do so by simply obeying the rules, and non-Jews can do likewise by converting to Judaism and observing the Sabbath. In the meantime, Sabbath legislation and custom create the structure for Jews to share a day each week in fellowship, worship, study, and family and communal gathering, making for a powerful element in Jewish group identity.[45] Even Asher Ginsberg ("Ahad Ha-Am," 1856–1927), a secular Zionist, wanted to maintain the Sabbath for communal, if not religious, reasons:

> A Jew who feels a real tie with the life of his people throughout the generations will find it utterly impossible to think of the existence of Israel

without the Sabbath. One can say without exaggeration that more than Israel has kept the Sabbath, the Sabbath has kept Israel. Had it not been for the Sabbath, which weekly restored to the people their "soul" and weekly renewed their spirit, the weekday afflictions would have pulled them farther and farther downward until they sank to the lowest depths of materialism as well as ethical and intellectual poverty. Therefore one need not be a Zionist in order to feel all the traditional sacred grandeur that hovers over this "good gift," and to rise up with might against all who seek to destroy it.[46]

Can one gain these advantages without law? Paul, especially in the New Testament's Book of Romans, thought so. He actually went further, claiming that law is in some ways detrimental to attaining spiritual goals. Much of Christendom has adopted his view.[47] In practice, however, Christian denominations often have specific rules. Historically these canons have been enforced with punishments as harsh as torture and death, and some groups of Christians still impose excommunication.

The Jewish tradition, in contrast, has consistently and unreservedly maintained that law is essential for the life of the spirit, in part for the reasons delineated above. Moreover, from the Jewish perspective, God demands obedience of the law. The content of the law may change over the course of time, but the corpus of the law, however it is defined in a given time and place, is obligatory.

The modern Reform Movement does not accept this binding character of Jewish law, and many contemporary Jews do not abide by it. For these people, Jewish law clearly cannot function in the ways described in this section. Only those who obey it can expect to reap its rewards.

For those who do abide by it, though, Jewish law remains a powerful mechanism through which one can learn of God's ways, be motivated to follow them, and come in contact with God. It transforms one's actions into a quest for the holy.

THE TRUTH VALUE AND WISDOM OF THESE THEOLOGICAL CLAIMS

The intent of this chapter is to explore the ways in which action can produce knowledge of ordinary things and of God. As examples of the latter, we have delineated some of the theological implications of the biblical commandments to honor and revere one's parents and to observe the Sabbath, and we have shown why these lessons must be encased in law if they are to affect our lives significantly. We have yet, however, to indicate how these implications constitute theoretical and practical *knowledge.* In what sense, in other words, do honoring and revering parents and observing the Sabbath inform us of truths about the world and about God? And how do we know that these prescriptions for action are wise? We have described how these actions bespeak specific convictions about life, but how can we test whether the claims behind these convictions are true and wise?

What the Examples Teach

In order to examine the truth status of the theological lessons we have derived from the commandments we have discussed, let us first summarize them. In obeying the commands to honor and revere one's parents, the Jewish tradition would have one learn the following about God:

1. Our parents are the bridge for us between human beings and God. They are not intermediaries between us and God, and they are not the medium through which we experience God and interact with the Holy One. In Judaism, no human being plays those roles; we experience God directly. From our parents, however, we learn proper attitudes and behavior toward others

and toward God. Indeed, by honoring our parents, according to the tradition, we honor and experience God.

2. Our very understanding of "God," in fact, is, in part, an extension of what our parents mean to us. Both God and our parents created and sustain us, care for us, have power over us, and teach us how to live. It is therefore no surprise that one of the traditional appellations of God is "our Father." By attributing these qualities to God, Judaism claims that they are not restricted to our parents, but rather characterize experience as a whole and the independent Being who creates it.

3. It is not clear whether Jewish law requires love of parents in addition to honoring and respecting them, but the tradition demands that one love God, even when faced with adversity.

4. Even parents are not to be treated as gods, and therefore God's commands must be obeyed in preference to conflicting demands of parents.

Carrying out the laws of the Sabbath can teach us the following about God and about the divine-human relationship:

1. We are to imitate God in both creating six days a week and desisting from creation on the seventh. In affirming our connection to God in this way, we add dignity to our work and, indeed, to our lives, for both our work and our rest follow God's example.

2. God created the world such that human effort can bear fruit. We can use our faculties for evil ends; God has given us the freedom and ability to do that. When we direct our energies toward good purpose, however, we imitate God's creation of the universe. Unlike God, we cannot create out of nothing; our creativity is limited to fashioning things anew. Since God has created the world such that we can succeed in many of our efforts, however, striving to be creative in a positive way is not

an activity necessarily bound for frustration. On the contrary, when human beings overcome obstacles and successfully create new, good things, they participate in a divine activity and are themselves regenerated.

3. God's creation of us and provision for us should evoke in us gratitude and obedience.

4. God owns the world; in the words of the Psalmist, "The earth and everything in it belongs to God, the world and all its inhabitants" (Psalm 24:1).[48] Human authority to manipulate the world is therefore delegated and limited. Hence not only one's own desires, but also those of any human master must be set aside in deference to God's commands.

5. Work is necessary and desirable for pragmatic, psychological, and theological reasons, but it is not, and must not become, the ultimate goal of life. We work so that we can sustain ourselves physically, psychologically, and spiritually in this world and help God create an ideal world, a "kingdom of the Almighty."

6. God is eternal, a divine characteristic which we can appreciate and share when we set aside moments in time.

7. Obeying God's commands (including, but not restricted to, the Sabbath) is the way open to humans to become as close to God as they can, to see and respond to the world as we believe God does, to be holy.

How These Lessons Function in the Life of the Jew

As we survey these statements, several things should be clear about them. First, those who honor and revere their parents and observe the Sabbath would probably not be aware of all of these lessons each time they act in these ways. At the same time, the implications described above would not seem strange to them. On the contrary, such people, when shown these dimensions of

their actions, would undoubtedly feel that the suggested interpretations increase the significance of their acts.

Second, the tenets listed above all fit into the Jewish worldview. Therefore when one interprets the Commandments in this
way, their import for the individual Jew increases. Jewish action
and ideology then reinforce each other. This confirms one's
commitment to both and gives one a sense of cohesion and
constancy. In a world that otherwise appears chaotic and senseless, one feels that some things, at least, are stable and meaningful.

Third, these tenets are not merely principles to be acknowledged and espoused intellectually; they are convictions that are
to pervade one's life, influencing both thought and action. They
therefore appear in many forms within the tradition—in stories,
proverbs, poetry, and commandments—so that they are easily
remembered. Stories and poetry are especially well suited to
making these tenets part of people's emotional structure,[49] and
the legal form, as we discussed above, is a potent mechanism to
define, communicate, and effectuate these principles.

Choosing an Appropriate Standard of Truth and Wisdom

But are these convictions true and wise? Yes and no. They are
not "true" or "wise" in the sense of being proved beyond a
reasonable doubt. Quite the contrary, reasonable people abound
who affirm the convictions of other faiths and philosophies,
many of which are inconsistent in whole or in part with the
statements enumerated above. On the other hand, though, Jews
find them both true and wise. They would claim, in fact, that
these tenets best articulate what our experience in these areas
reveals to us.

How does this happen? That is, how do the actions produce

knowledge in the first place, and how can reasonable people disagree about the content of that knowledge?

Twentieth-century philosophers such as Pierre Duhem, Willard Van Orman Quine, and Morton White have shown that each person's judgments of what is and ought to be are integrally related in a system of principles.[50] We form these beliefs as we grow up. Individuals with a philosophic bent later think about them long and hard, but most people simply adopt the world-view of those they know and love. In any case, the formation and evaluation of one's beliefs is always a procedure that involves one's full being, not just the workings of the mind. One's emotions, relations, and actions exert a significant influence on what one believes, and, conversely, one's beliefs affect what one feels and does and the relationships one chooses.

This process usually does not operate linearly. One does not know God, for example, and then decide deductively that this requires one to observe the Sabbath or to honor one's parents. Conversely, one does not observe the Sabbath or honor one's parents in the absence of some sort of supportive beliefs. The process, in other words, is not serial, but contextual, with beliefs, actions, emotions, and relationships all affecting one another in determining how we think, feel, and act.

Because this is the case, our beliefs can never be totally objective. The lenses through which we see issues in the first place, and the criteria with which we weigh them, are themselves the products of the perceptions and values we have assimilated over the years. We can and should make our judgments more objective than they otherwise would be by learning how and why other individuals and groups think and act as they do. But even this information we inevitably filter through the lenses of our own view of the world. As Judah Halevi noted, people generally prefer to see the world through the lenses they have used since childhood, particularly when those they love use the same lenses.

Indeed, in many areas of life, total objectivity is not an appropriate goal. Especially with regard to the broadest questions of perspective, there often is not one correct way of seeing things, but rather a number of possible ways, each with its advantages and disadvantages. Empathy and human understanding are at least as important in such matters as objectivity is.

These methodological points clarify what it means to evaluate the truth of the tenets implied by the commandments concerning parents and the Sabbath. It is *not* a matter of deciding whether these principles can be proved beyond a reasonable doubt. Indeed, that stringent criterion, while used in American criminal cases because of a strong presumption of innocence, is used almost nowhere else. Even scientists consider theories to be proven with probabilities of fifty percent or less. Demonstrating the truth of assertions also does *not* require that all intelligent, reasonable people would or should agree with them—especially if they concern nonphysical matters like values, interpretations, and perceptions. The appropriate question is rather the extent to which the assertions fit human experience and mold it into a coherent, good, and meaningful form of life.

Criteria for Making Judgments of Truth

This, of course, calls for a judgment to be made, and intelligent people will disagree. Their own personal and communal histories and characters will account for part of their differing views. Part of their disagreement, though, will be based upon factors which can be experienced and judged on intersubjective and intercommunal bases.

There are four components to such an evaluation. First, one

must define one's standards of judgment, including the relative importance one assigns to the values one holds. One may even provide some rationale for one's standards and one's relative weighting in an attempt to convince others to think and act likewise, but they may not concur. When they do not, one must simply stipulate one's own rating system.

Second, one must analyze the philosophy or religion in question for its strengths and weaknesses in terms of the criteria one has defined and adopted. Here, too, there may be disagreement; even those who share the same values and views may differ as to their application. If one carries out these two steps, however, one has fulfilled the obligations for making a *reasoned* decision.

Third, to make an evaluation not only reasoned, but *reasonable,* one must share it with others and be open to adjusting it on the basis of what they have to say. This surely does not necessitate accepting whatever someone else says, but it does require that one at least consider objections and be open to accommodating those which seem worthy. When done to the satisfaction of others who hold similar values, this step can persuade them of the correctness of a given way of thinking or plan of action, sometimes even despite original reluctance to concur.

Finally, when a judgment is not only shared with others, but tested by oneself and others in practice, especially over a long period of time, and when it continues to fit people's experience, we call it *true.* It is true to life as we know it. It may not ultimately be true: we may later discover refuting evidence. This, however, is the case for all areas of human endeavor, and it does not prevent us from applying the adjective "true" to those judgments that fit our experience to date. We say, for example, that the facts established by contemporary science are true even though we know that some of them will be restricted in application—if not confuted altogether—in the future.

In more complex areas of human life, we are prepared to call a judgment true even when we know that the judgment is not totally adequate. So, for example, we might say that an economic interpretation of the American Revolution is true even though we know that ideological, sociological, and geographical factors also played crucial roles. Similarly, "The early bird catches the worm" is true, even though "Haste makes waste." We recognize that when there are multiple elements involved, statements may be true, even if only partially so.

A Soft Perspectivist Use of These Criteria

Honor and respect for parents and observance of the Sabbath bespeak tenets that clearly articulate a perspective on life. This perspective Jews have embraced as their own for millennia. As such, they have special emotional attraction to Jews. Even nonreligious Jews who deny the existence of God would probably consider the tenets which do not directly invoke God as their own, forming part of their Jewish, ethnic identity. Such people would, for example, most likely acknowledge strong obligations to honor and revere parents as the ones who created and raised them. Religious Jews would find more sources of meaning in these commandments, but secular Jews might honor the letter and spirit of these duties to parents despite their denial of the tradition's theological foundation for them. Similarly, nonreligious Jews might adopt the Jewish attitudes toward creation, creativity, time, and labor expressed in the Sabbath without observing it—although, again, one who does follow its laws would be reminded of these principles weekly and would undoubtedly find more dimensions of meaning in them.

The reverse would be true for non-Jews. To the extent that these principles are also part of their own tradition, non-Jews would warm to them as well. To the extent that they are distinctly Jewish in either kind or degree of emphasis, however, their Jewish identity might well be, if anything, an emotional deterrent to non-Jews to accept them as true.

This does not mean that non-Jews would necessarily deny the truth of these tenets. In the language of Chapter 1, that would automatically be true only for those who embrace "hard perspectivism." It would, in fact, be a very hard version of that view, for it denies people's ability to see the truth of the principles held by others not only because the tenets are unfamiliar or difficult for them to understand, but because they do not even want to try.

That may be the case for some, but I have greater faith in people's ability and desire to understand others. For a "soft perspectivist" like me, the attachment of given principles to a specific group—in our examples, the lessons enumerated above concerning parents and the Sabbath, if associated specifically and exclusively with Jews—would only mean that other groups would not necessarily know the tenets, would not automatically be attracted to them, and would therefore be likely to question them more thoroughly than Jews would. Non-Jews could, however, learn the principles and could be convinced of the reasonableness and the truth of even some of them that were not antecedently part of their own religious or philosophical perspective. The same would be true for Jews investigating systems of belief and action different from Judaism.

There are limits to this, however. I am not a nonperspectivist. One's own views do play a role in judging the truth of others' claims and the wisdom of their ways of life.

Moreover, if one exposes oneself to many other people's religions and becomes convinced of the truth of other beliefs and the wisdom of other patterns of behavior, ultimately one will no longer be an adherent of the religion with which one started. Perspectives by their very nature *define* ways of thinking and acting, emphasizing some and *ruling out* others.

Oriental cultures are more tolerant of espousing multiple, inconsistent views. The Japanese, for instance, are commonly both Buddhist and Shinto. Western cultures, by contrast, are exclusivist, so that if one is a Christian, for example, one cannot be a Jew, a Muslim, a devotee of an Eastern religion, or an atheist.

My own position is not as liberal as Oriental views because I think that some claims preclude others, not only in logic, but in practice. One cannot get vigorously involved in the world and attempt to change it while simultaneously denying the metaphysical reality of the world and seeking to detach oneself from it as much as possible. If both of those stances bespeak elements of truth and wisdom, then one should not embrace either exclusively. One should rather try to integrate the strengths of both visions into a reasonably coherent system of thought and action and energetically devote oneself to that.

In this process, one can and should have a healthy sense of epistemological humility. That is, one should recognize that our lack of definitive knowledge in areas like religion, philosophy, morality, and social policy requires that we tolerate and sometimes even appreciate other people's beliefs and patterns of action.[51]

Such pluralism does *not,* however, collapse into nihilism, individualism, or relativism—that is, the positions that there is no truth or wisdom, or that it is totally a matter of what an individual or group says it is. Using criteria such as those described in the previous section, we *can* evaluate claims to truth and wisdom and then rank-order them, and we *can* simultaneously recognize that other intelligent people may assess the options differently. The proper epistemological position, then, is not relativism, but relativity—that is, not that the truth is whatever a community says it is, but that there is an objective reality that serves as the criterion for the truth of any system of ideas but that we can only know it from the perspective of a perceiving community. To maintain its beliefs responsibly, the community must continually strive to improve its fix on reality by testing its views through observation and action. Ultimately, though, we cannot rise above all perspectives and see the world objectively; we must content ourselves with perceiving the world through a perspective that seems to work.

The soft-perspectivist position I am espousing therefore amounts to this: You affirm your own approach as the best approximation of truth and wisdom of which you are capable; else why adopt it? You simultaneously deny that other approaches are the best candidates for truth and wisdom, at least as far as you can tell. You remain sincerely open, however, to criticism of your own position, and you acknowledge and appreciate that in *some* areas other ways of thinking and acting are as good or better than your own.

People who adopt this approach are thus principled pluralists. They consider the positions of others, recognizing and perhaps even adopting those perspectives' strengths. They affirm their own philosophy and pattern of actions, however, as the best overall, based at least upon their own evaluation of experience, if not also upon the judgment and practical experience of others.

Evaluating the Truth and Wisdom of Our Examples

Returning now to the principles learned from, and implicit in, the commandments concerning parents and the Sabbath, what shall we say of their truth?

Religious and, to a somewhat lesser extent, non-religious Jews consider them true. This is not only because these tenets express part of the content of Jewish identity, and not only because they bear the weight of the tradition, but also because they have fit Jewish experience over time.

While this may seem a rather rough-and-ready way of supporting the truth of these affirmations, one should note that the process of justifying the principles of science is not much different. A fundamental assumption of science, for example, is the principle of the uniformity of nature, according to which a ball rolling down an inclined plane today will have the same velocity as the identical ball that rolled down the same plane under the same conditions yesterday. Nature is "uniform" in that way. If that were not true, the fact that a given object behaved one way on a given day would say nothing about how it would behave tomorrow. Scientists could then never generalize over phenomena to describe the laws of nature. That would effectively make it impossible to learn anything from scientific research except what we see at this moment. The doctrine of the uniformity of nature is therefore essential to the entire scientific enterprise. When philosophers of science try to justify it, however, they ultimately rely upon the fact that it works.[52] Acting in accordance with the principle of the uniformity of nature has produced results that have accorded with later experience, and so nature seems to be constructed in that way.

Jews would claim the same thing about the principles embedded in honor and reverence for parents and in the Sabbath: seeing the world in accordance with these doctrines works. Those who adopt them are not continually frustrated in their perceptions as if they were constantly butting up against an impenetrable wall. On the contrary, they find that their ongoing experience supports and sustains these beliefs. The human being and nature at large therefore seem to be constructed that way. On the understanding of truth accepted in science, then, the principles underlying the Sabbath and honor of parents bespeak the truth.

Jews would also consider the commandments wise. They would contend that abiding by these laws enriches life. Individuals and society are better off when they use these rules to guide their lives; they get into trouble or, at least, forgo significant dimensions of meaning, when they do not.

Jews would also claim that, in several ways, such tenets can put them into contact with God. Human ego makes people prefer to see themselves as the masters of the world and the sole parties responsible for its benefits—in the words of Deuteronomy, that "My own power and the might of my own hand have won this wealth for me." We must, however, "remember that it is the Lord your God who gives you the power to achieve this, in fulfillment of the covenant He made on oath with your ancestors."[53] The essence of a religious outlook, in other words, is that we acknowledge our limits, our dependence upon physical, mental, and moral powers beyond us. The commands to remember and observe the Sabbath and to honor our parents encourage us to do this, by reminding us in concrete actions of our divine and human creators and the appropriate relations we should have with them.

A Jewish perspective further entails that we recognize that the God upon whom we depend entered into a lasting, covenantal relationship with us in which we became subject to obligations like honor and respect for parents and observance of the Sabbath. In fulfilling these duties, then, we can meet and acknowledge the heteronomous God who commanded them. Moreover, by following these commandments one becomes more Godlike, and one experiences a part of God's goodness and holiness.

Obeying the Commandments in and of itself, of course, will not necessarily provide us with these perceptions and interactions. One can mindlessly act out of habit—"religious behaviorism," Heschel called it. For the commandments to be a conduit to God, one must instead be open to their theological dimension and receptive to communicating with God through them.

That is, since our thoughts and actions affect each other, we must begin with a perspective that can at least accommodate a theological dimension to life in order to be able to recognize God when we come across Him. If we think in such a way, our actions help to inform us about where and how to discover God; they reveal theological truths, as it were. They simultaneously serve to justify the adoption of a theological perspective in the first place, for we find that it works in understanding our experience of reality.

Of course, as Buber reminds us, even if we are interested in communicating with God, we cannot force God to interact with us; God may hide from us and be in "eclipse"—just as any other human being may refuse to respond to an invitation for relationship.[54] Acting according to the commandments, however, constitutes such an invitation, one that God specifically indicated He would favor. Therefore, even though such action does not guarantee that we will experience aspects of God in the process, it holds great promise for such contact.

These, of course, are *Jewish* perceptions and actions. As I have tried to demonstrate above, though, they are open to analysis, critique, and denial or adoption by non-Jews. As such, they represent serious claims on the part of the Jewish people to both truth and wisdom. Jews with sufficient epistemological humility must recognize that intelligent, sensitive people may see the world and act in it according to other doctrines; that is one part of the soft perspectivism and pluralism I espouse. At the same time, they would insist that Jewish perceptions of the world and Jewish rules for acting in it are the best approximations available to human beings in their search for truth and wisdom.

4

Knowing God through Words of the Divine: Revelation

Understanding Revelation

Shared action is one prime way in which we learn about other people; verbal communication is another. Conversation often accompanies doing things together, but talking and acting can each be done without the other. They are, in other words, independent phenomena. Moreover, these two forms of human behavior produce knowledge of another person in different ways, each with its own distinctive philosophical strengths and weaknesses.

The religious phenomena parallel to human exchanges of words are revelation and prayer. As typically construed, in the former, God speaks to human beings; in the latter, human beings speak to God. Both are highly problematic from a philosophical point of view primarily because, as generally conceived, one of the communicators, God, is not available for direct, reciprocal communication as human beings are to each other when they

91

have a conversation. This raises many questions. For example, how do we know that it is indeed God communicating with us through revelation? On what basis do we accept one revelation over others, or one record of a revelation over others? Does God continue to reveal matters to us today? If so, how? When we speak to God through prayer, how can we ever be sure that God hears? Is it really communication or only extended monologues?

Learning about Others through Words

These problems of knowing God through revelation and prayer are immediately apparent to us. When we investigate our knowledge of other human beings through our communication with them, however, we find that some of the same questions apply.

The assumption of most human conversation is that others are telling us the truth. We know, however, that some do not, and some entire categories of people we presume to be dissembling. Used car salespeople and politicians, for example, have long been mistrusted. We do not even believe people who back up their words with visual demonstrations. Television advertisers in the middle of the twentieth century concentrated on giving visual proof of their products to their new, large audience. The present generation of young adults, however, grew up assuming that anything could be produced by visual effects. It therefore does not even trust what it sees. It presumes, in fact, that anyone selling anything may well be lying.[1]

If we do not know a person through any previous contact, it is even hard to determine whether we are hearing the truth about who he or she is. If we have something significant at stake (e.g., if we must decide whether to accept this person's credit card to purchase an item from us), we are likely to require identification. Since that can be falsified, we may even ask a third party who knows both of us and who can be trusted—in our example, a telephone credit check.

The chances of being deceived are even greater when the verbal communication takes place over the telephone or in some other way that prevents the hearer from directly observing the speaker. Mistakes are more probable when we lack visual confirmation of the identity and intent of the person talking. We learn to recognize the voices of the people we know, but sometimes even they can trick us into thinking someone else is talking as part of a ruse or practical joke. When we are not able to see another person's facial expressions and body language, we are more likely to confuse a jest for something meant to be serious (or vice versa).

The problems grow worse still when the verbal communication is in written rather than in oral form. Handwriting is an identifying mark, but it is sometimes open to dispute. Hence, the existence of contested wills and the need for notary publics. When the written words are typed or written by someone else, or when the document is unsigned, the reader's ability to identify the author and his or her intent diminishes yet further.

Even when verbal communication is articulate and accurate, we do not depend on it alone, for we recognize that people's words only afford us partial knowledge of them. So, for example, people who have been pen pals for years may know much about each other. Nevertheless, they often feel that they do not really know one another until they communicate in nonverbal ways by meeting and doing things together. Writing lacks the immediacy and spontaneity of personal contact, and so we are somewhat different people in writing than we are in person.

We must, in sum, learn to account for possible deceptions in verbal communication and to compensate for its insufficiencies through other means of contact. Only then can we use words as one means to learn about other people and interact with them.

Varying Jewish Conceptions of Revelation

When we apply these considerations to our knowledge of God, the problems we have with revelation and prayer become less awesome and less peculiar to religion. In this chapter we shall see how this analysis of human communication helps us to understand revelation, and in a subsequent chapter we shall apply it to prayer.

We do not rely exclusively on the record of biblical revelations for our knowledge of God. Our allegiance to the text, in other words, is not based solely, or even primarily, on an historical assertion about an event at Sinai over three thousand years ago. The meaning and significance of the Bible for us, including its ability to reveal God to us, instead derive from the vigorous interaction between the texts and the people who have applied them to their lives over the centuries.

From early in the biblical period some 3500 years ago to our own day, Jews have used the oral and written traditions that were later edited into the Bible to interpret their experience and to find instructions for living. They did so, in part, because they believed that the Bible expresses God's way of construing reality, and that, therefore, no other document could possibly be as knowing, wise, and authoritative. Moreover, the Bible has provided a context of perceptions and values to link current experiences with the many others of life, past, present, and future. It thus gives meaning to life by making it possible to understand contemporary experience in the framework of a larger pattern.

This commitment to the Bible would not have endured, however, unless Jews had continued to find the Bible relevant to new ages and ideas. By the middle of the fifth century B.C.E., they no longer sought to supplement the Bible with new revelations to determine how God wanted them to deal with new situations.

They had found no convincing way to discern true revelations from false ones, and they feared the potentially revolutionary implications of that genre of divine communication. At any time, after all, a new revelation could authoritatively overturn centuries of thought and practice—or claim to do so. For those reasons and others, the Rabbis narrowed the domain of revelation by refusing to recognize the legitimacy of revelations much after the destruction of the First Temple and by stressing the primacy of the revelation to Moses over the others which they did legitimate.[2]

They then interpreted the Torah in the light of their ongoing experiences. These experiences were seen, in turn, to confirm the worldview and value system of the Bible *as Jews came to interpret it*. *Midrash* (interpretation) indeed provides a formal mechanism whereby the ongoing experience of the people is invoked to confirm, refute, or modify the meaning and application of biblical revelation. Thus the very meaning of the Bible has been constantly changed through the process of rabbinic *midrash*—so much so that Judaism is really the religion of the Rabbis more than it is the religion of the Bible.[3]

Does this process reduce revelation to a wholly human phenomenon, in which human beings continually speak to themselves but pretend, for some reason, that it is God talking? Has revelation, in other words, effectively become simply the record of human experience with God, phrased in language that makes it seem like a communication from God?

How one answers this question depends on one's view of revelation, especially the source and nature of its authority. Reconstructionist Jews would indeed claim that the Torah is completely the work of human hands set to articulate the contemporary understanding of God's nature and will. Modern Jews can and should learn from "revealed" texts selectively,

retaining those elements of the ancient Jewish conception of
God that ring true with their own experience and discarding or
modifying the others.

As for revelation, according to Reconstructionists there was
no revelation at Sinai by a God external to nature; there was
rather human discovery of the character of the God of nature.
Human beings at the time expressed their discovery in the
contemporary, heteronomous language of revelation as if it had
been produced by a God outside nature. We should not be
swayed by this, however, because they also externalized the
descriptions of their own human actions. They said, for example, that God took them out from Egypt when they meant to
describe the fact that they had revolted and left Egypt. They used
the language they did because they did not understand the
notion of actions initiated by human beings independent of the
powers of nature, and because, in any case, the Exodus from
Egypt was a remarkable feat that could only have been accomplished with the help of the salvational powers of nature—that
is, God. After the Greeks, however, we have a clearer conception of what is autonomous action and what is not, and we,
therefore, no longer talk about the acts we initiate as if they were
produced by external forces. Similarly, we should no longer
think of God in such external terms but should rather translate
our ancestors' externalized language into our internalized expressions. Thus, "God revealed" becomes, for Reconstructionists, "We discovered."

At the other end of the spectrum, Orthodox Jews make two
fundamental claims about revelation: God spoke words at Sinai,
and the Torah which we have in hand is a verbatim transcription
of those words. This imparts direct, divine authority to the
Torah's stories and rules. Moreover, in theory at least, those
who believe this can enjoy the psychological security of
knowing with a certainty what is true and right.

In fact, however, Orthodox Jews argue vehemently among themselves about a whole host of issues. Thus, in practice the theory does not provide an unambiguous divine message or the emotional assurance which might accompany it. The Orthodox theory also fails to account for the history of the transcription of the Torah itself and the cross-cultural influences apparent in it. More importantly, it fails to take proper notice of the indispensable role of fallible human beings in understanding and applying the meaning of the Torah. When one takes account of that, one sees that neither the Torah nor any other document can offer divine, unerring truth and wisdom.

The Conservative and Reform movements take an historical approach to the Bible, applying the same tools of historical analysis to the Bible that one would use in probing any other text. These include comparative linguistics, comparative law, archaeology, history, techniques of literary analysis, and the like. When one uses such methods, one discovers that the Bible consists of a number of documents written long after Sinai and edited together even later.

Some Conservative Jews believe that God spoke in words at Sinai. They deny the second tenet of the Orthodox position, however. That is, they acknowledge the history of how the Bible was composed and its implication that we do not have in hand an immediate transcription of what God said.

Other Conservative Jews believe that the Torah's words may not be those of God directly, but the people who uttered them were divinely inspired. This inspiration was similar in form to that of a Mozart, a Shakespeare, or an Einstein in that the human beings involved have the experience that they are, as it were, being carried on a wave with powers beyond their own in creating their masterpiece. Religious revelation differs in content, though, in that it is directed to the expression of religious topics—specifically, the relationships between humanity and

God and what that means for human interaction, thought, and practice—rather than to the topics of music, drama, or science. This would mean that the words of the Bible were crafted by human beings but were not theirs alone, for in the process of writing the verses of the Bible these people were inspired (literally, "breathed into") by God.

Still other Conservative Jews believe that the Torah is the record of how the ancient Hebrews sought and met God. These people described their experiences and the meaning they ascribed to them in the literature we know as the Bible. The words of the Bible, then, are completely human in origin, but they stem from encounters with God that they try to articulate.

For all three of these Conservative positions, revelation continues in our day through the process of ongoing *midrash*. That is, Conservative Jews believe in continuous revelation.

The crux of the Conservative position is that although we do not have a verbatim communication of God's will in hand, Jewish law, as shaped by the rabbis of each generation, is binding. As articulated in the new, official formulation of Conservative beliefs, *Emet Ve-Emunah: Statement of Principles of Conservative Judaism,* "The sanctity and authority of Halakhah attaches to the body of the law, not to each law separately, for throughout Jewish history Halakhah has been subject to change."[4] The Conservative positions on the composition of the Torah and the compulsory character of law thus necessitate a sophisticated account of the law's authority, one which accounts for both its divine and human elements and for its constancies and changes. Such expositions are possible, and there have been a number, but they require time and thought to digest. They thus lack appeal to those who prefer the world to be more simply and easily understood.

Contemporary Reform Jews might subscribe to any of the theories held by Conservative Jews, but the original Reform position, still held by many, was that the Bible represents the original Jewish understanding of God's nature and will, but that our own revelations of God have progressed beyond that ("progressive revelation"). Contemporary Reform Jews do not all claim any longer that modern formulations of God's will are necessarily better than those of the past. They all do maintain, however, that the law was never intended to be obligatory for all generations and that it certainly is not so for us. Instead, each Jew must study the tradition and individually choose which elements of Jewish law to observe (if any), and how to do that.

In practice, there arc few Reform Jews who have the skills and knowledge to take this process seriously. The Conservative Movement also suffers from a gap between theory and practice, with a large, unobservant laity. There, however, formulation of the law is left to the rabbis, who have the knowledge and skills to do so. The extreme stress on individual autonomy in Reform ideology also makes it difficult, if not impossible, to define the Jewish community in terms of communal norms rooted in the tradition. Indeed, on this reading one wonders how any form of behavior could be ruled out as being unsupported or even antagonistic to Judaism. Reform Jews, though, would claim that any more coercive theory both misstates the tradition and ignores the realities of the modern world.[5]

How I Understand Revelation

My own view is based on a keen awareness that I do not know what happened at Sinai. God may have spoken in Hebrew words there, more or less as we have them recorded in the Torah, or Moses may have been inspired by God to articulate the divine message in his own words but in a given way, or the Torah may represent how our ancestors put their experiences with God into words. I affirm at least the last of those alternatives, and I remain open to the possibility of either of the former but not convinced of either of them. It is for this reason that I have titled this chapter "Knowing God through Words of the Divine," intentionally playing on the ambiguity of the word "of," so that "of the Divine" may refer to God's actual words but at least designates our words about God.

In any case, I accept the arguments of modern biblical scholars to the effect that the Torah itself is not a direct transcription of events at Sinai but rather represents a compilation of sources from a variety of times and places.[6] Moreover, even if the Torah were a direct recording of words spoken there, it would be a record by human beings according to their own understanding of those events, and that limits its credibility. As William Temple has pointed out,[7] classical theories of revelation claim that we can gain especially authoritative knowledge about the nature and will of God through a direct, divine revelation, but all of the major religions (even the fundamentalist ones) assert that that revelation must be *interpreted.* As soon as one says that, however, one has lost the claim to special, unerring authority that the revelation was supposed to afford because its interpretations will inevitably represent a *human* understanding of its contents.[8]

These considerations lead me to the following position:[9]

1. Human moral, intellectual, and aesthetic *faculties* distinguish human beings from other animals, in degree if not in kind. As such, these capabilities are a touch of the divine within humanity in the root sense of "divine" as power, for they enable human beings to know, feel, and do things that other animals cannot.

2. The structure of the world is an objective base that sets a limit to possible alternatives in thought and even more so in practice. The world's design can and should serve as a criterion

for the evaluation of any philosophic vision or moral code. Murder, for example, can become the norm for humanity only on pain of extinction of the human species, and wanton use of atomic weapons carries the same price. I hold that the world was divinely created, then, at least in the sense that its creation involves powers beyond our control. I therefore would be willing to say that God informed us about divinity and the world and gave us the Law in an *indirect* way by creating the world in such a way that certain formulations of thought and practice fit the pattern of creation much better than others.

3. I would aver, however, that the specific *content* of our theological ideas and codes of practice is of human creation and hence subject to error and change. For me, revelation occurs in events *that human beings interpret to be revelatory* of truths or norms of conduct. Thus, any event could be a source of revelation, although some may be more impressively so than others.

I would want to stress that within Judaism, it is the Jewish *community* of the past and the present that decides which events are revelatory and what the content and implications of that revelation are. This communal check prevents revelation from being simply the figment of one person's imagination, and it preserves the tradition's insistence that revelation must be affirmed by the rabbis of each era so that there will not be multiple Torahs.[10]

Especially on difficult issues, this process may not produce settled decisions as to what is revelatory and what is not until generations hence, and that undoubtedly will upset those who want indubitable, divinely authoritative rulings now. The reality, though, is that even if one thought that the Bible consists of God's actual words at Sinai, one can never know whether a given rabbi's interpretation of those words will have staying power for the Jewish community until many years later. In the meantime, for my view, as for the literalist view, the rabbi's interpretation is the authoritative expression of God's word if, and only if, the contemporary community sees it as such.

4. I then observe Jewish law (that is, Jewish law has authority for me) because it is the way *my people* have understood *the demands of God* in the past and do so now. Similarly, Jewish philosophic views from the Bible to modern times have special relevance to me because they represent the way my people have understood God, human beings, and the world. Both Jewish law and Jewish thought thus require attention to God, the Jewish people, and the interaction between them.

The identity of who within the Jewish people makes these decisions is unfortunately not as clear as it once was. Historically, it has been the rabbi of each community who exercised this authority because he had the education in the tradition to know its content and methodology and because the community who hired him thereby indicated that they trusted his knowledge and sensitivity to make such decisions for them. Even then, there were sometimes conflicts between what the rabbis said and what the community did, and so rabbis had to adjust their decisions to communal custom and thinking, and vice versa. Moreover, there always were discrepancies among the various Jewish communities worldwide in both thought and practice.

After the Enlightenment, however, the gap between rabbinic decisions and communal practice grew wider, and it still is so, even among the Orthodox. Similarly, the differences in practice among the Jewish communities of the world have also broadened. This makes defining the "community" of Jews relevant to making decisions in Jewish law and thought very difficult.

On some issues, my "Jewish community" refers to all Jews. Certainly fulfilling the obligation in Jewish law to redeem Jewish captives applies to Jews of all stripes. Even then, though, defining who is a Jew can be sticky: witness the experience of the

Israeli Chief Rabbinate with the Cochin Jews of India in the early years of the state, and consider the Reform position which no longer insists on matrilineal descent to define a Jew.

On many issues, then, the definition of whose ideas and practices count in defining God's will in our own time as Judaism understands it cannot include all Jews, however that is defined. Most lay Jews in America today either do not affiliate with a synagogue at all or they practice what sociologist Charles Liebman has called "folk religion." That consists of several seasonal celebrations, especially those marked by family meals (the Passover *seder*) or by the need to respond to the Christian environment in which we live (Hanukkah), life cycle events, contributions to Jewish and general causes, social action, attendance at High Holy Day services and perhaps several other services during the year, and other observances chosen at will.

Clearly, this kind of autonomous, eclectic choosing of what to adopt from the Jewish tradition and what not cannot serve as the definition of God's will in our time. It does not even pretend to be. Indeed, Liebman points out that even those who practice the folk religion see rabbis and others who are more serious about their Jewish commitments as the criteria for defining what the Jewish tradition says about any given topic. They see the legitimacy of their own folk religion to depend completely upon the validation they derive for it from the "elite religion"—that is, the form of Judaism lived by the rabbis and religiously practicing lay people in each religious movement.

Consequently, both to preserve consistency with the historical Jewish tradition and to reflect the sociological realities of contemporary Jews, I would define "the community" that determines how the tradition is to be interpreted and applied as the "elite" in each branch of Judaism. The seriousness with which the rabbis and some lay people take Judaism and their movement's interpretation of it gives them the right to count in the

determination of what should constitute the practice and ideology of the movement to which they belong. As in many areas
of life, those who accept responsibility enjoy concomitant
rights; those who do not, lose those rights.

Even then, there are sometimes differences among the elite of
a given movement. Among the Orthodox in recent decades, this
has led to vicious name-calling and even throwing stones at each
other. I would hardly endorse such methods—and I am sure that
most serious Orthodox Jews would not either. Significant disagreements, however, can and do occur within a given movement. Sometimes they even lead to a splintering of the movement into various divisions or a fracturing of the movement into
independent parts. As difficult as this may be to tolerate emotionally, in some ways this is a healthy sign, for it means that
people are taking their task of interpreting God's will and living
by it seriously.

Since I identify conscientiously as a Conservative Jew, the
"community" whose ideas and practices define God's word for
me in our time is the body of Conservative rabbis and lay people
who actively live Conservative Judaism in what they think, say,
and do. On legal issues this is defined by the decisions of the
Conservative Movement's Committee on Jewish Law and Standards, and on philosophical issues the parameters were defined
by the Commission on the Philosophy of the Conservative
Movement in its document, *Emet Ve-Emunah: Statement of Principles of Conservative Judaism.* Deciding matters of Jewish law and
thought within the context of a Jewish community narrower
than all Jews may not be ideal, but it is the way Jewish law has
been applied and practiced for most of its history, albeit with
greater coherence, and it is inevitable today.[11]

5. When a particular Jewish law is not moral or wise, however, I must be prepared to change it in consort with the rest of
my community, taking due regard of the weight of tradition in

the process. The same is true for a statement of Jewish thought: while I give special attention to biblical and rabbinic theology because it is the rubric of my people's thought, I accept the main thrusts of those theologies because I am convinced by them and must reject those portions which I find untrue.

Evaluating traditional laws and concepts must be done deliberately, and commitment to the tradition requires that the burden of proof rests with the one who wants to change it. Moreover, the need for communal concurrence should help to guard against precipitous changes. No mechanism can guarantee wisdom in such evaluations, however, and no simple rules can be applied to determine when to change an element in the tradition and when not to. Indeed, it is entirely possible that some feature of the tradition that is dropped or modified now for good and sufficient reason will reenter the thought and practice of our people several decades or centuries hence, and, conversely, something that is added now may be eliminated later. Human beings are not omniscient. Nevertheless, in both principle and practice, responsible commitment to the tradition requires that at times its adherents be prepared to change it.

This does not necessarily entail rejection of those truth statements and norms on which reason, morality, and experience are neutral or inconclusive. On the contrary, I would be interested in affirming the necessity to abide by many of the rationally unnecessary rules *(hukkim)* and by the decisions of the tradition in rationally ambiguous areas of thought because those are precisely the factors that identify the Jewish group most strongly, as the Rabbis recognized.[12] The identity and character of a society are largely a matter of its particular perspective and style, and I would not want to neglect those in affirming rational and experiential criteria for judging the content of revelation.

Jews have historically tolerated and exercised more individuality in theology than they have in Jewish law. This stems, in part, from the rabbinic view that one function of Jewish thought (Midrash Aggadah) is to make Jewish practice appealing to the individual.[13] Moreover, law is, by its nature, more systematic, for ultimately there must be a coherent rule of practice by which the society is going to operate. In contrast, societies can permit greater leeway in thought without incurring significant danger of disintegrating. This does not mean that any view of God or humanity can be considered Jewish, and it does not preclude describing a reasonably coherent Jewish view on most subjects. The degree of diversity countenanced in matters of thought, however, has historically been quite broad.

In our own time, Jews in large numbers have abandoned Jewish law as binding, choosing to adhere to whatever Jewish practices they wish. This certainly does not make for a recognizable, coherent Judaism. Like the tradition, I would embrace a pluralism in both thought and practice, but the former would be larger in scope than the latter.

In both law and ideology, then, respect for a traditional idea or practice requires Jews, in my view, to begin with a bias in its favor, but the ultimate criteria of acceptance are our own reason and experience as human beings and as Jews. I do not believe that we have ever been privy, even as coordinated communities, to an indisputably clear vision of God's nature or will that could substitute for those, and even those experiences which exhibited a relative clarity must be interpreted and applied by fallible human beings. We must, therefore, reject ideological or normative assertions that contradict our reason, moral sensitivity, or experience, even if they are based upon an interpretation of a text accepted as revealed.

We clearly use our own individual experience and reason when responding to the tradition, but, as indicated above, for Judaism to retain continuity and coherence, we must discuss our evaluations with the other members of our community and make decisions as a group. Fortunately, Judaism's reliance on an ongoing, communal tradition has largely eliminated conflicts between our religion and our contemporary context and conscience, and Jews must continue this salutary process of integrating the new with the old through communal interpretation and adjustment.

6. This view enables me to make a serious knowledge claim for revelation. Philosophers like Descartes and Kant have demonstrated that our sensations of the physical world are private to each and every one of us. As a result, the mark of objectivity and truth in every area of human thought has been that a given proposition withstands testing over a period of time by a variety of people—especially those with no vested interest in confirming the results.

The Jewish understanding and use of revelation follow this same pattern. Revelation, like sensory experience, is usually given to an individual. This makes it epistemologically suspect. Martin Buber, in fact, thought that encounters with God can produce no real knowledge—that is, data accessible and testable by anyone other than God and the person involved—because they are completely private to those two parties.[14] Medieval Jewish philosophers like Judah Halevi and Moses Maimonides tried to bolster the epistemological authority of revelation by emphasizing that the central revelation in Judaism occurred before 600,000 people, but David Hume and others have raised substantial doubts as to the veracity of the witnesses and their reports.[15] In any case, since the only record of the presence of that many witnesses is the Torah itself, the argument is circular, using the Torah to substantiate itself.

Through its strong commitment to a communal tradition, the rabbinic approach to revelation, which I have largely followed in my own conception described above, provides, I think, a much more effective answer to this epistemological challenge.

While the Rabbis claimed that everyone standing at Sinai interpreted this event according to his or her own understanding, and while there could be differing interpretations of God's revelation which are all "the words of the living God," they nevertheless insisted that revelation had to be mediated through the rabbis of each generation so that there would not be multiple Torahs.[16]

In other words, just as intersubjectivity serves as the criterion for objective knowledge of the physical world, so too Judaism requires an intersubjective testing of any reputed revelation. The mode of verification of the knowledge we gain by revelation is simply whether the community and the representatives of its tradition (the rabbis) accept the revelation in question, and the method of falsification is through the community's rejection of the proposed revelation. This is the process of midrash, through which the community shares, interprets, modifies, and either confirms or repudiates interpretations of its ongoing encounters with God. Through this process, revelation attains objectivity and confirmation, and Judaism can thus make a warranted claim for knowledge gained from it.

Revelation, of course, does not produce knowledge as verifiable as do our senses. While there are certainly philosophical problems in explaining how we acquire knowledge of objects from our sensory experiences, there are, as we have seen, further problems when we attempt to glean knowledge from our interpersonal experiences, and yet further problems when we try to apply these models to God. The differing *focuses* of religion and science produce disparate levels of verifiability. Nevertheless, the *logic* of religious discovery is structurally similar to the logic of scientific discovery. This makes it possible to assert for my understanding of the Jewish concept of revelation a claim to knowledge in a strict sense of the term.

7. The position I am taking captures much of the practical import of the Jewish tradition. The Torah itself equivocated as to

whether even Moses could encounter God directly.[17] It did
claim that God's *will* was revealed to Moses—a belief in which
the Rabbis concurred—but, as mentioned earlier, the Rabbis
were careful to limit the scope and authority of any other
revelation. Instead, it was the *midrash* of the Sages on the Torah
which was to be the basis of all Jewish law and thought. The
Rabbis were seriously interested in preserving a sense of continuity, and they certainly did not treat the Torah cavalierly or
wantonly. They were also aware, however, of the changes that
had occurred in the tradition and of their role in introducing
them. Since I too have emphasized the role of the community in
determining the identity and content of revelation, and since I
too stress the importance of introducing new laws and thoughts
as *midrashim* on the classical texts in order to preserve a sense of
tradition and rootedness, one who operates with my view of
revelation would function in much the same way as the Rabbis
did.

8. Having said that, I still must declare openly that my view
differs from theirs in regard to the origin of the Torah and the
reason for its authority. This raises two questions. First, why do
I maintain the concept of revelation at all? If the term as used in
Jewish thought normally denotes a communication of truths
and norms by God to man, and if I am hedging on affirming
belief in such an event and seeking instead to explain the
authority of Jewish ideology and practice in other terms, then
why bother to assert the concept at all? Second, since I admit
doubts about the nature of the original experience at Sinai, have
I not gone beyond appropriate limits to the reinterpretation of
the concept in claiming that what I have described is still
revelation?

In answer to the first question, I must admit that my initial
motivation for maintaining a doctrine of revelation is that it is
deeply embedded in the tradition that I cherish. In and of itself,
this would not suffice to commit me to the notion of revelation

because where necessary I am prepared, as I have stated, to revise ideas and laws in consort with the rest of my community, just as the Rabbis of the Talmud and Midrash did in their communities on many occasions and just as Jewish philosophers and legalists have done from their time to ours. In this instance, however, I prefer to retain the concept because I do think that we are the beneficiaries of continuous revelation, at least in the third sense delineated above—that is, in having ongoing encounters with God, the import of which we attempt to articulate in our developing law and theology.

This clearly does not mean that Judaism's understanding of life is the only possible one. There are obviously other traditions that claim similar authority for their philosophies of life and that have also undergone a long period of intersubjective testing. Judaism itself recognizes the existence of prophets and saints among non-Jews and does not require Jewish belief or practice of non-Jews, even with regard to attaining a place in the world to come.[18]

The Jewish tradition, however, has understood God and the implications of the divine element of experience for our lives in its specific way. It is my tradition, and, as Halevi noted, that in and of itself makes me partial to it. My attachment to Judaism, however, rests on other grounds as well. I find Judaism to be wise in most of its views of God, humanity, society, animals, inanimate nature, and the interactions among all of the above. I would imagine that this wisdom stems not only from the longevity of its experience, but also from the fact that the rabbis who shaped it functioned as judges. In this capacity, they saw human life in all of its foibles and triumphs. At the same time, they held onto the ideals that Judaism instills, such that the religion they fashioned is a remarkable blend of realism and idealism, one that I consider to be the right recipe for human life. I applaud Judaism's demonstrated willingness to adapt to new ideas and situations while yet retaining its basic perspectives and values. I think its legal methods are, for reasons described in Chapter 3, the most effective ways of accomplishing this balance between tradition and change. Those methods also translate Judaism's values to the actual contexts in which we live, thus making them real. I revel in the intellectual freedom Judaism fosters and in its emphases on family, education, community, and on improving this world. At the same time, I appreciate its insistence that all of these values make sense only if they are rooted in a broader, religious perspective of the relationships between individuals, society, the world, and God. All of these factors attract me to Judaism now and might well have done so even if I had not been born into it. I certainly think that Judaism reveals much of what life is all about to me in an ongoing, incremental way.

This leads to the second question: is the view I am advancing near enough to the traditional notion of revelation to warrant calling it that, or am I abusing the term? This, of course, is a matter of judgment. Fundamentalists and those who tend toward that position will be dissatisfied with my interpretation because it does not provide the kind of absolute assurance they seek. On the contrary, my account demands recognition of the doubts that surround the initial event at Sinai and the complex changes that have occurred since then. It also demands judgment in responding to those changes and tolerance of a variety of opinions as to the identity of "the words of the living God" in any age.

Most people will think that one or another interpretation of that revelation is the most accurate reflection of God's will in our time, and there are objective factors that one can call upon in supporting such a judgment. These would follow from a sensitive reading of the texts of the tradition, its method, and its spirit, together with an informed view of the contemporary circumstances to which the tradition is being applied. These objective elements can only serve as *grounds* for a specific interpretation, however, not as conclusive rationales which make all other interpretations logically impossible, and so, ultimately, one must make one's peace with the need to choose one interpretation that can be justified in varying ways.

This probably is not the biblical tradition,[19] but it is the rabbinic tradition on which Judaism is based. The Rabbis themselves disagreed as to whether every word of the Torah was given at Sinai or only the general principles, with Rabbi Akiba holding the former opinion and Rabbi Ishmael the latter. Some even claimed that Moses commanded 611 of the 613 commandments of the Torah at God's bidding and the people at Mount Sinai only heard the first two of the Ten Commandments directly from God. Thus, even the Rabbis recognized the human component in the process of communication between God and the people Israel.[20]

Consequently, despite the fact that my doubts about the nature of the original event and the fidelity of our record of it are greater than those of the Rabbis, I feel comfortable in calling this an account of "revelation." I do not know what happened at Sinai. The Rabbis believed that God spoke Hebrew words there, but even they disagreed as to exactly how they were spoken. They differed even more as to the content and implications of what was revealed there. In any case, I am asserting, as they did, that the authority of the tradition can stand under a variety of interpretations of that event. I am also claiming, as they did, that its import is determined by its ongoing interpretation and application within the Jewish community. I am affirming, then, much of the Rabbis' theory of revelation and virtually every aspect of their practice based on it.

Since the process of revelation is a pervasive element in the Jewish tradition, and since it serves as the principal medium for the transmission of God's authority to that tradition, religious Jews must come to terms with it, however problematic it may be. Moreover, the existence and wisdom of the Jewish tradition over centuries are a phenomenon that people seeking truth must acknowledge and attempt to understand. I have suggested that recognition of the problems inherent in gaining knowledge from human conversation and appreciation of the rabbinic understanding of revelation as ongoing together go a long way toward alleviating the philosophical problems raised by revelation. I have also described my own adaptation of the rabbinic position in an attempt to account for further questions and in order to provide an overall theory of revelation. I do not pretend that everything is neat and clean; indeed, I would be deeply suspicious of any theory that claimed total adequacy in explaining a phenomenon as complex as this. I have, however, attempted to articulate a conception of revelation that is in accord with both reason and tradition and that can motivate the religious life of a Jew.

EXPERIENCING REVELATION

When revelation is properly understood and applied, it can be a source of theological knowledge for us; it can be a path to God. All of this, however, is very cerebral. The *experience* of revelation, however, is quite different, at least in tone. It combines terror before an absolute Sovereign with the warmth of a loving God. Jewish theologies, in fact, differ at least as importantly in the emotions that they engender toward God as they do in the substance of how they portray God.[21] These emotional components of revelation, like the experience itself, are by no means rare or esoteric. On the contrary, they happen often for anyone who pays attention.

How I Hear God's Word: Study

The most direct way in which revelation continues to occur is through study. In fact, according to the tradition, *each time a Jew studies the Torah or its rabbinic commentaries and expansions, God is revealed anew.*

The Rabbis of the Talmud, who shaped what we today know as Judaism, made this clear when they proclaimed rabbinic interpretation of the Torah the new form of prophecy—indeed, superior to biblical prophecy:

> Rabbi Abdimi from Haifa said: Since the day when the Temple was destroyed, the prophetic gift was taken away from the prophets and given to the Sages [Rabbis].—Is a Sage not also a prophet?—[Clearly yes.] What he meant was this: although it has been taken from the prophets, it has not been taken from the Sages. Amemar said: A Sage is even superior to a prophet, as it says, "And a prophet has a heart of wisdom" (Psalms 90:12). Who is [usually] compared with whom? Is not the smaller compared with the greater?[22]

No longer, according to the Rabbis, did God's revelation take the forms, common in the Bible, of visions, voices, and signs; that ceased shortly after the destruction of the First Temple in 586 B.C.E.[23] Instead, Jews were to look for God in the Torah, the product of the original, public revelation at Sinai. "Turn it over, and turn it over again, for everything is in it."[24]

That which later prophets said, and even the new interpretations that students would suggest to their teachers for all generations to come, were contained in the revelation of God to Moses.[25] At the same time, each time Jews studied it, they would discover a new aspect of life and of God, for "Matters which had not been revealed to Moses were revealed to Rabbi Akiba and his colleagues."[26] That is, all later insights connected to the Torah and its later commentaries were already *implicit* in it, and yet each represented to the one studying—and perhaps to others too—a new revelation of God. God Himself, according to rabbinic legend, spends 25 percent of each day studying His own Torah;[27] even God can gain new understanding!

We have noted that the first and last three blessings of the *Amidah* throughout the year are the same; it is the middle section of this prayer which varies with the occasion. On weekdays (morning, afternoon, and evening) the middle section consists of thirteen blessings which bespeak our daily concerns. The very first of these blessings thanks God for giving us three kinds of knowledge: information, ability to understand and reason, and experiential wisdom. Without these, the liturgist apparently reasoned, we could not even begin to address God. Thanksgiving and petition require that we know for what to ask and thank God.

> You graciously endow mortals with knowledge, teaching human beings understanding. Grant us of Your knowledge, understanding, and wisdom. Praised are You, Lord, who graciously grants knowledge.

As soon as one has such knowledge, one recognizes one's errors and the need to ask for forgiveness before one can request anything else. Thus, the next two blessings appropriately ask that God help us mend our ways and forgive us for our transgressions before the succeeding blessings address other petitions to God. All of this interaction with God, however, depends, in the first place, upon the subject of the first of the middle blessings, religious knowledge. As Hillel said, "A boor cannot be reverent; an ignorant person cannot be pious."[28]

Before the middle of the twentieth century, though, Jews did not enjoy the economic wealth to permit many people to study for long periods of time. Females often received no formal education at all, and males commonly had to suspend school at age nine or ten to help the family earn a living. A few, of course, did manage to continue, and some became rabbis. When Jews think of the Jewish past, they often assume that, like a few famous rabbinic scholars, all Jews studied for many years. The lyrics from the opening number of *Fiddler on the Roof,* however, reflect what was the historical reality for the vast majority of Jewish sons for centuries: "At three I started Hebrew school; at ten I learned a trade." Moreover, before the advent of the printing press at the end of the fifteenth century, even if one had the time and ability, it was hard to procure the materials for study.

From biblical times, however, the Jewish tradition, unlike many others, did not restrict knowledge of God's nature and will to a clerical elite, but, quite the contrary, insisted that each Jew know it. Abraham was singled out, according to the Bible, "that he may instruct his children and his posterity to keep the way of the Lord by doing what is just and right," and ever since then, Jewish parents have been charged with the duty of teaching the Torah diligently to their children and grandchildren.[29] Most often this was accomplished informally, in the midst of fulfilling Jewish duties and through the liturgy. The Torah actually depicts this process with regard to some commandments, describing the child's question and the parent's answer.[30] Early in rabbinic times Jews also established schools to supplement family training with more formal education.[31]

How I Hear God's Word: Public Torah Reading

However effective such informal and formal modes of individual study might be, not all children or adults would be able to avail themselves of them, and certainly not during the entirety of their lives. The Torah therefore provides for a public reading of its contents once every seven years when all the people are assembled at the Temple in Jerusalem:

> Moses wrote down this Teaching and gave it to the priests, sons, of Levi, who carried the Ark of the Lord's Covenant, and to the elders of Israel. And Moses instructed them as follows: Every seventh year, the year set for remission [of loans], at the Feast of Booths, when all Israel comes to appear before the Lord your God in the place which He will choose, you shall read this Teaching aloud in the presence of all Israel. Gather the people—*men, women, children, and the strangers in the communities*—that they may hear and so learn to revere the Lord your God and to observe faithfully every word of this Teaching. Their children, too, who have not had the experience, shall hear and learn to revere the Lord your God . . . (Deuteronomy 31:9–13).

When the First Temple was destroyed in 586 B.C.E., the Jewish people were exiled to Babylonia, where most continued to live even after the Temple in Jerusalem was rebuilt some seventy years later. The people living outside of Israel could not be expected to attend the Temple's sabbatical rites and were not obligated to do so. This meant, however, that they would not hear the Torah reading prescribed in Deuteronomy. Moreover, Jews living outside the land of Israel as a minority among a pagan majority needed to be formally reinforced in their faith more often than once in seven years.

Jews, therefore, began to read a section of the Torah in the synagogue at least four times each week—an innovation ascribed to Ezra, who lived in the middle of the fifth century B.C.E. Every Saturday afternoon, Monday morning, and Thursday morning a brief section would be read, and each Sabbath morning a longer selection would be read. Customs varied, but during the course of one to three years, the entire Torah would be read, and then the process would begin again. Rabbinic sources speak of an official who would translate the reading into the vernacular after each line was read to make sure the people understood. As the Rabbis said, "Just as the Torah was given to Israel by God through an agent [Moses], so must we always give the Torah to the people through an agent."[32]

Both the Temple and the synagogue Torah readings had two related but distinct objectives. One was to communicate the substance of the Torah to the people so that they would know how God had interacted with their forebears and what God expected of Jews for all generations. In addition to this educational goal, there was a more narrowly religious one: the people were to feel the awe of God. As the verses cited above from Deuteronomy put it, "that they may hear and so learn to revere the Lord your God and to observe faithfully every word of this Teaching." From the Torah reading, one was to learn to *revere* and to *observe*.

That is true also of the Torah reading in the synagogue: the member of the congregation is not only to hear God's word, but to come into contact with God. If the former were the only goal, then now, when we have multiple means of mass communication, we could convey God's word much more efficiently than the public Torah reading does. One could even argue that Jewish leaders *should* dispense with the public reading of the Torah. Since most Jews living outside Israel cannot understand the Torah's Hebrew, if the Torah were only read to communicate the message of its words, Jews could certainly use the time to better Jewish profit.

Jews obviously do engage in many educational activities and use books, films, television, and computer programs as tools to teach the Jewish heritage, but it is the second goal that explains why educational activities and devices cannot replace the synagogue's Torah reading. The Jew needs to experience God's presence. He or she can do that to an extent through individual or group study, but the revelation *par excellence* in Judaism was not communicated to individuals or to small groups, and it was not conveyed in written form.

At Sinai the whole people was assembled. There is some ambiguity in the Torah as to whether they all heard God proclaim the Decalogue or whether, due to their fear of hearing God in unmediated form, either they or God insisted that Moses announce it to them. To reconcile these stories, and to account for the fact that the first person singular is used with reference to God only in the First and Second Commandments, one of the Rabbis claimed that the people heard directly from God only those two sections of the Decalogue.[33] Nevertheless, the impression conveyed to Jews from their earliest training through their adult years is that revelation was experienced by all of the Israelites.

It was also fully awesome, preceded by days of preparation and accompanied with "thunder and lightning, the blare of the horn and the mountain smoking" (Exodus 20:15), an event in which "the Presence of the Lord appeared in the sight of the Israelites as a consuming fire on the top of the mountain" (Exodus 24:17) and the Lord spoke to them "face to face on the mountain out of the fire" (Deuteronomy 5:4). One must remember that in the Jewish tradition as well as in most others, Scripture is historically and fundamentally oral. It was only later reduced to written form. Oral traditions are told by living people with much more punctuation, interest, and power than any text can possibly convey. Printed texts are venerated in many traditions, and their abiding presence supplies a sense of security and makes possible the pleasures of studying them; but oral transmission enlivens religious sensitivities and sensibilities as no text can.[34] Hearing the Torah orally in the synagogue enables one to feel part of the People Israel standing at Sinai, imbued—indeed, overwhelmed—with the presence of the heteronomous God and the words they heard God as saying.

This drama is embodied in the very words surrounding the communal reading. A prescribed number of people are called to the Torah to recite blessings before and after a section of the Torah is chanted. Each uses a traditional formula that makes it clear that revelation happened in the past and *also occurs now, each time the Torah is read.* Pay attention to the tenses of the verbs in the traditional blessings:

> *Before the Torah is read:* Praised are You, Lord our God, Sovereign of the universe, who has chosen us from among all peoples by giving us His Torah (or, "and has given us His Torah"). Praised are You, Lord, who gives the Torah.
>
> *After the Torah has been read:* Praised are You, Lord our God, Sovereign of the universe, who has given us the Torah of truth, planting within us life eternal. Praised are You, Lord, who gives the Torah.[35]

God *has given* the Torah, but God *gives* the Torah anew each time it is read publicly in the synagogue. *The Torah reading, then, becomes nothing less than a reenactment of Sinai, one that we should approach with respect, wonder, and even trepidation.* In reading the Torah, we are coming into contact with God's heteronomous and authoritative will. We may and must interpret it in human categories, and the process of interpretation makes it more comprehensible and applicable to us—indeed, more human. Nevertheless, at the moment the Torah is read, we have—and should have—an experience of the *mysterium tremendum,* the power, mystery, and sheer awe of God.

To recapture some of that, Jewish law and custom surround the public Torah reading with a number of requirements. The Torah itself, for example, must be made of parchment and must be handwritten by a pious scribe trained to write its letters in a specific kind of Hebrew print with crowns on the top of some letters. Detailed rules prescribe what must be done during the service and thereafter if an error or blotch is discovered while reading a Torah scroll. The Torah cover is a work of art, as is the cover of the table on which it is read. The Torah is not simply opened and read; it is taken from the ark when the congregation is standing and singing appropriate biblical verses, and it is carried around the congregation before it is returned to the table where it is to be read. Although a system of voweling notation was already in use by the ninth century, the Torah scroll does not include that, and so the reader must prepare in advance to know how to pronounce the Torah's words correctly. He or she must also memorize the notes by which the verses are sung. There must not be any error in reading God's word to the congregation, and so two people stand at the table with books open, ready to correct the reader's mistakes. This whole ceremony can only take place if at least ten Jewish adults are present, since it must be a communal reading.

If the only aim of the communal reading of the Torah were to convey its contents, many of these rules would be totally impractical. Their existence proves that that is not its sole objective. All of these requirements are designed to impart a degree of fear, caution, and amazement to the proceedings. Their very impracticality adds to that: this is not to be a normal hearing of information, but an unusual event, embroidered with enigmatic ritual. One listens to the Torah being read not only with attention, but with reverence and deference. This is not like reading any other text, and it is not even like reading the Torah itself for purposes of study; this is a reenactment of Sinai, with all of its power and mystery. One comes into contact not only with God's will, but with God.

Revelation as Exodus, Torah, and Covenant

Revelation may inspire dread and humility; it may reinforce our awareness of the transcendent gap between ourselves and God.

And yet, for Jews, revelation also entails warmth and benevolence, for it is the substance of God's ongoing relationship with the People Israel. Actually, in Jewish tradition revelation is not one theme, but three: God led the Jews out of slavery from Egypt, gave them the Torah, and created a covenant with them.

The Exodus from Egypt is repeatedly mentioned in the Bible and Jewish liturgy. In part, this is because the Exodus shows that God can be trusted to keep promises. God promised Abram to redeem the People Israel (Genesis 15:13–16), and so He did.

This, though, is just one example of a more fundamental belief of Judaism which the Exodus demonstrates—namely, that God acts in history. God did not create the world and forget about it, but rather takes an active role in determining events.

Probably the most important reason the Exodus is emphasized so much in Judaism, however, is because it is the beginning of the Jewish People. The descendants of Abraham and Sarah were not galvanized into a nation until they left the slave existence and mentality of Egypt. Human beings are always concerned with beginnings because we correctly feel that much of the character of a person or people is already evident at birth. Because this is so, we celebrate birthdays of both individuals and nations as a way of expressing our appreciation for their existence.[36] The Exodus marks the birth of the Jewish People, and Jews celebrate their existence as Jews by often mentioning their birth in the Exodus and by associating it with some of the most important Jewish perceptions, values, events, and practices.

The Exodus gave the Jews physical existence as a nation, but it was the revelation at Sinai that gave the Jewish People its distinctive character. The whole purpose of the redemption from slavery was to enable the Israelites to receive the Torah and act according to its precepts. Consequently, God threatens to annul the Exodus by destroying the entire nation when they flagrantly disobey by building the molten calf (Exodus 32–33).[37] Conversely, since receiving the Torah was the goal of the Exodus, the Sabbath, which is described in Deuteronomy's version of the Decalogue as a celebration of the Exodus, is fittingly devoted to an extended, communal reading and study of the Torah.

The revelation, however, was not only a unilateral dictation of God's commands; it was a confirmation of the ongoing relationship between God and Israel articulated in the Covenant between them. This, of course, was not a contract in the usual, human sense of the term, in that Israel's accession to the Covenant was not completely voluntary. Both the biblical and rabbinic traditions recognize the compulsion under which the Israelites assented to the Covenant. According to the rabbinic legend, God held Mount Sinai over the people and told them to accept the Covenant's terms or else God would drop the mountain on their heads to bury them! Nevertheless, both the Bible and rabbinic literature assert that the Israelites were given a choice and proclaimed "We shall do and we shall hear" (Exodus 24:7).[38] This is not as strange as it sounds: in both sovereign-subject and parent-child relationships, there is a similar combination of the voluntary and involuntary.

The revelation, in any case, records the history of the relationship between God and Israel, their mutual promises, the consideration each party gains in the agreement, the penalties for violating the agreement, and expressions of genuine affection between the parties. It thus contains the substance of the Covenant between God and Israel. As such, revelation is a phenomenon which Jews associate not only with awe and fear, but also with God's care, concern, wisdom, and love.

Since the Sabbath, according to Deuteronomy's version of the Decalogue, was motivated by the Exodus, it functions as a symbol of all three themes intertwined with it—the Exodus itself, the revelation at Sinai, and the Covenant that resulted from these events.

While Passover is the symbol of the Exodus *par excellence,* the liturgy does tie the Exodus to the Sabbath as well. This appears especially clearly in the sanctification over wine (the *Kiddush*) on Friday evenings, where the Sabbath is not only "a reminder of Creation," but also "the first among our days of sacred assembly which recall the Exodus from Egypt."

As we have discussed, the most potent symbol of Sinai in the Sabbath rites is the extended reading and study of the Torah on Saturday morning and the continued Torah reading and study at the Saturday afternoon service. The Sabbath liturgy, though, also refers to Sinai, appropriately in the Saturday morning *Amidah* before the Torah is read:

> Moses rejoiced at the gift of his destiny when You declared him a faithful servant, adorning him with splendor as he stood in Your Presence atop Mount Sinai. Two tablets of stone did he bring down, inscribed with Sabbath observance. . . .

Of these three themes linked to revelation, though, the Sabbath is preeminently the symbol of the Covenant. The phylacteries *(tefillin)* are described in the Torah as the sign of the Exodus (Exodus 13:9, 16), of God's commandments (Deuteronomy 6:6–8), and of God's enforcement of the commandments (Deuteronomy 11:13–21). On the Sabbath, though, wearing the *tefillin* is unnecessary and inappropriate because the Sabbath itself is 'a sign of all of those elements of the Covenant. The Sabbath in rabbinic thought is the sign of all of the commandments.[39] Even before the Rabbis, the prophet Ezekiel repeatedly singles out the Sabbath as the litmus test of the extent to which Israel was observing God's law and the strength or weakness of the whole relationship between God and Israel:

Ezekiel 20:10–20:

I brought them out of the land of Egypt and I led them into the wilderness. I gave them My laws and taught them My rules, by the pursuit of which a man shall live. Moreover, I gave them My Sabbaths to serve as a sign between Me and them, that they might know that it is I, the Lord, who sanctify them. But the House of Israel rebelled against Me in the wilderness; they did not follow My laws, and they rejected My rules—by the pursuit of which a man shall live—and they grossly desecrated My Sabbaths. Then I thought to pour out My fury upon them in the wilderness and to make an end of them; but I acted for the sake of My name, that it might not be profaned in the sight of the nations before whose eyes I had led them out. However, I swore to them in the wilderness that I would not bring them into the land flowing with milk and honey, the fairest of all lands, which I had assigned to them, for they had rejected My rules, disobeyed My laws, and desecrated My Sabbaths; their hearts followed after their fetishes. But I had pity on them and did not destroy them; I did not make an end of them in the wilderness.

I warned the children in the wilderness: Do not follow the practices of your fathers, do not keep their ways, and do not defile yourselves with their fetishes. I, the Lord, am your God: Follow My laws and be careful to observe My rules. And hallow My Sabbaths, that they may be a sign between Me and you, that you may know that I the Lord am your God.

And just as the Covenant is specifically between God and the People Israel, so, too, the Sabbath, its symbol, is exclusively God's gift to the People Israel:

Exodus 31:16–17 (used in the Friday evening and Saturday morning Amidah):

The Israelite people shall keep the Sabbath, observing the Sabbath throughout the ages as a covenant for all time. It shall be a sign for all time between Me and the People Israel. . . .

Mekhilta Ki Tissa (on Exodus 31:17):

"It is a sign between Me and you," that is, and not between Me and the other nations of the world.

Sabbath morning Amidah:

Lord, our God, You have not given it [the gift of the Sabbath] to the other nations of the earth; You, our King, have not bestowed it upon those who worship idols, and the uncircumcised [i.e., non-Jews] do not enjoy its rest. Instead You have lovingly given it to Israel, Your People, the descendants of Jacob, whom you have chosen.

Revelation as God's Gift

This last theme, that the Sabbath is God's gift to Israel, also applies to the Torah as a whole and to revelation, the process by which Israel received it. In Hebrew, in fact, there is no classical word for "revelation"; instead the phrase used is *matan Torah,* "the giving of the Torah." Israel feels grateful not only for the gift of the Torah, but for being aware of how precious a gift it is. As Rabbi Akiba said,

> Israel is beloved, for a precious instrument was given to them. As an extra measure of love, it was made known to them that they were given a precious instrument with which the world was created, as it is written, "For I give you good doctrine, forsake not My Torah" (Proverbs 4:2).[40]

The overriding feeling of Jews regarding revelation, then, is one of gratitude. This feeling is expressed many times in the liturgy, but it is perhaps best articulated in the two versions of the paragraph before *Shema* in the evening and morning services. The law is certainly not an impossible burden or the command of a God who knows only justice: it is nothing less than a prime expression of God's love.

> *Evening version:* With constancy You have loved Your people Israel, teaching us Torah and commandments, statutes and laws. Therefore, Lord our God, when we lie down to sleep and when we rise, we shall think of Your laws and speak of them, rejoicing in Your Torah and commandments always. For they are our life and the length of our days; we will meditate on them day and night. Never take away Your love from us. Praised are You, Lord, who loves His people Israel.

Morning version: Deep is Your love for us, Lord our God, boundless Your tender compassion. You taught our ancestors life-giving laws. They trusted in You, our Father and King. For their sake graciously teach us. Father, merciful Father, show us mercy; put it in our hearts lovingly to understand and discern, to listen, to learn, and to teach, to observe, to perform, and fulfill all the words of the teachings of Your Torah. Open our eyes to Your Torah, help our hearts cleave to Your commandments. Unite all our thoughts to love and revere You. Then we shall never be brought to shame. . . . Praised are You, Lord, who loves His people Israel.

Revelation, then, is awesome, but it is also enlightening and beneficent. One experiences it each time one studies and each time one hears the Torah read. Its meaning is at once always the same and always new. Its significance remains unchanged, since it is both the source of wisdom for our lives and the gift which God gives the People Israel in love.

5

KNOWING GOD THROUGH
DIVINE ACTION

The people of the Torah learn of God through the words heard at Sinai. They have known God before then, however—and at least as impressively—through the Ten Plagues and the Exodus from Egypt. This chronology should not be surprising: actions are usually more graphic and convincing than words. Actions, in fact, undergird our belief in words. In the Exodus story, for example, the people undoubtedly trust God's words at Sinai not only because of the overpowering setting in which they are delivered, but also because the Israelites have been primed to believe in the God of their deliverance by the events through which they had just passed.

When we moderns try to use God's actions to know God, however, we immediately run into trouble. In the human world, we can usually identify the agent quite easily by recognizing his or her body. Mystery stories, in fact, gain much of their intrigue from subverting that assumption and forcing us to guess who did the act on the basis of less direct evidence. What is mysterious and unusual in the human setting becomes the norm in theology: since God does not have a body, we must always use indirect means to identify events as the work of God.

THE RELATED PROBLEM OF EVIL

The problem of evil makes this all the harder. Briefly stated, it is this: If one believes that (1) God is one, (2) God acts in human history, (3) God is all-knowing (omniscient), (4) God is all-powerful (omnipotent), (5) God is good, and yet (6) there is unjustified evil in the world, then one is involved in a self-contradiction. An all-knowing, all-powerful God who is also good, after all, could never allow unjustified evil to exist and would never need to.

Aside from raising a fundamental issue concerning the nature of God, this severely complicates the problem of recognizing when God produces an act, and when not. If we could claim that God does only good, then we would have a clear criterion by which to know when God is acting. Restricting God's action to the good, however, compromises divine unity and power, for who or what else is then responsible for the evil we experience? On the other hand, if God does produce evil, what are we to make of the claim of divine goodness?

How we identify God's actions depends, to a degree, upon how we resolve the problem of evil. To do that, one must deny—or at least soften—one of the premises listed above.

One classical Jewish approach restricted God's power (assumption #4), claiming that "all is in the hands of Heaven except the fear of Heaven."[1] That is, God *could* control everything but *chose* not to do so in order to grant to human beings the freedom to make some decisions and the ability to carry them out.

Rabbinic legend records that God hesitated in creating such a being, for surely human beings would at times use their freedom to violate the divine will. When consulting the angels, God even hid from them mankind's potential to do evil so that they could not use that persuasive argument against the creation of human beings.[2] This story underscores that God knew full well that people would sin and *nevertheless* created humanity with this ability.

Why did God do this? In part, perhaps, because God knew that free will is at the heart of what it means to be human. Only with such capacity can we gain the joy and dignity of being independent, creative beings; without it we are but machines. Therefore God is not evil in giving us the capacity to choose; on the contrary, that gift gives meaning to life and enables us to be partners with God in perfecting the world.

Human free will not only defines what it is to be human; it also defines God's relationship with us. God gains more prestige—and is indeed a greater God—if He can persuade a being with free will to act in accordance with divine desires rather than program an automaton to do so. Human analogies make this clear: assuming that a person and a machine can do the same thing, it is a much greater feat to convince the person to do what you want than to turn on a machine to do so. The machine has no choice in the matter; the person does. This rationale for creating human beings with free will is consistent with a general theme oft repeated in both the Bible and rabbinic literature, namely, that God created the whole world, and especially the angels and human beings, for His glory.[3]

In any case, because we *can* choose to do right or wrong, we bear *responsibility* for our choices. Human free will, thus, makes people, rather than God, the culprits for much of the evil we experience in this world while yet explaining how God remains good.

There are, however, several problems with this resolution of the problem of evil. First, innocent people suffer when others abuse their free will. How can a benevolent God allow this?

Apologists often claim that this result, however unfortunate, is the price we pay for free will. Our capacity to choose is genuine only if we can *act* on our evil choices just as we can effectuate our good ones. Therefore God *logically* could not have given us free will while yet preventing us from inflicting harm on one another. God's choice was either to permit us to cause pain and death, or not to give us free will at all. We cannot, as it were, "have our cake and eat it too." As a result, human beings, and not God, are culpable for much of the evil we see and suffer.

This "free will defense" for God becomes questionable, though, when the evil inflicted by others is extensive and cruel, as in the Holocaust. Again invoking the parental example, good parents will step in at some point if the damage to be done by their child's choices will be too great, and one would expect the same of a benevolent, divine Parent.

When children reach their late teenage years and beyond, of course, parents lose power to determine their children's choices, although often they still exert considerable influence. Applying the parental analogy in this stage to God, however, would seriously impugn God's power and simultaneously flatter us human beings. Have we indeed grown up to that degree in our relationship with God?

Some think so, primarily, although not exclusively, as a result of God's apparent inaction in the Holocaust.[4] They claim that that event is totally a human product into which God could not intervene without compromising our adult level of freedom. The very fact that God did not prevent the Holocaust, in other words, forces us to recognize the reality of this new status of God and human beings and this new relationship between them.

I personally wonder whether God is so impotent and whether we are so mature. Moreover, this approach does not explain why innocent people suffer and die in situations where no human will is involved, as in natural disasters such as disease and earthquakes. In some such cases, prior human choices to adopt bad health habits or to ignore proper earthquake construction standards make the human beings involved at least partially responsible, but there are many instances in which no human choice even remotely affects the occurrence. Floods, hurricanes, earthquakes, and many diseases do their damage regardless of human action, and many morally good adults and innocent children suffer in the process. How could a good, powerful God allow this?

Because of such weaknesses in this approach, rabbis and philosophers within the Jewish tradition, in search of other explanations, have sometimes denied or restricted one of the other assumptions entailed in the problem of evil. So, for example, the Bible and the rabbis of the Talmud variously adjusted the last assumption—that there is evil in the world. Along these lines, they sometimes claimed that people deserve the suffering they endure, whether or not they recognize this, and thus the pain they feel, while certainly unpleasant, is not evil.[5] They also maintained that people pay for the sins of their parents, and therefore the suffering, while possibly unwarranted by the children, is, in the larger scheme of things, retribution for past wrongs.[6] A major rabbinic adjustment of the last premise was that God rewards and punishes not only in this world, but in a world to come, and there the accounts of unpunished malefactors and unrewarded benefactors will be rectified. God's justice and goodness are thus preserved, despite present appearances.[7] Maimonides even went so far as to deny existence to evil, maintaining that it is only the absence of good.[8] However difficult this may be to swallow in the face of the pain felt by many, it too rescues God from responsibility for evil. If there is none, nobody can be blamed for it!

Jewish naturalists like Mordecai M. Kaplan, Milton Stein-

berg, and Harold Kushner have instead preferred to restrict
God's actions to the good, consciously giving up God's omnipotence in the process. Thus Kaplan claims that "earthquakes and
volcanic eruptions, devastating storms and floods, famines and
plagues, noxious plants and animals . . . are simply that phase of
the universe which has not yet been completely penetrated by
godhood," for "the modern conception of God" follows the less
frequent rabbinic opinion according to which, "The Holy One,
blessed be He, does not associate His name with evil, but only
associates it with that which is good."[9] Similarly, Harold
Kushner, in a moving, popular book, has maintained that all
excuses for an omnipotent God become untenable in the face of
senseless, personal tragedy and that we must consequently affirm that God, though good, is not all-powerful.[10]

Even Kaplan admits that his position "involves a radical
change in the traditional concept of God" because it undermines
divine omnipotence and omniscience.[11] It also understates the
reality of evil. Kaplan specifically affirms that evils exist,[12] but it
is hard to take them seriously if the power of God is behind the
good but does not participate in perpetrating evil. God, after all,
is our symbol for ultimate reality. Therefore, restricting God to
the good, as Kaplan and Kushner have done, makes evil meta-
physically unreal. It is a conceptual way of pretending that evil
does not have any permanent existence, that it is, at worst, what
Steinberg depicts—the areas of the universe that God has not yet
reached. We might *wish* this were so, and we might warm to
thinkers who tell us that it is; but ultimately this only deceives
us, for evil is as real, as permanent, and as powerful a part of our
experience as good is. It therefore behooves us to build that
reality into our conception of God.

Of the various ways of doing so, the extreme positions on
both ends of the spectrum were already articulated in ancient
times. One is that strain of biblical and rabbinic literature that

maintains that we must simply accept the evil we experience as an act of God which we cannot understand, that God, though good, sometimes does things which defy understanding in their arbitrariness. Nevertheless, we must continue to believe in God and carry out the divine commands.[13]

The opposite position, classified as foolish and heretical in classical Jewish literature, can no longer be cavalierly dismissed. Richard Rubenstein has argued that the Holocaust demonstrates once and for all that there is no God who acts in history, that there is only the overpowering, amoral God of nature. Massive overpopulation—the cause of world poverty, insufficiency of medical services, and unemployment—and the nuclear threat have together underscored this even more. Jewish ritual and fellowship can aid us in huddling together and supporting each other against the ravages of this God, and they can enable us, as they always have, to find psychological support and emotional expression in life-cycle events, but the only philosophically appropriate prayer is silence. Rubenstein underestimates the positive experiences of life, and his view wrecks havoc with our moral expectations and practice—both of which are equally part of the world we know—but he has honestly and courageously forced his readers to focus on the hard realities at the core of this prime objection to theism.[14]

Between these extremes, a variety of positions have been proposed. They each shy away from divorcing God from evil, on the one hand, and from making God amoral, on the other. Typical of intermediate stances on any issue, these positions lack the conceptual cleanness of the extreme views described above, but they capture more of the intellectually messy reality of our experience. In that sense, they are probably closer to the truth.

What we really want, of course, is some way to satisfy our emotional need to make sense of instances of evil in our lives and to acquiesce to them intellectually as somehow appropriate. We also want reassurance that such instances will not happen again, that our world is ultimately not a threatening place. Kushner's response probably comes closest to speaking to the emotional need; but his theory, as we noted above, comes at the expense of making God irrelevant to evil, thus evading the metaphysical reality of evil and threatening the unity of God. It also entails other problems that we shall describe below.

The wisest response to this emotional need is, I think, what the Rabbis of the Talmud advanced long ago in developing the mourning rites—namely, a time dedicated to crying openly and unreservedly about the hurt, to voicing our worries about the future, and, eventually, to turning our attention to how we are going to cope with this loss or malady in the future—all in the context of the presence and support of those near and dear to us. Ultimately, emotional needs require responses that speak directly to those emotions.

There is an intellectual part to our dilemma, however, and it is a serious one. The depth of our emotional distress in the face of evil, in fact, is at least partially due to our inability to make sense of occurrences of evil—especially, for believers, in the presence of a powerful, benevolent God. After all, we are not bifurcated beings; our emotions and our intellects are interrelated. A rational explanation of evil would certainly not eliminate our need to express the grief, fear, anger, and dismay we have when confronted with it, but it would at least give us a sense of its place in our universe. This would reaffirm our sense of order and security in the world, which are precisely the emotions we need to regain in order to carry on. As long as we recognize, then, that rational deliberation can never substitute for the outpouring of emotion required to cope with emotionally trying circumstances, the quest for a theory that adequately accounts for our various experiences in the world, both good and bad, is not only intellectually necessary, but emotionally beneficial.

Fusing Conceptions of God

My own philosophical approach to these issues, then, will follow this line of development: To devise a sound theory to identify and account for God's role in evil, we must first recognize a basic ambiguity in the Jewish concept of God. Once we decide what we mean by the term "God," many of the questions will no longer be so perplexing, and religious faith will become not only possible but plausible. Moreover, in the process, we will discover some fundamental commitments of the Jewish approach to life.

A wide variety of conceptions of God have emerged in the course of Jewish history. The most prominent Jewish thinkers have included rationalists like Hermann Cohen and mystics like Luria, naturalists like Mordecai Kaplan, supernaturalists like Samson Raphael Hirsch, and even total secularists like Ahad Ha'am. This variety was possible, in part, because of a feature of the Jewish tradition that we have seen earlier in the context of law and which applies equally to theology. That is, the Jewish tradition, from talmudic times on, substituted Midrash for revelation, claiming that revelation ceased with the destruction of the First Temple and that, in any case, the Sages learned more about God through their methodology of Midrash than prophets could ever learn through revelation.[15] Jews, therefore, had great latitude in their attempt to describe God and to make Judaism an intellectually lively and rich tradition.

The diversity in Jewish conceptions of God is not, however, an unmitigated blessing. Aside from the problems of authority that it raises, it causes confusion when people try to combine elements from different sources and discover that not all of the conceptions are coherent. One such classical confusion that we have discussed at some length above was pointed out centuries ago by Judah Halevi and reiterated in a different form and for a different purpose by Mordecai Kaplan: it is the confusion which results when we graft the original Hebrew notion of God, conceived individually as a superhuman Person, onto the Greek notion of God, conceived generically as the concept of godhood.[16] Richard Rubenstein called attention to another synthesis which is even older. It is the Torah's synthesis of the God of nature with the God of history.

I would like to point out another fusion similar to Rubenstein's and yet distinct from it, namely, the God of power with the God of goodness. It is similar to Rubenstein's synthesis in that the God of nature is often manifest in displays of power and the God of history in interventions to assure a good outcome. Rubenstein's distinction and mine, however, are not equivalent, for sometimes power is associated with the God of history and goodness with the God of nature. The Ten Plagues, for example, were intended, according to the Torah, specifically to exhibit the power of Israel's God of history, and Jews praise the God of nature in every weekday morning service for bringing both light and crops.

Both Halevi and Rubenstein endorse discarding one of the conceptions of God they note in favor of the other. I have argued that we must retain both of Halevi's conceptions of God, distinguishing what we mean in the various contexts in which we use the term, "God." I would say the same for Rubenstein's two views and for the related pictures of God as powerful and good.

Before describing how such an approach would affect the problem of evil and the difficulty of identifying an act as God's, however, let us first describe each of the two conceptions that the tradition affirms and combines. T. H. Meek maintains that power is the original meaning of most biblical terms referring to God and that God was associated with goodness only subsequently in the Jewish tradition.[17] Whether or not one agrees with this, it is certainly true that power is a significant part of what we mean by "God." We even use that sense in common parlance, as when lawyers say that an event was "an act of God." In such contexts "divine" means "superhuman" or "beyond human knowledge and control." In asserting the existence of divine phenomena in this sense of "divine," we stress that we human beings are not all-powerful or all-knowing, that, on the contrary, we are vastly limited in our knowledge and control of even the most fundamental conditions of human existence and welfare, and that we should, therefore, have the humility to appreciate the good things in life and to fear the bad. Traditionally, a Jew is supposed to utter one hundred blessings each day, for blessing God for something calls attention to our dependence on God's power.

The realization of the existence and omnipresence of such superhuman powers can, of course, make one very much afraid. After all, what is out of one's control can potentially be dangerous and harmful. From its beginning, however, the Jewish tradition trusted that the presence of the divine in the world was primarily a benevolent one. God might become manifest in very negative ways, but that was not considered the norm. On the contrary, the Jewish assumption that God is good and just is so deeply rooted that, throughout history, Jews have protested vehemently and eloquently whenever events reveal God to be unjust or malevolent. Such protest makes sense only if one first assumes that God can be expected to be just and good. When things did not go well, Jews usually reacted with the conviction that the situation would improve. Ultimately, Jews trusted, we will reach the eschatological, messianic age in which all human limitations, frustrations, and sinfulness will be eliminated. Jews could reasonably have that faith because they believed that within God, justice and goodness are fundamental.[18]

A second sense of the term "God," then, means good. God is thus "the savior" who has mercies without end, as we daily recite in our prayers. In fact, the *Shema* demands that we *love* God and, unless we are masochists, that demand makes sense only if God is good and, hence, an appropriate object for our love. In this sense the word "divine" is used to express extreme approval of qualities or acts, including those of human beings. Thus, when we refer to love, care, and concern as divine qualities, we mean that they are very good, that they make people godly, in contrast to bringing out their animal nature.

Why the ancient Hebrews combined power with goodness in their conception of God is a matter of conjecture. It might have been because their assessment of the conditions of life was optimistic and that they honestly thought that all would work out well in the end. Alternatively, it may have been because they viewed life pessimistically and, therefore, created a conception of a benign God in order to alleviate their deepest fears. More traditionally, it was because they had immediate, personal experience with a benevolent God.

Whatever their reason, the Holocaust has made it clear (if it was not before) that the powers-that-be in the world, whether natural or human, do not always work for human good. In other words, our experience has shown amply that the combination of power and goodness that the ancients built into their conception of God is an inherently incongruous and unstable combination. Consequently, if we are going to be able to make any sense of the relationship of God to the Holocaust, we are going to have to sort out, once again, the two elements of power and goodness.

DIFFERENTIATING THE TWO DEFINITIONS OF GOD

Specifically, when asking whether or not God had a role in the Holocaust, the answer depends upon which sense of "divine" is being used. If divinity means goodness, then, by definition, God was not in something as horrible as the Holocaust. If divinity means power, then God most assuredly had a hand in that overwhelmingly gruesome event.

The first alternative, identifying God exclusively with goodness, saves God's benevolence and reassures us of the ultimately benign nature of life. It is, however, wishful thinking. We obviously would *like* to say that there is a God who is totally good, but that does us a disservice because it hides a large part of our experience. The fact simply is that there *is* evil in this world.

One could agree that there is evil but determine to leave God out of it, as Kaplan, Kushner, and others have done. This would save God's reputation for benevolence, but only at a great price. Specifically, dissociating God from all occurrences of evil immediately compromises God's omnipresence and omnipotence. Depending upon how one explains the origin of evil, this approach might also subvert God's unity. It would not do this if one claims that evil occurs where God has not yet reached, as Steinberg does, but then one is left with the problem of identifying the source of evil. If one imputes evil to some active agent outside God, then, effectively, one believes in at least two gods. Even without such a dualistic assertion, a God who does not cause evil is a very pallid God, one divorced from much of our experience and irrelevant to it. Such a God would be, in fact, a mere personification of our desires and/or our moral values. Besides all these problems of this option, eliminating God from evil also diminishes and distorts the reality and power of evil.

As a result, to account for the role of God in evil, I would prefer to use the first notion of God described above, the one in which the "divine" refers to superhuman qualities and events, whether they be good or bad. I would then affirm that God *is* in the Holocaust. In this way I would be denoting that the events of the Holocaust went far beyond the normal conception of human power, psychological maneuverability, and morality.

The immediate problem with my view, of course, is that it makes God responsible for evil as well as for good, and, as we saw before, there is at least some support in the tradition for denying that evil derives from God. I would like to point out, however, that there is also traditional support for the view that God is responsible for evil, and that may well be the mainstream position. For instance, according to Isaiah, God proclaims: "I form the light and create darkness: I make peace, *and create evil;* I, the Lord, do all these things."[19] When the Rabbis used this verse in the morning prayers, they changed it to: "Blessed art Thou, O Lord our God, who forms the light and creates darkness, makes peace and *creates everything.*" As they themselves explain, however, they did this because of the need for a more felicitous expression suitable to the language of prayer, *not* because they wanted to deny that God creates evil.[20] Moreover, Satan, the personification of evil, is always portrayed in biblical literature as an instrument of the Divine, and the Rabbis followed suit.[21] The Rabbis even claimed that Jews must *thank* God for whatever evil befalls them and not just for the good things they enjoy:

> Do not behave towards Me as the heathens behave toward their gods. When happiness comes to them, they sing praises to their gods . . . , but when retribution comes upon them they curse their gods. . . . If I bring happiness upon you give thanks, and when I bring sufferings give thanks also.[22]

The Sages went further yet: Jews must *bless* God for evil as they bless God for good. We love God much more profoundly, according to the Rabbis, when our love is not restricted to appreciation for the good but encompasses the acknowledgment that God generates the bad, too.

> A person is obligated to utter a benediction for the bad just as one utters a blessing for the good; as it is said, "And you shall love the Lord your God

with all your heart and with all your soul and with all your might"
(Deuteronomy 6:5)—"with all your heart," i.e., with your two impulses,
the good and the evil impulse; "with all your soul," i.e., even if He takes
your soul; "with all your might," i.e., with all your wealth. Another
explanation of "with all your might" is that with whatever measure He
metes out to you, return Him thanks.[23]

And, finally, God inflicts punishment. Sometimes that punishment is deserved, in which case God's justice is at work. But
sometimes God punishes people contrary to all human understanding of when punishment is called for, as in this famous
example:

> Rab Judah said in the name of Rab: When Moses ascended on high, he
> found the Holy One, blessed be He, engaged in affixing crowns on the
> letters of the Torah. Moses said: "Lord of the Universe, why are these
> additions necessary?" He answered: "There will arise a man at the end of
> many generations, Akiba, son of Joseph, by name, who will expound upon
> each tittle heaps and heaps of laws." "Lord of the Universe," said Moses,
> "permit me to see him." He replied, "Turn around." Moses went and sat
> down behind eight rows [of Rabbi Akiba's disciples and listened to the
> discourses upon the law]. . . . Thereupon he returned to the Holy One,
> blessed be He, and said, "Lord of the Universe, You have such a man, and
> You gave the Torah through me?" He replied, "Be silent, for so I have
> decided." Then Moses said, "Lord of the Universe, You have shown me
> his Torah, show me his reward." "Turn around," said He; and Moses
> turned around and saw people weighing out his flesh in the market [after
> he had been executed by the Romans]. "Lord of the Universe," cried
> Moses, "such is his knowledge of Torah, and such is his reward?" He
> replied, "Be silent, for so I have decided."[24]

This story, it seems to me, precisely articulates our problem
with the Holocaust, for it deals with specifically that type of evil
that is the suffering of the innocent. The Rabbis unequivocally
make God responsible for it in this passage. Of course they also
tried to exonerate God elsewhere by taking refuge in divine

omniscience: perhaps the slaughtered and the suffering did, in fact, sin, even if such sins were hidden from us, and God's punishment is, therefore, appropriate and perhaps even benevolent.[25] They were aware, though, that in many cases such a line of argument would simply not do. There *is* a residue of evil in this world, there is undeserved suffering, and God is responsible for it. This is, after all, precisely what we should have expected from the Rabbis, given that they waged an unceasing war against the Zoroastrian notion that there was a separate power which caused evil. That, they knew, would violate God's unity:

> "I, even I, am He, and there is no God in addition to me; it is I that kill, and it is I that make alive; I wound and I heal" (Deuteronomy 32:39). This verse is an answer to those who say, "There is no Power in heaven," or to those who say "There are two Powers in heaven," or to those who say, "There is no Power who can make alive or kill, do evil or do good."[26]

All of this, then, indicates that for the rabbinic tradition, too, the root sense of "God" did *not* assume divine absence from evil. On the contrary, God created evil and inflicts punishment—sometimes contrary to all human understanding of when punishment is deserved.

GOD'S JUSTICE AND GOODNESS

This bring us to the second problem with affirming God's complicity in the Holocaust. The tradition, after all, maintains that God is both just and good. This belief gave moral courage and hope to thousands of our ancestors because it justified decency in the face of gross indecency. God would ultimately punish the wicked and bring triumph to the righteous in a

messianic age, and so it makes sense to act morally and constructively despite all appearances to the contrary. But if God was at
least partially responsible for the Holocaust, how can we any
longer believe in such ultimate justice and goodness?

The Rabbis themselves were hard put to defend the apparent
lapses in God's justice, and sometimes they simply admitted that
we cannot understand His acts.[27] The Holocaust, it seems to me,
makes it totally impossible to ignore any longer the great mass of
evidence against this tenet.

Nevertheless, my attitudes toward life are virtually the same
as those who believe that God is just. That is, despite the
evidence of the Holocaust, I still believe that justice, morality,
and compassion are crucial, even if they are not rewarded.[28] We
simply have to advance our thinking to a point that some of the
Rabbis had already reached—namely, that doing the right thing
for the sake of reward is really not the proper motivation and
often does not work out anyway, and that in the end the only
reward for performing a *mitzvah* is having done it and the
impetus that that gives to performing another *mitzvah*.[29]

Similar considerations apply to God's benevolence. I certainly
would agree that there *are* positive phenomena in our experience
and that we must be as honest about those as we are about
negative events like the Holocaust. I would go further: I would
say that if the evidence of negative versus positive is roughly
even, we should accentuate the positive, choosing to describe
the glass as half-full rather than as half-empty and to act constructively on the basis of that view.[30] And I would even endorse the stance of Job and of many of our ancestors who
maintained their commitment to Judaism in the face of horrible
demonstrations of the evil that occurs from time to time in this
world, for I do think that, if necessary, the Jewish way of life is
worth dying for.

What gives me trouble is the tradition's conviction that all will be right in the end. I certainly *wish* that humanity could be cured of at least some its more grievous afflictions, such as its propensity to make war. Moreover, I think that Jews have a positive duty . to *try* to free humanity of such maladies, based on our generally positive attitude toward the world and the ample evidence that exists in our experience to support it. I also think that ultimate emancipation is beyond human ability to achieve; to attain it, we will need God's help, as the tradition emphasized.[31]

Past human history, however, and especially the Holocaust, has made me too skeptical to believe with a complete faith that in the future we will be completely relieved of all of these limitations. The evil manifestations of both God and humanity have been too rife. I *hope* that good will triumph, but it is a hope and not a conviction for me, since, despite my desires, I entertain considerable doubt that it will happen.

The tradition had no such misgivings. The tradition's conviction referred to messianic times, however. Moreover, I do want to affirm the pragmatic upshot of the doctrines of God's benevolent and redemptive character, namely, that we must act constructively while still realizing the limits of our ability. Thus, my position is not so far from the traditional one, although it certainly is not identical with it.

One last point must be made here. When I maintain that God played a role in causing the Holocaust in the first sense of "God" and when I affirm that the second sense is a separate meaning which is at times inconsistent with the first, am I just enunciating a softer version of Richard Rubenstein's philosophy? I think not, because I *am* affirming the second sense as well as the first. That is, I am agreeing with the classical Jewish commitment to constructive action in this world through both the ritual and moral *mitzvot*. That commitment is based on the faith that our action can make a difference, that the conditions of life are not incorrigibly beyond remedy. I may have doubts about whether the human condition is ultimately and fully redeemable, but I do, nevertheless, adopt the tradition's optimistic and enterprising philosophy of life regarding the possibility of more modest improvements. I do so because I think that it is both consistent with past experience and a wise formula for our future action. It is this conviction that is expressed in the second sense of "God," and I would affirm it as I would avow the first.

TRUTH AT THE PRICE OF CONSISTENCY AND FANTASY

I have tried to show that the traditional concept of God involved a combination of power and goodness, two elements that our experience has shown to be often discordant. Consequently, clarity about God's role in the Holocaust demands that we sort out these two factors in what we mean by "God." This does not mean that we should deny either one of them; it merely means that if we want consistency, we must separate these two attributes which the tradition ascribed to God. On the other hand, if we want our concept of God to express the crucial elements of our experience, we must allow both the powerful and the good to be parts of God, however incongruous they may be. Here, as usual, rabbinic tradition preferred to tolerate inconsistency in order to encompass truth.

If one takes this approach, one understands more deeply the truth behind our ancestors' perception of God's acts in history. We come to know God every time we experience the incredible power of nature. Even if we understand the biological processes which produce a new baby, for example, the experience of seeing one born is literally awesome. It demonstrates to us the limits of our own power and knowledge while at the same time revealing the presence of God.

Sometimes that revelation is not a pleasant one for us. Some babies are born with defects, and some years the rain does not fall in the amounts we need. Sometimes we experience not only the absence of what we want, but the presence of what we do not want. These active manifestations of evil occur both in natural phenomena and in human relations. Human beings are indeed at fault in some such cases, but at least as often we must see the hand of God in these negative events. The ancient Israelites did not flinch from this, and neither should we.

On the other hand, like them we should also appreciate and thank God for the good we encounter. Earthquakes and the Holocaust are no more of a theological problem than are abundant food and actions on moral principle. Both types are features of our world which we alone cannot cause or prevent. We may be more aware of God when things are not going well for us, just as we notice our skin only when it is cut or bruised. This, however, is a fault in our cognizance, for God is present in our ongoing sustenance and well-being at least as much as in our privations and distress. Indeed, the Jewish tradition, by claiming that God's chief attribute is goodness, asserted that, on balance, we have much more to thank God for than to complain about. We must, in any case, note and appreciate God's presence in the good as much as we cry out and protest to God for the bad. God is manifest in both sorts of divine actions.

Neither of these conceptions will, on its own, speak to the emotional turmoil engendered by occurrences of evil in our lives. For that, we should resort to the emotional means of release and comfort crafted by the Rabbis long ago in the rites of mourning. Our distress will not be alleviated for long by pretending that we understand unjustified evil in our world or by divorcing God from it; denial can be beneficial for a brief time during mourning, but ultimately it is not healthy either psychologically or philosophically. We must instead face the ultimate ambiguity of our existence with the commitment to truth, the faith, the strength, and the good sense of Jews over the ages.

6

KNOWING GOD THROUGH HUMAN WORDS: PRAYER

EXPERIENCING GOD THROUGH PRAYER

The Quandary: I Cannot Pray, but I Must

Most people periodically find themselves wanting to pray and actually engaging in prayer. This especially happens at critical moments in their lives, when they yearn to express exuberant joy, deep sorrow, or overwhelming needs. Their prayer may not be liturgically appropriate, and it probably does not come out of a thoroughly developed theology, but the instinct to pray is universal and natural for all.

Contemporary Jews who take an interest in Judaism, however, typically begin their exploration not with prayer but with trying to perform one or another of the other commandments. They do this, in part, because they simply do not know how to address the theological basis of prayer. From the point of view of the tradition, all of the commandments are deeply rooted in the experience of God. Carrying out commandments other than prayer, however, often can be rationalized on the basis of concomitant humanistic dimensions of meaning, and so engaging in them does not require immediate assent to theological claims.

The same cannot be said, however, for prayer, another human activity through which the Jewish tradition would have us learn about God. Prayer seems to be inextricably bound to belief in God. To whom, after all, does one pray if not to God? It would seem, then, that, unlike other Jewish actions, prayer from the start commits one to belief in God, and that is precisely what many Jews cannot handle.

That is not the only reason why many modern Jews avoid prayer. They lack the skills of Jewish worship, and thus prayer is strange and unfamiliar. Yet they feel that they should be able to pray, and so prayer is also threatening and humiliating. For many, these mechanical and emotional obstacles, together with the sheer time and energy required, explain why they do not pray.

The philosophical issues, however, if not the primary reasons why a Jew does not pray, generally lurk in the background. Why should one pray? Is there a God who hears prayer in the first place? Even if there is, why does God need our prayers? After all, the omniscient God of the tradition should know our needs and thoughts without our voicing them. We certainly should not have to repeat them over and over again, as the liturgy bids us do. Moreover, how do we know whether a prayer of petition is successful? God can presumably say "No!"—and there are occasions when doing so is benevolent. For all of these reasons and more, many Jews do not pray.

And yet prayer is at the root of Judaism. In biblical times the primary form of worship was animal sacrifice, but the Bible includes public prayers which accompanied sacrifices and the performance of other commandments, some personal prayers, and, of course, the Book of Psalms, much of which was probably used in a variety of liturgical settings.[1] Since sacrifices were restricted to the Temple in Jerusalem by the end of the First Temple period, the destruction of the First Temple and later of the Second Temple spurred the development of liturgy together with theological rationales for the substitution of prayer for sacrifices.[2] By the time the Mishnah was edited (approximately 220 C.E.), the basic structure of Jewish liturgy was already established.

Prayer also pervades Judaism. The tradition ordains prayer three times each day, with four services on Sabbaths and Festivals and five on Yom Kippur. Jewish life-cycle events are likewise surrounded by prayer. Even daily activities such as rising in the morning and eating are occasions for Jewish prayer.

Moreover, people who are really at home with Judaism find prayer both natural and meaningful. They see themselves commanded to pray, and they do so often. Even if nonpracticing Jews know very little about prayer, they correctly sense one crucial theological truth about it: Judaism loses much of its impact in the absence of prayer.

Most important, though, is the fact with which we began: many deeply want to pray. I certainly did, even as I was going through decades of severe doubt about God. While one can for a time set aside the various problems involved in prayer and just plunge in, as it were, at some point one must confront the issues. Bifurcating your intellect and your religious life is both psychologically and religiously unacceptable, for you can love God "with all your heart, with all your soul, and with all your might" only if you have taken the trouble to try to understand and integrate your religious impulses and activities.

The Skills and Levels of Prayer

The first step in dissolving some of the discomfort with prayer is to correct a common misconception. Jews commonly assume that, like breathing, one should be able to pray automatically. When they find that they cannot do this, they are disconcerted and annoyed. Prayer, however, is a skill; it does not usually come spontaneously to people. Some people do indeed have a gift for being able to pray, but most of us require extensive training and practice to master the skill of prayer.

Actually, prayer requires a number of skills. Some of them are evident. To participate fully in traditional Jewish prayer, one needs to be able to read Hebrew. Jewish law accepts the legitimacy of prayers offered in one's native language, but even with the best of translations, without Hebrew one is always a step removed from the vital spirit of Jewish prayer. An active, conversational knowledge of Hebrew is not required, but it certainly helps to be able to read and understand at least some of the key words of the *siddur,* the Jewish prayer book.

Jewish prayer is not only spoken; it is chanted. The Jewish heritage of liturgical music is one of the oldest and richest in the world. It is easy to see how this makes Jewish prayer beautiful, but the music can, and often does, do more. In many circumstances, it contributes immeasurably to the depth of feeling in Jewish prayer and to its very meaning. We communicate, after all, not only in what we say but in how we say it. Consequently, to experience the full impact of prayer one needs to learn the various modes used on specific occasions for chanting both the services and the scrolls as well as the particular melodies sung in a given congregation.

Jews not only say and sing their prayers; they move with them. There are times when it is proper to stand, sit, bow, bend the knees, and take steps forward and backward. Ashkenazic Jews, those descended from the Jews of Eastern Europe, often sway back and forth ("shuckle") while they pray. We communicate with our bodies at least as much as we do with our words, and so this liturgical choreography enhances the experience of prayer.

So do the clothes we wear. Here again, there are several skills to be mastered and questions to be answered. When and how is the *tallit* (prayershawl) worn? When and why are its fringes kissed? How does one put on *tefillin* (phylacteries) and take them off? Is head covering necessary? If so, why? Why do some people wear white gowns and sneakers on Yom Kippur? Are any of these symbols available to women—or required of them?

There are skills and areas of knowledge involved in Jewish prayer that are less obvious than those mentioned so far. One is the ability to discern the multiple levels of meaning of the prayers' words. Much of Jewish liturgy is based on material from biblical and rabbinic sources. To one who knows these sources, the lines of the liturgy reverberate with allusions and associations that enrich the cognitive and emotional meaning of the prayers. This is especially true of the poetic sections of the prayer book, but the prose was also crafted with great literary skill and with extensive usage of traditional themes and language. For one who understands these, the prayer book becomes an artistic weaving of the sources of the Jewish tradition to express the mind, the heart, and the soul of the Jew.

There is yet more to be learned. The meaning of Jewish prayer does not stem from the individual prayers alone; much of the impact of the prayers is a product of their order. The prayer book is what its Hebrew name says, a *siddur,* an ordered liturgy. The prayers are arranged with the intent to create a veritable symphony of prayer, with emotional highs and lows. By following the course of the set liturgy, the Jew is taught and reminded of some of the primary values and tenets of Judaism in the context of emotionally inspirational words and music. This enables Jewish prayer to be morally and educationally enriching as well as emotionally expressive.

The most difficult skills of prayer are those that touch its very heart. Prayer, after all, concerns a person's beliefs, values, conscience, historical associations, emotions, and hopes. To pray, we must cultivate the ability to think in abstract terms and to deal with the nonconcrete, or the "spiritual" side of our lives. Developing physical skills is difficult enough; learning to handle and foster our spiritual natures is harder still.

The many skills involved in Jewish prayer may seem overwhelming, but they are not if another misconception is recognized as such and dispelled. Many Jews assume that prayer is one type of experience, and one either has it or does not. That, however, is false: prayer is a multifaceted experience that exists in a variety of forms and on many different levels. Some types and levels of prayer are more fulfilling than others, but all have value. Consequently, a Jew who is not fully competent in the skills described above can have important, meaningful experiences of prayer while acquiring the skills to deepen and broaden them. Such people should take comfort in the fact that even those who have considerable experience and skill in worship succeed in their prayers on the various occasions in which they pray to differing extents and in many different ways.

In this respect, prayer is very much like baseball. Both require skills. Some people are naturally talented, and for them the acquisition of the necessary skills is deceptively easy. It would be a mistake, though, to conclude from watching such people function that everyone should have the same ability. That would only produce embarrassment and frustration when one tried it oneself. It would also be a mistake to deduce that natural talent in and of itself is enough; even the most gifted must practice. It would be an even more serious error to think that only people to whom prayer or baseball comes easily can accomplish these tasks. Quite the contrary is true; for the vast majority of us, praying well demands the time and effort of extended preparation—just as deft baseball playing does—but, with that, both can be effectively done by almost everyone.

Prayer is also like baseball in that even professionals attain their goals to differing degrees each time they engage in the practice. Sometimes even people who have prayed daily for years strike out in prayer. They cannot concentrate at all on what they are doing and perhaps even resent the time they devoted to prayer that day.

At other times, prayer is the rough equivalent of a walk in baseball. On such occasions, the person praying is not moved by any of the prayers but, nevertheless, is glad to have spent the time in prayer. It was, at least, a brief time spent away from the hectic schedule of the day. Even if one's mind wandered throughout the time one was saying the words of the liturgy, the exercise still carved out some time for meditation. Moreover, one might appreciate that, in more attentive moments, these prayers articulate some of the most significant aspects of one's life. Today's experience of prayer was thus worthwhile even if it was only a walk through the prayer book.

Sometimes one gets the equivalent of a base hit. A particular prayer, or sentence, or even phrase happens to hit home. That may be because it speaks to the particular problems one has at the moment, or because it stimulates one's thought, or because it reminds one of an important value, or because it adds a bit of beauty to the day, or because it gives one a sense of the meaning of being a human being and a Jew. In other words, just as one can get a base hit in baseball by hitting the ball to a variety of areas within the ballpark, so too one can score a base hit in prayer through a variety of different experiences. What makes them all a base hit is that one of the prayers has enabled the person praying to reach one of the goals of prayer.

At other times one achieves the equivalent of a double or triple in baseball. Several of the prayers hit their mark, perhaps in very different ways, and one is left with an awareness of how important it was to pray. One's day, one's week, and perhaps even one's life has been enriched.

And then, once in awhile, one hits a home run. It would not be realistic or fair to expect a home run each time one is at bat in prayer any more than it would be in baseball. Those who pray very little often make that mistake. A home run in prayer, like one in baseball, requires much practice, many trials and errors, and, ultimately, consummate skill. Even that is not enough. One needs some luck, too. The conditions have to be just right, and one's body, mind, and emotions have to be perfectly attuned to one another and to the task at hand. This does not happen very often.

Moreover, one should not pray only in hopes of having such an experience—any more than one plays baseball only for the times one hits a home run. In fact, some of us will play baseball all our lives and never hit a home run. Indeed, if our praying or baseball playing were to succeed on every level each time we tried, we would be very different individuals and societies from what we know, and prayer—and baseball—would have to be restructured to speak to our needs. The fact that prayer (or anything else) cannot remake us into ideal human beings does not negate its value, however, for prayer *can* remind us what to strive for and motivate us to try. Although it cannot move us in all its dimensions every time, it *can* affect us on some level on many occasions. It thus can be a valuable practice even if it is not always or totally successful.

The Spiritual Content of Prayer

But what constitutes "success" in prayer? Even if we do not expect to hit a home run immediately, for what should we aim? We know where the outfield fence is in baseball, but what kind of experience is a home run in prayer?

When one looks at the traditional prayer book, one finds prayers of petition, thanksgiving, confession, praise of God, and emotional expression, as well as provision for periods of study.

There are, in other words, many ways to hit a home run, often independent of one another, just as there are many directions in which a home run in baseball can be hit and many places in which the ball can cross the outfield fence.

These varied forms of worship together develop the spiritual side of our being. Indeed, in contrast to the frenzy of the cults and the solitary meditation of some Oriental religions, Jewish communal prayer and study are the major repositories of Jewish spirituality.

Some modes of Jewish prayer place the individual praying at the center of consciousness, while others are more God-centered. This explains why people who have not developed a clear conception of God can nevertheless gain meaning from many aspects of Jewish worship. They can focus on the more person-centered aspects of Jewish prayer at first and then gradually move toward the more God-centered elements. As we shall discuss in greater detail later, this, in fact, is a prime way in which prayer informs us about God: we begin thinking about ourselves and find ourselves drawn by prayer into thinking about God. To achieve this, we do need to be willing to set aside our intellectual conundrums for awhile and jump into the dialogue with God, but this is no different from many other aspects of life in which we must engage in the experience before we have a clear conception of what we are doing. Indeed, we cannot expect to do accurate and adequate theology without such experience upon which to build our thinking—just as we cannot hope to do accurate or adequate science without concrete experimentation first. The experience is, in other words, a prerequisite for the thought.

The common denominator of all forms of Jewish prayer, however, is that one goes beyond oneself or recedes within oneself and turns to the Holy One to at least some degree. One acknowledges one's dependence upon God and seeks to renew and strengthen one's relationships with the Eternal. As such, all forms of prayer constitute worship. Moreover, they all are necessary, for a broad relationship with God requires varying degrees of emphasis on the self. Sometimes we *need* to express our own particular wishes or feelings; on other occasions, we *need* just as urgently to bury ourselves in God. Nothing is too personal, and nothing too sublime for prayer.

The multiplicity and variety of the elements of our spiritual being addressed and cultivated by prayer make it the crucial and enriching experience it is. On any given occasion, in fact, a Jew can gain spiritual meaning from prayer in any or all of the following ways:

1. Expression of Our Desires

People often mistakenly assume that prayer succeeds if, and only if, one acquires what one requests. This is an error on two counts: most prayers in the traditional prayer book are not petitions, and thus, the tradition clearly assumes that prayer can succeed in many other ways; and a benevolent God would not grant all petitions, any more than a caring parent would.

Indeed, one must recognize that petitionary prayer raises some of the thorniest of theological problems. How, for example, are we to understand the relationship between God's response to our petitions and the laws of nature? Presumably, since God established and governs the natural order, the Holy One has the power to alter the normal rules of the world in response to our prayers, but would that not challenge divine foreknowledge of our desires and God's own response to them? Conversely, if God does interrupt the laws of nature in answer to our petitions, how is it that we can depend upon nature to be consistent so that we can study it, predict it, and shape it to our benefit through science?

Moreover, how are we to recognize when God has indeed

answered our prayers? When we get what we want? But then how can we reconcile such a criterion with our awareness that sometimes a benevolent God should say "No!"? On the other hand, can we ever know for certain that God has not answered our prayers? Would, for example, the fate of Jews in World War II count as such an instance?

These problems are perhaps especially evident to Jews living in a scientific, post-Holocaust age, but they were also apparent to the Rabbis who shaped the Jewish tradition in the first five centuries of the Common Era. Rabbinic literature records two somewhat different responses to these questions.

The mainstream view, recorded in the Mishnah, the Tosefta, the Babylonian Talmud, and the later codes, is that one may request of God to act in a given way only with regard to that which has not yet been determined. Thus, the Mishnah forbids petitionary prayers to change the gender of a fetus or the identity of a house burning in a distant fire, and the Tosefta prohibits asking God to transform a hundred volumes of grain or wine into two hundred.[3]

The other rabbinic position, reflected in the Midrash and the Palestinian Talmud, sees every petitionary prayer as a request for a miracle. Since God can clearly intervene in nature, asking God for a miracle is not theologically unreasonable. It is, however, religiously interdicted because God wants us to accept the world we experience as given. Therefore, since we do not see a fetus, it is legitimate, according to these sources, to ask for a change in its gender, but such a prayer ceases to be permissible when the child becomes part of our experience—that is, when it is born.[4]

Both of these views mark a rather radical departure from the Bible. To prove that Baal is not god and the Lord is, after all, Elijah asks God to send a fire from heaven to consume his sacrifice, and Joshua asks for nothing less than the delay of sunset so that his troops could prevail. By comparison, the prayers prohibited by both of these rabbinic positions ask for miracles which are relatively minor. Nevertheless, for the Rabbis, "We may not rely on a miracle" for "The world pursues its natural course" *(olam keminhago noheg)*.[5] God, in the rabbinic view, might choose to work a miracle but cannot be expected, or even properly asked, to do so.

The resultant rabbinic position—that we may ask God only for those things which are not yet determined—accords nicely with contemporary science. Seventeenth-, eighteenth-, and nineteenth-century scientists and philosophers believed that nature operated like a giant machine in which everything was determined by fixed laws. Prayer for God's intervention, therefore, could not possibly change anything but a person's feelings—and those, according to Spinoza, were ephemeral and misleading. Twentieth-century science, however, has discovered an inherent uncertainty in nature, not because of human ignorance or failure to measure carefully, but because nature itself is, in important ways, indeterminate. There are, of course, many regularities in nature that we can learn and use. Indeed, our knowledge of such regularities has had an immense effect on our lives. Yet, in accord with the findings of contemporary science, in the many matters which could, in full agreement with the laws of nature, proceed poorly for us or to our benefit, it is reasonable to ask God to intervene on our behalf.[6]

Making requests of God is not only theologically legitimate and intellectually reasonable; it is also religiously valuable. The Jewish tradition clearly thought so. Thus, even though prayers of petition, in comparison to other types of prayer, occupy relatively scant space in the *siddur,* they are placed at the very center of the *Amidah,* one of the two main prayers of the weekday morning and evening services and the central prayer of the afternoon service. Moreover, while personal petitions may be made of God at any time, they are specifically invited as part of the last blessing of the middle section of the *Amidah*. Clearly, then, the tradition treats petition as an important element of prayer, one which is actually required.

Why so? In part, this is because prayers of petition can clarify and express our hopes and even motivate us to work to accomplish them. The prescribed petitions repeated three times each day also enlarge the range of our concerns: we willy-nilly pray for things the tradition says we *should* want, even if such things are not now the focus of our attention. These prayers additionally expand the beneficiaries of our pleas: since the prayers are phrased in the plural, they make us think of *other people's* needs. Moreover, voicing our desires within the context of the liturgy forces us to test the validity of our wishes by the values of our tradition and its concept of God. As Jakob Petuchowski, a leading Reform theologian, has suggested:

> True prayer cannot very well voice strivings and aspirations which run counter to the very nature of God as we conceive of Him. This seems to be the profound truth behind the rabbinic requirement that the creedal element of the Jewish worship service, i.e., the recitation of the *Shema* and its Benedictions, *precede* the prayer of petition.[7]

In Abraham Joshua Heschel's words, "It is in moments of prayer that my image is forged, that my striving is fashioned."[8]

By their very nature, prayers of petition express our dependence upon God. Despite our pretensions, we find that we cannot gain what we need by ourselves, and so we ask God. We cannot force God to respond as we want; that would be magic. As Martin Buber has pointed out, it would also be to treat God as an It rather than the Thou God always is.

> Magic desires to obtain its effects without entering into relation, and practices its tricks in the void. But sacrifice and prayer are set "before the

Face," in the consummation of the holy primary word that means mutual action: they speak the *Thou,* and then they hear.[9]

We must, in other words, first overcome our haughtiness, our presumption that we can accomplish whatever we want on our own. As Heschel put it, "Our first task is to learn to comprehend why prayer is an ontological necessity. God is hiding, and man is defying."[10] In verbalizing our wishes, we recognize that we are not self-sufficient, open ourselves to God, and seek to influence God's actions. We *can* do this, according to the tradition, because God listens to prayer.

Since prayers of petition often emanate from our fondest desires and address the Divine as a compassionate and concerned parent, they can be an emotionally powerful link to God. As with human children and parents, what begins as an expression of need can become an opening for communication on many matters and, ultimately, for empathy and love. Similarly, even though we must shed our arrogance in asking God for what we cannot gain ourselves, the experience often is, ironically, a reassurance of our divine value. As Rabbi Dudley Weinberg put it, a man in prayer "can be humble without being humiliated, because he is loved and he *knows* that he is loved."[11]

Thus, in providing us words to express our desires, the liturgy forces us to test them by what the tradition considers legitimate aims, to think of others, to acknowledge our dependence on God, and, to the extent we can, to see the world as God does. It thereby shows us that God *has* answered prayer and still *does* so. We *individually* may not gain more knowledge, health, food, or other goods than we have now, but God has provided these commodities to us and to other human beings in some measure and deserves to be praised as such. Our wishes, of course, are inexhaustible; we always want more of life's goods, and we often think we deserve them—sometimes with justification. The liturgy, however, helps us to restore perspective by shifting our attention from our latest, personal wants to the needs of others and to the reality that God has provided much already. Thus, the liturgical formula for petition sets it in the plural ("Grant *us* peace . . .") and expresses our petition as part of the praise of God. After requesting healing, for example, we say, *"Praised* are You, O Lord, who heals the sick." Professor Petuchowski is again instructive:

> It is the peculiar genius of Judaism that many of its petitionary prayers— and all of the petitionary prayers which have gone into the making of the Eighteen Benedictions [*Amidah*]—conclude on a note of praise. . . . They are, in fact, *benedictions,* that is, praises, as much as they are petitions. They praise God for what He has done, for what He can do, and what He will do. And the recipients of God's "answer" are mentioned in the plural, not in the singular. The individual thus learns to look upon himself as a part of the whole faith-community of Israel. The concerns and the woes of his people become his own woes and concerns, even as the hopes and aspirations of the group become those of the individual. In the process, the individual Jew begins to see his own needs from a larger perspective—a perspective which enables him, even in moments of personal distress, to praise God as well as to petition Him, to thank as well as to plead. . . . Once we understand this, we may also understand the daring statement in the Talmud that "The Holy One, praised be He, is longing for the petitionary prayers of the righteous."[12]

Through petitionary prayer, we may not get all we want, but we give expression to our desires. In the best of circumstances, we also learn in the process to recognize what we should want, what we ourselves can do to achieve it, what we already have, what others need, and what God's role has been and should be in answering our petitions.

2. Perspective, Appreciation, and Meaning

The liturgy includes numerous praises of God. These undoubtedly must seem redundant and obsequious to the first reader of the prayer book. Indeed, Jews who rarely attend services often point to this aspect of the prayer book as the one that most alienates them. The surfeit of praises of God conjures up images of lowly servants in an ancient royal court, and moderns do not like to think of themselves in that abject posture. Moreover, the excess of praises makes one seem insincere; in the words of Shakespeare, "M'lady doth protest too much."

Greater attention to the human condition, however, will reveal that the Rabbis were probably wise in including so many praises of God in the standard liturgy. We inevitably must view everything from our own perspective ("our egocentric predicament"). This philosophic fact is coupled with the psychological fact that we are concerned most for ourselves. These features of our existence are not, in and of themselves, bad. We have no choice but to see the world from our own viewpoint, and the Rabbis proclaimed that we *should* first save our own lives in preference to those of others.[13]

Inevitable egocentrism in outlook and legitimate self-interest, however, all too easily lead to selfishness. Praise of God can act to counteract this danger. By focusing attention on God rather than on ourselves, we can come as close as possible to seeing the world as God sees it.

This is important philosophically because it restores proper perspective to our vision of the world. Expressions of gratitude to God help us recognize that we can neither understand, produce, nor take for granted the many prerequisites of life on which we depend. This should induce appropriate epistemological humility as it expands our vision of reality.

Praise of God is also important psychologically. It serves to underscore that we are not the source of all value, no matter how much we would like to think so. We are each minuscule in the ultimate scale of value, for, as the biblical Book of Kohelet (Ecclesiastes) underscores, our lives are short and our impact small.

At the same time, though, since God created us and loves us, each one of us, no matter how destitute or debased, is supremely valuable. Both of these evaluations of our worth are *simultaneously* true. As the hasidic *bon mot* has it, a person should always carry two pieces of paper in his pockets. On one should be written "For me the world was created," and on the other, "I am but dust and ashes."[14] Therefore the way in which we gain clarity of vision must not undermine the value of human knowledge and existence while it simultaneously reminds us of its limits. Praise of God is uniquely suited to communicate both messages at once, for it makes us acknowledge our limitations by comparing us to God while actually reinforcing our sense of worth by calling attention to the identity of our Creator and Lover.

Praising and thanking God thus help us to combat our epistemological and psychological egocentrism. By focusing on God, we recognize that the world is much larger than what we see, and we are motivated to acknowledge that it is not only we that count, either individually or collectively.

Since the very structure of our being makes us sorely tempted to fall back into such mistakes, the liturgy's multiple repetitions of God's praise should now make sense. We need to be reminded of the limits of our vision and our worth over and over again. Our egos dominate what we see and what we do all too extensively and all too often. At the same time, we must not lose sight of the importance of what we know and the significance we all bear as creatures of God. Frequent praise of God enables us to achieve and maintain this balance, thereby helping us to attain nothing less than truth and psychological well-being.

By doing this, such prayers add meaning to our lives. Praise of God gives us perspective, thereby helping us identify proper goals and attitudes; the daily cycle of Jewish prayer assures that our awareness of these aims will not be occasional and fleeting but rather will be repeated and enduring. By lauding the Eternal we continually reorient ourselves to God's view of the world, clarify our objectives, measure our current activities by them, change course when necessary, and gain an appreciation of the significance of our specific acts.

3. Communal and Historical Roots

Our inescapable egocentrism presents yet another problem: we are separate and lonely.[15] We must form our own individual personalities to be psychologically healthy, but we must also create many ties to others.

Jewish worship is specifically designed to do that. Almost all of the prayers are phrased in the first person plural (even the confessionals), and the clear preference in Jewish law is that one pray as part of a *minyan,* a community of ten or more. The text of the liturgy, moreover, helps one feel ties to the Jewish people—past, present, and future—and to God. It speaks of God as the God of our ancestors, and it invokes memories of God's care for them in the past as an indication of the continuing relationship contemporary Jews have with God and as the theological foundation for our prayers for Jews in distress now. All of these features of Jewish worship provide a powerful sense of community and rootedness.

Moreover, prayer is one of the fundamental religious acts that Jews do with other Jews. Jewish communal life is expressed, of course, in common educational and social endeavors too, but prayer historically has been a critically important experience in shaping the character of the Jewish community. It is there, after all, where the group voices its essential views, values, associations, commitments, and hopes. Prayer is, in other words, the arena in which Jews together as a community recall and renew their souls.

4. Knowledge of the Tradition

Sometimes prayer is effective because it teaches us something about our heritage. Popular opinion commonly dissociates prayer from learning, but the Jewish tradition makes study a part of the service and even considers it a form of worship.[16]

This is most apparent in the formal, educational parts of the service, including the Torah readings four times each week and on Festivals, and the sermon or communal discussion of the Torah reading. But the education afforded by Jewish worship takes place more pervasively and subtly through the liturgy itself, which introduces the Jew to many selections from biblical and rabbinic literature.

Moreover, the Rabbis, recognizing that Jews are supposed to pray each day, used the opportunity to expose the entire community on a daily basis through the *siddur* to some of Judaism's central beliefs and values. They created, in other words, a book of theology for the Jewish people as a whole. Indeed, the *siddur* is the closest thing Jews have to a creed, and serious study of it is probably the best way to know the heart and mind of Judaism. Jewish prayer, based upon the *siddur,* thus engenders a continual renewal of one's Jewish orientation and commitment.

5. Aesthetic and Emotional Effectiveness

Because the worship of God is an important matter, Jews strive to make it beautiful. Jewish law requires that we pay attention to the physical setting to insure that it is attractive and clean. While customs vary in regard to proper attire for services, the general principle is that it should be reasonably modest and clean. The one chosen to lead the prayers must not only be exemplary morally, but must also know both the words and proper melodies and must have a pleasant voice. Sometimes choirs or instruments are used. All of these steps are taken to enhance the aesthetics of worship, and a service may succeed for people merely because it is beautiful.

This, however, is a tricky factor to evaluate and effectuate. Sometimes music and other aesthetic touches do not heighten worship, but actually interfere with it. This is clearly the case when the music is calm and serene and one wants to be wild and ecstatic, or vice versa; but even when the music fits one's mood, it might detract from one's concentration on the prayers. Similarly, artistic work in the sanctuary or the architecture itself may enhance the experience of prayer for some and diminish it for others.

Rabbi Eliezer Berkovits has even warned that magnificent, contemporary synagogues may actually be a reactionary throwback to the Temple of yore. There the emphasis was on the cultic acts performed by the priests, who were removed from the congregation to inspire awe in the acts they were performing. In creating the synagogue, the classical rabbis consciously moved the architectural and ceremonial focus to the center of the room. They instituted this and other changes to democratize the service and to stress its goal of changing people's behavior in accordance with God's will.[17] To retain this atmosphere is a real challenge for large, modern congregations.

On the other hand, prayer may succeed in religiously and emotionally moving some people precisely because of the efforts made to augment its meaning by making it artistic. Much of the liturgy is not written in emotionally neutral, matter-of-fact sentences but in exclamatory, charged language, for one of the functions of prayer is to help people articulate how they feel, what they fear, and what they hope for. It fulfills this purpose when it tears a person up as much as when it calms one down. Prayer has these effects most noticeably at turning points of life such as birth, adolescence, marriage, and death, but it can do this any day of the year.

Part of the reason for this is that artistry in the service is not, for the tradition, an aesthetic value alone; it is a *religious* concern. The verses used to justify attention to this aspect of the service specifically tie aesthetics to our relationship with God. We embellish our surroundings, the liturgy, and the music by which we pray not only to enhance and deepen our own emotional involvement, but also to show our respect for God. Thus, in commenting on the verse, "This is my God and I will glorify Him" (Exodus 15:2), Rabbi Ishmael uses an alternative meaning of the Hebrew root *n-v-h* and explains it as "This is my God and I will beautify Him." How so? "I shall be beautiful before Him in the performance of the commandments. I shall prepare before Him a beautiful palm tree, a beautiful booth [both for the Feast of Tabernacles], beautiful fringes [for the prayershawl], and beautiful phylacteries [for daily morning prayer]."[18] Attention to aesthetics is part of the way we honor God.

It is also a way to show gratitude to God. As the Midrash says, "If you have a pleasant voice, lead the congregation in the recitation of the *Shema* and the Eighteen Benedictions [*Amidah*] . . . to fulfill the verse, 'Honor the Lord with your substance' (Proverbs 3:9), that is, with that which He has graciously granted you."[19] Beautifying the service and its surroundings thus not only adds to our pleasure, but also bespeaks important aspects of our interaction with God.

This theological aspect of aesthetics has yet another dimension: worship is a primary way in which we spend time with God. It is, in anthropological language, a "game" that we enjoy together with God. Thus Romano Guardini notes that

in a precise sense, it is impossible for liturgy to have a practical "purpose," for the simple reason that, as a matter of fact, it does not exist for the sake of man, but for the sake of God. . . . To play before God, to *be,* not to create a work of art, that is the innermost essence of liturgy. That is why we have the exalted mixture of profound seriousness and divine happiness in it. Only he who is able to take art and play seriously can understand why liturgy so carefully prescribes in a thousand regulations the nature of the words, the movements, the colors, and the vessels.[20]

Clearly, in a Jewish context, God is God with or without our worship. Equally as clearly, prayer serves in roles besides the aesthetic. The play function, however, *is* one important way in which prayer operates. Three times a year, the Torah commands us to "celebrate *for Me*" Passover, Shavuot, and Sukkot. On these three "pilgrimage festivals," every male was required to "appear before the Sovereign, the Lord" in the Temple to thank God and rejoice before Him, "and they should not appear before Me empty-handed" but rather bearing gifts for God according to their means. This was, in part, to show gratitude for the bounty God had bestowed, but it was also to insure a joyful festival time with the Holy One. The Second Tithe, in fact, had to be brought to Jerusalem and consumed on these festivals, thus assuring plenty of food to grace this divine-human party.[21] In this role, as Guardini says, liturgy does not have a practical purpose for us; we do not engage in it to "get" something else. Instead, in this aspect of prayer we *are* before God, interacting with God in activities we both enjoy. Students of Martin Buber will immediately think— correctly—of the I-Thou relationship we are to have with God. As Buber described it, that too is without "practical" value; it is rather a pure relationship into which both God and we enter because we need and want each other's companionship.[22]

Aesthetics are part of the medium of such a relationship; we "enjoy" things together. This is not frivolous or trifling; it is a serious component of the relationship, one that makes it possible for it to come to fruition. This explains why the Torah takes great pains to describe in detail the building of the Temple and the acts in it, and it also clarifies why later Jewish tradition did the same for its substitute for the Temple rite, prayer.

While people commonly associate prayer with emotional expression and judge a service solely on this basis, prayer can succeed in any of the ways described in this section, and more. Moreover, as Abraham Heschel reminds us, the purpose of prayer is at least as much to learn how God feels about things ("prayers of empathy") as it is to give voice to our own feelings ("prayers of expression").[23] Nevertheless, prayer clearly accomplishes one of its goals if it is emotionally effective, enabling us to experience beauty and to express our feelings while at the same time, as far as we can tell, enabling God to enjoy spending time with us.

6. Moral Effects

Prayer can also affect the morality of our thoughts and actions. For one thing, it reminds us of the full gamut of Jewish values. Since values are not physical and concrete, we forget them easily. Prayer—like ritual objects and acts of all sorts—helps us to remember our commitments so that we have a better chance to make them a part of our lives. This purpose of prayer and ritual is clearly enunciated in a paragraph of the Torah about the fringes of the *tallit,* which is both a ritual object and an integral part of prayer. The paragraph, used as the third section of the *Shema,* states that we should wear fringes on our garments so that we shall "look at them and recall all the commandments of the Lord and observe them so that you do not follow your heart and eyes in your lustful urge. Thus you shall be reminded to observe all of My commandments and you shall be holy to your God."[24] Since prayer is required three times each day, it reminds us continually of our moral commitments.

Prayer also helps us to atone for the wrongs we do. The Hebrew word for prayer may, in fact, mean, "to judge oneself." We take account of what we have done and express our regret for the sins we have committed. This is important morally in at least two ways: it relieves the guilt we feel for our wrongs so that we are not stymied by our sins; and it enables us to regain a clear vision of what we ought to do so that we can make a fresh effort to improve. We have not completed the process of *teshuvah,* "return," until we act more appropriately when we are tempted to commit the same sin the next time a similar situation arises, but prayer is an important vehicle for enabling us to do that. Only if we can overcome our guilt through prayer, apology, and restitution (if possible), and only if we can gain a better sense of what we should do, can moral improvement take place. Prayer thus plays a vital role in enabling us to improve our moral character.

Worship can also make us aware of moral issues and give us insights into moral problems we face. The liturgy or Torah reading may serve these purposes, and the homily or sermon is often specifically designed to do so.

Finally, prayer can stimulate us to act as we should. The exhortative sections of the liturgy, Torah readings, and sermons can motivate us to correct the bad, and the inspirational aspects of prayer can arouse us to strive for the ideal. The regimen of prayer forces us to stop our normal activities and to take a serious look at life, and that alone may enable us to strengthen our moral resolve. Heschel captures this element of prayer eloquently:

> A word uttered in prayer is a promise, an earnest commitment. . . . We . . . face a claim, an expectation. God reaches us with a claim. . . . Prayer is meaningless unless it is subversive, unless it seeks to overthrow and to ruin the pyramids of callousness, hatred, opportunism, falsehoods. The liturgical movement must become a revolutionary movement, seeking to overthrow the forces that continue to destroy the promise, the hope, the vision.[25]

7. Fulfilling a Mitzvah and Coming into Contact with God

For many, all of the functions of prayer described above are desirable *results* of prayer, but the primary *reason* to pray is because

Jews are obligated to do so. For reasons discussed below, even when we are not in the mood to pray, the tradition requires that we do. Since it is not always possible to pray enthusiastically, fulfilling the tradition's command to engage in daily worship inevitably entails that at times one must pray mechanically.

On occasions when people are able to involve themselves more deeply in their prayers, however, this legal requirement is transformed into a vibrant link between God and the people praying. They learn about themselves and about God through such an interaction. Moreover, the covenantal relationship between God and the People Israel, and the individual's part in that relationship, are renewed and reinvigorated through such prayer. This is the type of living communication with God that most of us imagine prayer to be.

Since petitionary prayer is the most egocentric, Maimonides regarded it as the lowest form of worship. We may be addressing God in such prayer, but we are concentrating on our own, selfish desires and, thus, on ourselves. The highest form of prayer, according to Maimonides, is that in which one loses sight of oneself and focuses completely on God.[26]

While fervent communication with God is surely a crowning glory of the experience of prayer, it is important to remember that prayer can be meaningful for any or all of the reasons described above, and for others as well. What is significant for one person may not be for another. Some may engage in prayer for one or more of its beneficial effects, whereas others seek to fulfill the relevant commandments and still others pursue a living link with God. Furthermore, on successive occasions a given individual will succeed in prayer in disparate ways and to varying extents.

One should further understand that virtually *everyone*—including rabbis and others who pray daily—often feels oneself to be a failure at prayer. For many, the reason for this is, in part, that we cannot have full knowledge of God and therefore can never quite know whether we have attained contact with God. Even for those confident in their faith, prayer is *an overdetermined activity,* with so many dimensions and goals that one cannot possibly probe their depths totally and continually. Either or both of these factors often lead people to be disappointed with their life of prayer.

One should recognize, however, that this frustration follows from setting one's goals too high. Because of the inevitable limits to our knowledge of God and the overdetermined nature of prayer, it is simply impossible to achieve every possible goal in prayer. It is also all too easy to lose sight of what one has, in fact, accomplished in a specific act of prayer. For the Jewish tradition, one *succeeds in prayer* if one simply fulfills the relevant commandments; one succeeds all the more if one is moved by some of the many modes of meaning in prayer. Prayer, certainly, is not exclusively the plea of the weak, as is commonly supposed; it is more often the expression of the strong, integrated personality of a person and a community who face life more realistically, actively, and sensitively because they pray.

Hebrew as the Principal Language of Jewish Prayer

Jewish worship may include prayers in the vernacular, but traditionally Jews pray in Hebrew. Moreover, there is an established liturgy that one is supposed to pray at specific times. This, of course, makes it difficult, if not impossible, for Jews who do not know Hebrew or the liturgy to participate in Jewish prayer. It also transforms prayer into a fixed, obligatory act rather than the free, voluntary expression that contemporary Jews often assume it should be. It is not uncommon, then, for Jews to object to both the language and the prescriptive nature of Jewish prayer.

Why is it important for a Jew to pray in Hebrew? In one sense it is not essential. According to Jewish law, one's obligations to pray can be fulfilled in any language.[27] Nevertheless, Jews have prayed in Hebrew throughout the centuries, and most of that time Hebrew was not their native tongue.

Accuracy of meaning is one rationale for this insistence on Hebrew. English, for example, is a Christian language. Historically it developed among Christians, and to this day most of the people who speak it are Christian. Consequently, it should not be surprising that English words relating to religion have Christian connotations. "Salvation," "holy," and "Messiah" immediately evoke Christian images in the mind of the native English speaker, and even "prayer" is misleading, its etymology emphasizing petitionary prayer over the forms that are most prominent in Jewish liturgy. Each of these words is the correct translation of a Hebrew word, but the meaning is seriously distorted in the process of translation.

Richness of meaning is another consideration. Rabbi Louis Jacobs has listed thirty different, traditional interpretations of Deuteronomy 6:4, used as the first line of the *Shema* prayer, most of which are lost in even the best translation.[28] If that is true for declarative prose, it is even more true for the poetry and other literary devices used in the liturgy. As Bialik put it, "Whoever knows Judaism through translation is like a person who kisses his mother through a handkerchief."[29]

Historical rootedness is another reason for using Hebrew in prayer. Over the centuries, Hebrew was not the native tongue of most Jews, and it still is not. It is, however, the language of the Bible, the Mishnah, and the *siddur*. These texts are at the heart of Jewish civilization both in time and in content, and consequently Hebrew was generally the second language a Jew learned, if not the first. Praying in Hebrew thus renews and strengthens ties to the roots of Jewish culture, and it contributes as well to the perpetuation of Judaism. It is a link to the ideological core of

Judaism and to the Jewish people's interaction with it throughout the ages.

It is also a bridge to the rest of the contemporary Jewish community. When Jews enter a synagogue anywhere in the world and discover they can join in the words (and often even the melodies) of prayer, they have powerful evidence of what it means to be part of a universal Jewish community. They may not know the spoken language, but praying together with the residents in Hebrew can quickly unlock doors. People immediately recognize each other as kin.[30] This feeling affects praying at home too, for you sense that your people for centuries and all over the world joins you in these hallowed Hebrew words.

Finally, Hebrew is "the language of holiness" *(lashon ha-kodesh)* for all Jews. One comes into contact with the transcendent and with eternity when one prays in Hebrew, in a way that cannot be duplicated in translation. The ancient Aramaic language of the *Kaddish* and *Kol Nidre* prayers has this effect on the most marginal of Jews, partially because of the settings of those prayers, but also because of the mystery and majesty conveyed by the language. Ironically, as Franz Rosenzweig pointed out, this feature of Hebrew prayer may be more potent for those who do not speak it regularly than for those who do; for without the familiarity and the secular concerns of common usage, Hebrew is more clearly an eternal language.[31]

At the same time, contemporary leaders of prayer cannot ignore the fact that many Jews cannot read or understand Hebrew. Such people will be willing to listen to Hebrew prayers only for so long. Moreover, there are limits to the religious goals a service can accomplish if it is in a language that most do not understand. People might, in fact, be led to free-associate in ways that are downright *contrary* to the import of the liturgy. Conversely, some Jewishly effective prayers have been written in English and in other languages, and there is no reason to deprive ourselves of this form of Jewish creativity. The appropriate practice, then, is to employ the vernacular for some traditional prayers and for some new ones, but to teach the Hebrew of the prayer book to children and adults and to use Hebrew for most prayers. This balance acknowledges the legitimacy and potential creativity of praying in the vernacular while preserving the many values of praying in Hebrew.

Keva *and* Kavvanah: *A Fixed Liturgy versus Expressive Prayer*

For many Jews the fixed aspects of Jewish prayer are very troubling. The obligatory nature of Jewish prayer and the set liturgy in which it must be done are undoubtedly the most surprising and vexing features of Jewish prayer to people used to Enlightenment notions of freedom of religion and voluntaristic views of prayer.[32] Why does Judaism treat prayer as an obligation that Jews must perform? Prayer should be more spontaneous than that. And why does it establish a set liturgy? Prayer should be more individualized and flexible than that.

1. The Obligation to Pray

To some it may come as a surprise that prayer is obligatory at all. Specifically, Jewish law demands that a Jew recite the three paragraphs of the *Shema* (Deuteronomy 6:4–9; 11:13–21; and Numbers 15:37–41) twice daily, once in the morning and once in the evening, each time with specific, accompanying blessings before and after it. In addition, one must recite the *Amidah* in place of each of the communal sacrifices in the Temple of yore, i.e., the morning sacrifice *(Shaharit)*, the afternoon one *(Minhah)*, and the additional one *(Musaf)* following *Shaharit* on Sabbaths, Festivals, the High Holy Days, and New Moons. (On weekdays the *Amidah* consists of nineteen blessings with accompanying prose, on *Musaf* of Rosh Hashanah it has nine blessings, and on all other occasions seven.) For at least the last thousand years, it has also been customary to recite an *Amidah* after *Shema* during the evening service even though there was no evening sacrifice.

The tradition cites several sources for the obligations to say these prayers. The Rabbis derive the general duty of worship from Deuteronomy 11:13, the opening verse of the second paragraph of the *Shema,* according to which Israel is "to love the Lord your God and to serve Him *(ule'ovdo)* with all your heart and with all your soul." The Hebrew word for "serve" is the same root used to denote the sacrificial cult. The Rabbis therefore ask, "What kind of service *(avodah)* is it which takes place in the heart?" They answer, "It is prayer."[33] The Torah's demand that we serve God with all our heart is thus, for the Rabbis, a command to pray.

The obligations for the specific, required prayers derive from two sources. Deuteronomy 6:4–9, used as the first paragraph of the *Shema,* says, in part: "Take to heart these instructions with which I charge you this day. Impress them upon your children. Recite them when you stay at home and when you are away, when you lie down and when you get up. . . ." Although the Torah probably meant that we should take *all* of God's commands to heart and repeat them often, and although the Rabbis clearly agreed with that, the Rabbis used this verse as the basis of the duty to say the *Shema* each evening ("when you lie down") and morning ("when you get up"). Strictly speaking, this is not a command to *pray,* but rather to *recite* the *Shema.* Early on, though, the Rabbis attached blessings to be said before and after the *Shema,* and over the course of time the recitation of the *Shema* was linked to the *Amidah*—so much so that one is not supposed to interrupt the flow of the one into the other.

The other obligatory sections of the liturgy are based upon the sacrifices in the ancient Temple. When the Temple was destroyed, the Rabbis used the service *(avodah)* of the heart to replace the service *(avodah)* of the Temple. Specifically, the *Amidah* substitutes for the ongoing communal sacrifices—one in the early morning and the late afternoon each day, and an additional one for the supplementary communal sacrifice which the Torah requires to mark Sabbaths, Festivals, and the High Holy Days as special occasions. Since there were no sacrifices at night, the evening service should not include an *Amidah,* and, indeed, there is no public recitation of the *Amidah* then. People do recite it privately, however, a *custom* which, according to Maimonides, Jews the world over have accepted upon themselves "as though it were an obligatory prayer."[34] There are thus biblical and customary roots to the obligation to pray.

Jakob Petuchowski has suggested that this may explain how moderns who do not accept the authority of Jewish law may nevertheless acknowledge and fulfill the obligation of Jewish prayer.

> Even without assuming that God thundered down from Mount Sinai the commandment that man pray, and without necessarily feeling bound by the specific manner in which the ancient Rabbis construed such a purported commandment, the modernist Jew could still relate to the prayer tradition of his people "as though it were obligatory." He might do so because he is sufficiently impressed by the devotion which the Jewish people has lavished, everywhere and at all times, on the very minutiae of worship.[35]

Petuchowski also points to the survival value of prayer for the Jewish people and to its spiritual values for the individual to ground the obligatory nature of prayer. We have seen above how these factors (and others) might motivate an individual to pray and might even suggest a duty to pray. The interesting argument here, though, is that the modern Jew, unimpressed by what the tradition considered divine commands, might, nevertheless, recognize and act on a duty to pray due to the sheer power of custom and the emotional attachments of rehearsing what our ancestors did and loved for centuries. This probably will not result in prayer three times a day, as the tradition demands, but it may be enough of an inducement to engender daily, or at least weekly, prayer.

There can, in fact, be many sources for the obligation to pray, as there are many sources for legal and moral duties in general. Judaism has always recognized this. That God stands behind the commandments has always been the core of their authority, but the Bible and the Jewish tradition thereafter have additionally recognized other rationales for obedience.[36]

Whatever the source of the obligation to pray, the very fact that it is an obligation helps us to pray. As Abraham Joshua Heschel noted,

> I am not always in a mood to pray. I do not always have the vision and the strength to say a word in the presence of God. But when I am weak, it is the law that gives me strength; when my vision is dim, it is duty that gives me insight.[37]

Moreover, for Jews, only if prayer is accepted as an obligation to God can it truly be divine service. That is, the obligatory nature of prayer affects its very character, distinguishing it from being exclusively the expression of our emotions and desires and making it genuine worship of God. Rabbi Eliezer Berkovits has perhaps put this best:

> When a man, overwhelmed by the impact of a specific experience, seeks the nearness of God or bursts forth in halleluyah or bows down in gratitude, it is prayer but not service of God yet; it is a human response to a potent stimulus. But when he prays without the stimulus of a specific occasion, acknowledging that man is always dependent on God, that

independently of all personal experience God is always to be praised and to be thanked, then—and only then—is prayer divine service of the heart.[38]

Berkovits may be stating the point too strongly: it is not "only" when one acts out of a sense of duty that one worships God. One can, I think, have a strong sense of serving God in prayer even without knowing that Jewish law requires that we do so or that we morally owe God such gratitude. Even so, Berkovits is certainly correct in saying that when one is conscious of such an obligation as well as the grounds for it, one's prayer is most clearly an act of divine service.

2. Set Times for Prayer

Clearly, Judaism would prefer the ideal in prayer—that is, that people pray regularly and that they pray with feeling. The Hebrew word for the fixed, regular aspect of the service is *keva* (set, established); the Hebrew word for fulfilling a commandment with the proper intention is *kavvanah* (intention, attention, devotion, purpose) from the root meaning "to direct (one's mind, emotions, will)."

One strain of thought in the tradition requires *kavvanah* throughout the service to fulfill one's obligations of worship. The law recognized, however, that it is difficult, if not impossible, for people at all times to control their inner thoughts, and, moreover, that the law cannot regulate them. Consequently, Jewish law concentrates on the act of prayer rather than on the intention. It does require the proper intention, though, at several crucial parts of the service, specifically, the first line of the *Shema* and the first blessing of the *Amidah*.[39] At all other times simply mouthing the words of the liturgy is sufficient, although greater *kavvanah* is certainly desirable.

Keva in both the times and content of prayer is important for several reasons. Even with the best of intentions, people who decide to pray only when the spirit moves them generally pray very little. Fixed times for prayer insure that we do pray, so that our commitment to this important activity in our lives is expressed in action and not just in resolutions. Like most other things in life, prayer happens most assuredly if it becomes part of our schedules.

By making prayer a frequent activity, Jewish law motivates us to learn the liturgy. *Keva* is important, especially in the early stages of one's experience with prayer, for learning liturgical skills so that we can call upon them when we really want to pray. *Keva* also affords us a community for prayer. The day and time one person is in the mood to pray is not likely to be the day and time when many others want to pray. Setting a fixed time for prayer provides a community for both those in the mood and those who are not. This enables the community to discharge its obligation to pray while also enhancing the prayer experience of everyone. As the Talmud says, "One who has a synagogue in his city and does not pray in it with the community is called a bad neighbor."[40]

Setting a fixed time for prayer also adds meaning to life in general. Life gains significance when we have goals and work toward their achievement, but it also acquires meaning by having a rhythm. People who abide by Jewish law may not be able to articulate objectives for their lives, but they know that there are weekdays and the Sabbath; holidays unique to specific seasons of the year; rituals marking the turning points of life, from birth through adolescence, marriage, and death; and, each day, *Shaharit, Minhah,* and *Ma'ariv.* Conversely, many moderns find life meaningless because it is unmarked and therefore unnoticed as it passes by. The fixed times for prayer are one of the ways in which Judaism calls attention to specific times in our day, week, month, and year, thereby imparting a rhythm to life and making it more meaningful.

Underlying these educational and functional goals is a theological one: prayer is our recognition of, and our response to, the transcendent reality we call God. It is a reality that we all too often neglect in the rush of our daily affairs. It is also a reality that we prefer to ignore as we pridefully claim that we alone are to be credited for our achievements and that we alone are masters of our destiny. The Torah knew this human penchant for self-glorification and warned against it:

> Beware lest your heart grow haughty and you forget the Lord your God . . . and say to yourselves, "My own power and the might of my own hand have achieved these great things for me." Remember that it is the Lord your God who gives you the power to achieve, in fulfillment of the Covenant He made on oath with your ancestors . . .[41]

Fixed times for prayer each day remind us of our place in God's universe, thereby instilling in us appropriate humility, appreciation of the divine value of human beings and of God's world, and responsibility for each other and for ourselves. At bottom, daily prayer is required because God must be looked for, recognized, and served in all we say and do.

3. An Established Liturgy

Keva in the other sense, a fixed liturgy, is also a bone of contention. People feel constrained, put upon, and sometimes simply bewildered by the formal, bound prayer book that they are handed in the synagogue.

Such people can take comfort in the fact that they are echoing classical rabbinic sentiments. The Rabbis of the Talmud, in fact, considered those who write down prayers to be as reprehensible as those who burn the Torah![42] Moreover, they warned that one should take care not to make one's prayer a fixed routine *(keva)*, which Rava defined as the prayer "of anyone who is not able to say anything new in it."[43]

In line with this, the Rabbis prescribed only a short outline of blessings and paragraphs around which the worshipers and their leaders were to weave prayers of their own. So, for example, the morning service, which is the longest daily service, requires only two blessings before the *Shema*, the three paragraphs of the *Shema*, one blessing after it, and the nineteen blessings of the *Amidah*. (On Mondays and Thursdays a brief Torah reading is also prescribed.) Reciting the necessary prayers—even with adding the two paragraphs of the *Alenu* prayer, with which all services have customarily concluded since the fourteenth century—would take someone familiar with the words about ten or fifteen minutes.

Ultimately, though, there is an established liturgy, however short. Since the first written order of service was published in the ninth century, the prayer book has grown considerably to include many embellishments of the essential sections, prose and poetry that became popular over the centuries as vehicles to express the same themes more fully. The length of the present service certainly exacerbates the problem, but the question is essentially the same even if our current liturgy were the original, short version: Why have a fixed order of prayer at all?

Put briefly, a settled liturgy exists so that prayer can accomplish its goals. Some of the experiences described above are more directly dependent upon a fixed liturgy than are others, but all of the spiritual objectives mentioned there benefit from it. Without a prescribed liturgy, it is hard to transcend ourselves sufficiently to gain the perspective that prayer can afford; our natural inclination is to include only prayers of expression and to neglect prayers of empathy. The traditional prayer book makes communal prayer possible; without it, we would not have a common language of prayer and may not even be able to pray together, let alone evoke and reinforce our ties to our people in the past, present, and future. The liturgy exposes us to our literature and our values and reminds us of them; individually created texts generally are much less successful in these tasks. Much of the emotional impact of prayer stems from the words and melodies that resonate through us; even the most articulate among us can seldom express themselves more fully, especially at the very moment they want to pray. The liturgy gives us a vehicle for emotional expression; it makes our dumb mouths sing. And finally, while there is much more latitude for altering the liturgy than is usually realized, some elements of it are required by Jewish law. The fixed liturgy therefore enables Jews to fulfill obligations to God as formulated in Jewish law, as it infuses a divine perspective into our lives.

This, however, does not preclude the creation of new prayers and new ways to say and sing them. As our ancestors did before us, we have both the right and the duty to enhance Jewish liturgy in whatever way we can so that it more adequately accomplishes its goals. This may mean dropping some of the *siddur*'s prose or poetry that no longer speaks to us, as well as adding our own. It may mean including new readings or lyrics in the vernacular as well as in Hebrew. We may also sing the traditional words with new melodies to add new zest to their message. All of these changes are part of the Jewish historical tradition of liturgical creativity and are to be encouraged as such.

Because of such variations, introduced to make prayer live for contemporary people, congregations differ in their services. For that matter, a given congregation may vary the form of its worship from time to time or offer alternative services. These are not new or regrettable facts on the synagogue landscape. On the contrary, synagogues throughout history have differed from each other in many features of worship, and the variety of services available then, as now, enables Jewish worship to speak to the spiritual needs of many diverse people.

To retain the Jewish character of the service, however, and to benefit from the effects of an established liturgy, innovations should be woven into the fabric of the *siddur,* preserving the few required sections and altering that which is not part of the fixed structure. Moreover, to preserve a sense of the history of our people and its liturgy, it is also worthwhile to retain at least some of the embellishments written down over the centuries. Many of these added prayers recommend themselves to us yet today, not only for the historical associations they provide, but for their sheer spiritual power. For effective prayer, then, both the individual and the congregation must artfully incorporate and balance all aspects of both *keva* and *kavvanah.*

THE PHILOSOPHICAL PROBLEMS AND PROMISE OF PRAYER

Prayer in the Absence of Unequivocal Belief

The language and the prescribed form of Jewish prayer are matters at issue for a large number of contemporary Jews, but their fundamental philosophical problem with it centers around their lack of belief in God. Many Jews are professed agnostics or atheists, and most of those who believe in God have moments of doubt, sometimes lasting for a long time and penetrating to the core of their beings. My own belief in God has certainly not been immune to such periods of doubt. How, then, can one engage in prayer without a firm, fairly specific, belief in God, when both the act and texts of Jewish prayer assume it?

Part of the answer stems from the fact that prayer is a multifaceted phenomenon, as described above, and some of its features are less directly tied to its underlying theology than are others. Without a belief in God, one can clearly reaffirm communal and historical roots, and one can also learn about the tradition and its texts. Even some of the moral and emotional effects of prayer are independent of faith in God.

But the answer lies deeper than that, as we will see if we consider one of the relationships between actions and words. We can learn much from the words of others about experiences we have not had. We can learn about skiing, for example, from people who have skied and from the accounts of some of them in books, even if we ourselves have never tried the sport. The degree to which we can glean information from such secondhand descriptions, however, depends upon the extent to which we can relate them to our own experiences. The most deftly poetic descriptions of the experience of skiing down a mountain in the cold, brisk, clean air of a sunny day can never capture all the nuances and feelings involved in the experience. The closer we come in our own lives to the objects and events being depicted, the greater our understanding will be of the words we read or hear, and the greater our ability to imagine their impact. Ultimately, we glean most from such descriptions if we have had the experience that the other person is describing—in this case, if we try skiing. Then we can evaluate and feel the force of other people's words by considering our own experiences, and, conversely, we can deepen our understanding of our own experiences through the other perspectives that such descriptions offer. In other words, the extent of our comprehension of other people's words depends upon the richness of our own lives and upon our ability to link what we hear from others to our own histories.

This is true of prayer too. Prayer is not primarily a philosophical statement; it is a religious act. Like all other acts, prayer may be easiest to understand and explain if one first knows and accepts the beliefs that underlie and justify it, but in prayer, as in most other areas of our lives, most people do not function that way. Instead, we act first and then discover and probe the beliefs that arise out of our actions. Put more generally, the experiential and educational order is the reverse of the logical order. That is, the philosophical structures that we create—the concepts through which we see the world—are motivated and tested by the experiences we first have as both observers and actors.

Applied to our topic, this means that we must pray for a substantial period of time before we can adequately appreciate and evaluate any attempt to describe its meaning in words. Indeed, an important part of that meaning is the experience with God, and *prayer is one of the ways in which we gain knowledge of God.* Once we have reached God through prayer, we have a basis in experience for our thoughts about God. We must first pray, however, even though this means plunging into the act of prayer without having first justified doing so intellectually. Our experience of prayer then undergirds our attempts to understand it and continually emerges in our minds as we do so. Prayer, in other words, is a foundation for theology. Heschel compares this to a palimpsest, a parchment that has been written upon several times, the previous texts having been imperfectly erased and remaining, therefore, still visible.

> Authentic theology is a palimpsest; scholarly, disciplined thinking grafted upon prayer. . . . First we sing, then we understand. First we praise, then we believe. Praise and song open eyes to the grandeur of reality that transcends the self.[44]

For prayer to serve as a ground for theology, though, people must be willing to pray without having a clear idea of the act or a firm belief in the object of the act, God. They can do this without encountering logical difficulties or dissembling about their beliefs if they consciously decide to keep the philosophical questions in abeyance, understanding that the resolution of those problems is partially dependent upon openness to the experience of prayer in the first place. In the process, they can adopt a variety of *provisional* views of God and prayer, letting themselves test these views by continuing experience with the nuances one learns in repeated and varied acts of prayer.

In sum, then, honesty and the demands of a genuine faith require that at some point people must address their questions straightforwardly and thoroughly, but a fully developed theology is not a prerequisite to authentic encounters with God in prayer. Conversely, those who do not pray may well become atheists because they are closing themselves off from one of the primary experiences of God, a crucial element in the justification of belief. Their abandonment of prayer, indeed, is as much a cause of their atheism as a result of it.

In addition to this philosophical point, several features of Jewish prayer should make it acceptable, and even helpful, to the philosophically undecided or skeptical. The prayer book includes widely varying views of God, sometimes in the same prayer. For example, the poem "V'khol Ma'aminim," written by Yannai in the seventh century as part of the High Holy Day liturgy, combines concrete, almost physical images of God with highly abstract descriptions. As Judge, God searches our most hidden secrets, opens His gate to those who knock in repentance, waits for the wicked, and before Him the great and small are alike, but God is also "I am who I am," whose name is the Immutable, who is all-powerful and all-perfect, and who dwells in mystery in the shadow of the Almighty. These disparate images permit the elite and the folk—and the elite and the folk elements in each one of us—to pray the same prayer, resonating to what moves us at the moment.

It is not only in the plain meaning of the liturgy that theological latitude is manifest: flexibility inheres in the process of interpreting traditional texts too. Therefore, people with beliefs as variant as Maimonides' rationalism and Moses de Leon's mysticism have been able to pray with the same prayer book. There is even evidence that some sections of the service were consciously formulated as they are, so that they could be interpreted to accommodate varying beliefs.[45]

New prayers might be written to express specific experiences and views of God, but people with no theological axe to grind have contributed to the liturgy in every age, better to express what God means in their lives. Once in awhile, especially in the last two centuries, people such as the early leaders of Reform Judaism and Reconstructionism have eliminated or revised major portions of the traditional prayer book to reflect their specific ideologies. More often, though, the necessary meanings have been attained without excision or substitution through reinterpretation. This elasticity in understanding the liturgy has enabled Jews to use the prayer book accurately and meaningfully as they struggle to speak of and to God.

Judaism tolerates not only varying theologies, but undetermined theology as well. The Jewish tradition was wise enough to recognize openly and honestly that there are serious limits to human knowledge of God. Consequently, lists of doctrines never fared well in the history of the Jewish religion. In contrast, the liturgy, which has endured, strikingly proclaims the conflicts in our theological perceptions. God is portrayed in one prayer as the universal Creator, and in the very next prayer as the particularistic giver of the Torah and lover of Israel. God is just, but merciful. Human beings are nothing, but yet worthy of being God's covenanted partners. God decides on Yom Kippur who shall live and who shall die, but because we have free will, repentance, prayer, and good deeds can avert the severe decree.

By stating these antinomies in juxtaposed sentences and paragraphs, the liturgy condones and even encourages a degree of indeterminacy in our conceptions of God. It is saying that we should not be too definite and self-assured about our beliefs but rather open to the complexity of life and of God. In that way it is making a powerful, antifundamentalist statement: we cannot legitimately proclaim dogmas about God as if they were clear, certain, and unqualified. We must rather assert the truths about God that we learn from the various parts of our experience while recognizing that they do not produce an adequate or even a consistent conception. God, according to the Jewish tradition, is, after all, beyond human understanding, and thus any attempt to capture God's essence in any fixed formula is both inaccurate and un-Jewish.[46]

I do not want to overstate the point. It is clearly easiest to pray with the traditional prayer book if one believes in some version of rabbinic theology, and it may well be that one can feel the full effect of Jewish prayer only in the context of that belief. Jewish liturgy, after all, was largely written by people with that faith, and consequently using it while believing in something else often feels inappropriate, if not downright jarring. It is nevertheless possible to pray with the traditional prayer book and to open oneself to meaningful experiences with God if one suspends judgment on the philosophical issues for a time and/or adopts provisional answers. Moreover, it is desirable to do so because the experience of prayer itself provides important data that should be incorporated into one's understanding of God.

Identifying the God We Wish to Know

As soon as we probe the phenomenon of prayer to reap what it can teach us about God, however, we encounter the disparate images of God that our faculties produce. As explained in Chapter 2, when we try to detach ourselves from the world and learn what we can as dispassionate, "objective" observers, we learn a great deal. Such knowledge has shaped virtually every aspect of our lives in this scientific twentieth century. In the realm of theology, detached reflection generally leads thinkers to abstract concepts of God, making God similar in many respects to the forces and features of nature.

Our experience, however, is not limited to what we gain in our function as observers of the world. We also interact with it. At such times all of our rational, physical, emotional, moral, aesthetic, and conative powers come into play, and we become personally involved with other segments of reality. We then encounter a personal God who loves us, gets angry with us, enters a Covenant with us, commands us, and accompanies us throughout our individual and collective lives.

If it were only that our intellect says one thing and our emotions and will another, we could conclude that the latter represent what we wish were the case, but that we should act on the hard facts we learn in the careful deliberation of the former. But our intellect, emotions, and will do not exist separately within us; they *interpenetrate*. Consequently, we *learn objective facts* about ourselves and the world in which we live at least as much when we relate to people and objects outside us as when we stand back to examine them in a detached way. That is, our personal experiences are just as true and objectively verifiable as our detached, cognitive experiences. We therefore can, do, and should learn from the former as well as the latter, and our conception of God should incorporate what we learn.

This consideration becomes especially important in prayer, for there the personal side of God is most in evidence. God, as perceived by the tradition, hears our praises and appeals. People as simple as Tevye, the milkman, can talk with God. In contrast, the detached God conceived as an impersonal force or moral principle does not hear prayer. This is a major drawback to the theologies that emerge from such thinking, for the warmth generated by one-to-one contact with a personal God is then lost. Prayer is a format by which the community is brought together for purposes of comradeship, education, celebration, mourning, sensitivity training, and moral stimulation; but if there is no personal God with whom we interact in prayer, then all of the noble functions just listed are not enough to sustain our interest. Without a personal God, prayer loses its soul.

The Difficulties and Lure of a Personal Conception of God

Why, then, do we sometimes hesitate to ascribe personal characteristics to God?

Medieval Jewish rationalists were embarrassed by the biblical and rabbinic depiction of a personal God because they thought that attributing personal traits to the Deity compromises God's infinity and eternity. Physical characteristics like a hand or foot would limit God's being, for presumably that which is beyond the outer edge of the hand or foot is not part of God. Moreover, all of the hands and feet we know are mortal, and so attributing such bodily parts to God may jeopardize divine permanence. Even emotional traits like anger and love would be limiting, at least if they were to be manifest in our world. God would then have to descend into the realm of the finite and become entangled in the world of transient, finite beings.

Abraham Joshua Heschel and others have demonstrated that such dilemmas were based upon Greek assumptions, for it was the Greeks who defined perfection in terms of completeness and immutability. For the Jews, in contrast, divine perfection actually *requires* personal involvement, with all the concern, love, anger, surprise, and change of direction which that entails. Divine being and power may have to be contracted to enable human beings to exist and interact with God in such a way, but that is a price which biblical and rabbinic theologies were willing to pay, for Israel's God was first and foremost a God who cares.[47]

What troubles moderns about ascribing personal characteristics to God is at once more straightforward and at the same time more profound. Put simply, such traits do not seem to fit. We normally expect that a personal being will speak to us, answer our questions, and communicate love, concern, and anger. When we try to apply these attributes to God, however, we have great difficulty. We have no experience of such interactions, at least not clear-cut ones.

Did God speak to us in the past? The Rabbis of the Talmud thought that he did, but they restricted divine utterances to the biblical period, substituting in their stead interpretation of God's one authoritative communication, the Torah.[48] This takes due recognition of the human element in receiving divine messages, and it frees one from the need to distinguish true prophets from false ones; but it put God one step removed from us. Nobody hears or sees God directly any more; we must rather rely on the opinion of the community of Israel and its rabbis, philosophers, and poets to determine what God's revelation in the past means for us today.[49]

Does God answer prayers? If so, how? Clearly people become strengthened and relieved through prayer, but not by a verbal response from God. Elements of the Christian tradition believe in such responses, but Judaism has not acknowledged and authenticated the reports of people who claim such divine messages. To conclude that God replies through action rather than speech raises the problem of how to recognize an act that is meant to answer a prayer—especially, as we have noted, since God can presumably answer "No!"

And how does God show concern for us? We are clearly the beneficiaries of miracles each day, as the traditional prayer book reminds us, for most of us are able to regain consciousness after sleep, to function reasonably well mentally and physically, and to enjoy the support of the nutrients we gain from the world. We are, however, also the victims of suffering, disease, crime, natural disaster, and other evils. Are these signs of divine anger and manifestations of God's kind and just discipline of us, as Deuteronomy suggests? Then we would expect a *quid pro quo* relationship between our actions and God's responses, as the Deuteronomist envisaged; but children dying of cancer and innocent victims of gang warfare demonstrate that this is not the case.[50]

In the face of these difficulties, we might say that God has a personality that expresses itself in ways that are radically different from human personality. This, however, would be a pyrrhic victory because then that which applies to human beings by virtue of their personalities would not necessarily apply to God, and vice versa. Use of the term "personality" in such significantly different ways is not only unhelpful in understanding God, but downright misleading.

In light of these difficulties, some theologians, such as Mordecai M. Kaplan and Richard Rubenstein, have abandoned the concept of a personal God altogether. As rabbis with deep commitments to the Jewish tradition, the two thinkers mentioned certainly did not do so lightly, but the problems involved in believing in a personal God, in their opinion, left them no choice.

Most of us, though, persist in ascribing personality to God, and we do so for at least three reasons. One is historical. Personal characteristics are so central to the classical Jewish conception of God that one wonders if any theology which drops them can deservedly be called Jewish. It is, of course, possible that our tradition erred on this issue throughout its history. In that case, a reevaluation and reformulation of this tenet would be necessary. Even if such action is justified—and I do not think so for the reasons delineated below—it would certainly be wrenching. For better or for worse, Judaism historically has defined God as personal.

The second reason is moral. God has always functioned within Judaism as a model for human behavior.[51] Consequently, if, in our conception of God, we eliminate personality, we are in effect denying its importance in human life. Judaism has always emphasized care and concern for oneself and for others. These traits of a personal being must, if anything, be even more underscored in our largely depersonalized, modern world. We are therefore reluctant to let go of these aspects of God lest Judaism lose its moral meaning.

The third reason is epistemological, one that goes to the heart of our philosophical discomfort with the dissonance we experience between our thinking and our prayer. Our interpersonal experiences give intersubjective evidence of the reality of human personality, and our attempts to relate to God seem to follow the same pattern. Although these attempts may be a manifestation of our tendency to anthropomorphize God, many thinkers in the Western traditions have found that their relationship with God is best expressed in personal terms. Halevi was certainly correct in affirming that the religious experience is not abstract and cerebral but rather concrete and total, involving the whole of a person's personality as an individual and as a member of a group. Buber expanded on this description by pointing out that the religious person forms a bipolar relationship with God, such that God is no longer a distant absolute Being, but our partner.[52]

This view, of course, may be a misrepresentation or even a total delusion. All humanity once thought that the earth was flat, after all. Human knowledge, however, can never rise above the intersubjective testing of the human community of knowers. We can push ourselves to experience new aspects of the universe and to approach it in different ways, and we can expose ourselves to the experiences and perspectives of other people; but ultimately we can never divest ourselves of the inherent limitations of human experience and see the world transparently, as it were. Therefore, the large number of people who find personal terms most adequate to interact with God and the commonality of their descriptions that arise from such interactions mean that the religious experience of a personal God can and does serve as a basis for serious knowledge claims.

Oriental experiences, of course, are very different, especially in Hinduism and Hinayana Buddhism, but I would suggest that this is due to the fact that personality (especially its element of free will) is viewed as an illusion and an entrapment in the East, while it is a reality and a blessing (indeed, an imprint of the divine) in the West. This distinction results in totally different kinds of religious experience and worship: religious training and practice in the East aim to rid us as much as possible of our sense of individuality, while in the West we are taught to relate to God in both word and deed in an active and intensely personal way. If we are to maintain the Western evaluation of personality in nontheological matters, however, then we should not be embarrassed to build it into our theology as well.

On the contrary, we should feel ourselves compelled to do so. For Halevi, the God of the philosophers and the God of Abraham were radically distinct because he understood philosophy to include only the knowledge gained in trying to *describe* experience in as detached a manner as possible. But since we learn objective facts about the world when we *interact* with it as well, it is *intellectually justifiable* to include that element of our experience in our concept of God. Moreover, it is *intellectually necessary* to do so because otherwise our image of God neglects a major part of our experience. Indeed, it may be the case that experiences of love, anger, hope, fidelity, and the like are logical prerequisites to an adequate understanding of God; it is certainly true that sensitive souls have told us as much about the nature of God as great minds have.

Reconciling Rationalist and Religious Images of God

But how can we harmonize the strongly personal image of God we glean from prayer with the abstract picture of God which theoretical reasoning produces? Several possibilities emerge. We can, as Halevi suggested, simply dissociate the two concepts, claiming that the God of the rationalist philosophers and the God of Abraham, Isaac, and Jacob have nothing to do with each other. This would rescue the traditional, personal God from all rational attack, for reason would be held to be blind and misleading when it tries to fathom the nature of God.

While this might give comfort to some believers, I find it objectionable on both religious and philosophical grounds. It reduces our religious commitment, since it excludes the rational side of our being from the experience of God. We might still have considerable religious fervor; indeed, since such faith would be unleashed by reason, it might generate even greater enthusiasm, as many of the fundamentalist Christian sects demonstrate. It would lack, however, the scope, the depth, and the responsibility which reason imparts to faith. Philosophically, bifurcating the rational and the religious concepts of God removes religion from the sphere of intellectual analysis and criticism. This encourages superstition.

Another option is to mix the two concepts. This is precisely what Jews have done historically: they grafted their original notion of God, conceived individually as a superhuman Person, onto the Greek depiction of God, conceived generically as Godhood. They did this to show that Jewish theology was in no way inferior to the best that philosophy had to offer, that, indeed, the Jewish concept of God included all that the philosophers had to say about the divine, long before they articulated their positions. This sort of grafting, however, results in hopelessly confused theology, plagued by many difficulties and contradictions. An abstract, infinite God is simply not the same as the personal, particular God of the Bible. To this extent, Halevi was right.

In order to arrive at a Jewish theology that is at once intellectually convincing and religiously meaningful, we must instead *integrate* the various elements of our experience into a coherent worldview. We must interweave what we glean from our two disparate approaches to God—the God of Halevi's philosophers, whom we experience as passive observers, and the personal God whom we find in interaction with the world around us, in revelation, and in prayer—in a way that takes account of their differences and yet explains why they are both part of our image of God. Only then can religious faith be truly a matter of "all your heart, all your soul, and all your might."

Integration through Metaphors

As one can imagine, interweaving the conceptions of the two approaches is easier said than done. It is not, though, a problem new to moderns. The same medieval rationalists who, in their philosophical treatises, persistently maintained that "He is not a body and has no body"[53] employed traditional anthropomorphic symbolism in prayer, including, for example, "Open Your hand and satisfy every living thing with favor" (Psalm 145:16, used in the early part of the morning service) and "Exalt the Lord and worship at His footstool" (Psalm 99:5, which is said when Jews take the Torah from the ark).

Maimonides set the pattern of this school of interpreting such language metaphorically. God does not really have a hand or foot, but we depict God in such human terms to make the divine comprehensible to us. Moreover, since people generally think

only of corporeal entities as real, describing God in physical
terms conveys the reality of God:

> The masses perceive nothing other than bodies as having a firmly estab-
> lished existence and as being indubitably true. . . . That, however, which is
> neither a body nor in a body is not an existent thing in any respect,
> according to man's initial understanding, particularly from the point of
> view of the imagination. . . . Since with regard to us [human beings] . . . all
> these acts are only performed by means of bodily organs, all these organs
> are figuratively ascribed to Him. . . . For instance, an eye, an ear, a hand, a
> mouth, [and] a tongue have been figuratively ascribed to Him so that by
> this means, sight, hearing, action, and speech should be indicated.[54]

This method of resolving the dissonance between the abstract
and personal conceptions of God creates a most uneasy truce
between them. It is only human intellectual weakness that ne-
cessitates thinking of God in human terms; the reality of God is
something else. Since all of us are subject to this weakness,
though, even Maimonides must pray to a God described in human terms. One thoroughly convinced of the metaphysical ab-
stractions with which Maimonides described God, though,
would surely not choose to pray to a personal God. This approach thus binds its adherents to a philosophically precarious
blend of the abstract and the personal. One must pray and act as
if God personally rules the world, expressing that personality in
ways known and practiced by human beings, even though one
knows that God in reality is beyond all human conception and
quite different from anything human beings describe in their
metaphors.

This approach also fails to capture the insight and commitment of biblical and rabbinic literature. That literature describes
God in human terms without any of Maimonides' embarrassment. God is beyond human conception, but what we know of
the divine can most appropriately be described in personal

terms. It is not only that our limitations allow us to do no better; it is that the reality of God comes closest to what we know as personal characteristics. For Maimonides, human traits would compromise God's perfection; in the Bible and Talmud, God's humanity is a crucial expression of His perfection. The thoroughgoing personalism of the God of the biblical and rabbinic tradition—a personalism from which even Maimonides could not entirely free himself—is not just a compromise with human intellectual constraints, but a conception of God borne of the stubborn evidence of a personal God which emerges from practice, especially in the context of prayer.

Integration through Recognition of Disparate Contexts

In fact, in settings like prayer we actually *must* let the intellect recede into the background, for we come to services hoping to activate the emotional and conative parts of our nature. Jewish prayer does include intellectually stimulating material, but it is a *separate* part of the service, centering around the Torah reading and the attendant lesson or sermon. Even there we expect to learn about our emotional or moral life, and we come away disappointed if we have been given a strictly academic treatise. It is not that the lesson or sermon should be intellectually sloppy, but we expect a different style and focus of teaching in services than we do in a college lecture, or even a synagogue adult education course. Thus, we pray to a personal, largely anthropomorphic God, if only because the context of prayer seems to require that we relax those standards of intellectual rigor that are appropriate to the realm of cogitation.

That our conceptions of God should depend, at least in part, upon context has some cogency, for that surely is true of our notions of human beings. Our perceptions of a teacher, for example, are altered drastically the first time we meet him or her outside an academic environment, and during family vacations parents often acquire a different image from that which they have at home. Even the rules of interaction change somewhat in these new settings. Our vision of the teacher or parent becomes richer: we have seen a new side to these otherwise familiar people, and we have interacted with them in new ways. The same applies to God: we know more about God when we experience the divine in a variety of different settings.

In the human cases cited, however, we are usually able to add our new information to what we knew before with ease. It may at first be *surprising* that teachers exist outside the classroom and parents outside the home, but it is not inconsistent with what we knew before. This, however, is not true of God. Appealing to the God of the philosophers in one context and the God of Abraham, Isaac, and Jacob in another involves us with not only additional facets of God, but conflicting ones.

How, then, can we reconcile our experiences of a personal God with our doubts about such a being? Ultimately, I think, we cannot. We must affirm the personal God of prayer because to refuse to do so would be to deny the validity of such experiences, even though there is intersubjective testimony to confirm them. On the other hand, to assert the existence of the personal God of the Bible and Talmud unequivocally is to ignore crucial questions concerning God's existence and nature.

Thus, it seems to me to be most honest and most adequate, both intellectually and religiously, to express myself in personal terms in prayer and other contexts of *relating* to God while admitting openly that this personal expression represents an extension of what we learn from a detached, critical analysis. Here, as elsewhere, we have not been able to fit all of our various experiences into a neat, systematic whole. Under such circumstances I would prefer truth to consistency.

Scientists do the same. Since light manifests characteristics of both waves and particles, physicists alternately use each of them to describe the behavior of light, while pointing out that these are only *analogies* from common experience to assist our understanding. They are not claiming that light *is* a wave or a series of particles; the phenomena of light simply do not lend themselves to neat categorization. Therefore, rather than ignore any of their experiences of light or interpret them in a forced way, scientists will use one analogy in some contexts and the other in others. They continue to strive to reconcile all of the facts into one, internally consistent picture; but they recognize that, failing this, rather than concocting a consistent picture that ignores or distorts some of their results, they are better off reporting all that they see.

Similarly, our experiences of God cannot be described in compatible, clearly understood, human terms. By denying the existence of some of these phenomena or by explaining them in a farfetched way, one could assert a clear, harmonious image of God, but that would be to tell a lie. The authors of the books of the Bible and the Rabbis of the Talmud instead reported and affirmed all of their experiences of God, even if those experiences did not fit into a neat pattern. Biblical and rabbinic literature thus make the Holy One the universal God of all humanity who yet has a particular relationship with the People Israel. God is just, and yet His mercy can overcome His justice—and sometimes He can punish in cruel and inscrutable ways. God is all-powerful, and yet human beings have free will. God is all-knowing, and yet He changes His mind. If they could not have both, Jewish classical texts thus preferred truth to consistency, and I would follow suit.

The import of philosophy of religion several decades ago was that different activities may well call for different rules of language usage and different procedures of justification.[55] Critics of that approach noted that, after all is said and done, we are

integrated human beings, and consequently there must be some
connections between the various languages we use. Clearly this
is correct, but it does not negate the fact that we do use language
differently in disparate contexts.

Our case is another example of this. What we are willing to
express in prayer we are not willing to assert in detached,
intellectual discussions, at least not with the same degree of
conviction; and what we maintain unequivocally in such discussions proves inadequate for prayer. We have different *purposes*
when we engage in these varying activities, and therefore we *use
language differently* in these pursuits—even to the extent of in-
tending different meanings by the same words when we use
them in both contexts.

John Herman Randall, Jr., was, to my knowledge, the first to
pinpoint this distinction. All religious people, he noted, use
religious symbols such as God as a loving Father, a stern Judge, or
as the Thou of an I–Thou relationship in religious practice. They
use such symbols to reveal something about the world in which
they function and to share with each other specific emotional
responses and appropriate activities in response to what has been
disclosed. Religious symbols serve, "not as instruments of a
'knowledge' based on an experience of what the world has done,
of how it has behaved and acted in the past, of the resources it has
been found to provide for men;" that is the function of scientific
and historical symbols. Religious symbols serve instead "as
instruments of 'insight' and 'vision,' of what it [the world] could
do, of what it might offer, of what it might become and be. . . .
They do not tell us that anything is so, they rather make us see
something." They also unify the experience of a community in
terms of its organizing concern, its vision of the divine. "To faith
the Divine is one."

When religious symbols *reveal* aspects of experience and *unify*
it in the framework of a fresh perspective, they provide us

knowledge in the model of what we called, in Chapter 2 above, "nonhypothetical discovery." That is, they disclose aspects of the world to us, not on the basis of new information that has been unearthed, but rather as a result of seeing the familiar facts in a different light, one that comes from a novel perspective that coordinates what we know in an innovative way and gives it new meaning.

> Religious "knowledge" is not mystic intuition, it is not the awareness of values, it is not the encounter with "the Holy," it is not existential commitment to the will to believe. It is rather a technical skill, an art, a "know-how." Within a broad "knowledge" we shall then distinguish between propositional knowledge, which must be either true or false, and "know-how," which is neither true nor false, but adequate and effective for its purposes or not. And thus the revelation which is the distinctive function of religious symbols, including religious beliefs, turns out in the last analysis to be the disclosing of a "know-how," a revelation of how to become aware of the world's religious dimension, of how to see God and enjoy him forever.

On the other hand, *some,* but by no means all, religious people also use *theological* symbols. In Western thought, such symbols have included, for Platonists, God as the Logos or objective, rational structure of the cosmos; for Aristotelians, God as the Prime Mover; for philosophers of idealism, God as the Absolute or Unconditioned; for Whitehead, the "principle of concretion," and so forth. In each case, these symbols are not invoked in the course of practicing religion, but rather in the process of thinking about it. Their purpose is to introduce intellectual consistency between people's beliefs in science and philosophy, on the one hand, and their religious and moral insights, on the other. "In each scheme," Randall says, "the highest object of knowledge has been identified with the highest good; and thus has been achieved, for that philosophy, a harmony between men's moral and religious faith and their way of understanding the world, between 'faith' and 'reason.' "

Theological symbols have a religious function only in the lives of those intellectually oriented, religious people who want to understand the relationship between their religious commitments and their scientific ones. Even for them, the religious function of these theological symbols is *different* from the role served by properly religious symbols: the former are needed to understand, the latter are used to practice, one's religion. As a result, says Randall, "The two sets of concepts of God we have been distinguishing both perform necessary and fundamental religious functions. But the two functions are so different that they do not compete."[56]

This may not be ultimately satisfying. The philosopher in each one of us wishes that all of our ideas would fit together neatly. In the context of this discussion, we want the conceptions of God which arise out of our practice and our intellects to be consistent. Disparity in the images which emerge from those two sources betrays the limits of our theological knowledge; if we truly knew God, we would have a consistent conception of the Holy One. And we desperately long to know the unknowable God.

Ultimately, though, we must face up to our lack of omniscience. Our only choice is to make do with the partial knowledge we can achieve. When we do that, however, we find that Randall is right, that our religious and theological images of God are not only dissimilar, but incompatible. This occurs because in religion, as in many other areas of life, the intellect, the emotions, and the will interpenetrate in varying proportions according to our aims.

In theology this difference in purpose between our thought and our practice means that the God of the philosophers is not identical with the God of Abraham, Isaac, and Jacob. This, however, depreciates neither the one nor the other. On the contrary,

as I have tried to demonstrate, both are legitimate and complementary conceptions of God, and we need both to be true to the
totality of our experience as human beings and as Jews.

Prayer as a Source of Knowledge of a Personal God

Prayer is one of our chief sources of knowledge of the personal
God of the Jewish tradition. It is in prayer, after all, that we
interact with God most intensely. In contemplating God rationally, in discovering God in the various forms in which the Holy
One is revealed, and in perceiving God in history, we notice
God. In performing the commandments other than prayer, we
act in response to God. Since such responses entail our body,
will, and emotions as well as our minds, they evoke more of our
internal being than do the other modes of knowing God, but
such actions still are done in answer to God's command. Only in
prayer do we express *ourselves* to God. Prayer thus involves more
elements of our being than do any of the other routes to God.

It is precisely such interaction, though, that most characterizes
the other personal relationships we know best—namely, our
personal relationships with each other. Thus, it is in prayer that
we find the strongest evidence for a personal God. No wonder
why people who pray regularly or who deeply want to pray find
it impossible to abandon their conception of God as personal.

On the other hand, this strong personal factor in prayer is also
a large part of the reason why it is so difficult for moderns to pray.
In highlighting the personal nature of God, prayer also underscores all of the problems involved in believing in such a God.

Our analysis of the cognitive issues involved in prayer, however, points us in the direction of a solution. Prayer, as we have
described it, is a crucial source of evidence for a personal God. In
the absence of prayer, the grounds for belief in such a God
drastically diminish. Prayer certainly does not resolve all of the

cognitive problems involved in conceiving of God as a person, but it establishes the reasons why we cannot easily abandon such a conception. If reason by its generalizing nature pushes us to believe in the God of the philosophers, prayer by its personal nature demands that we believe in the God of Abraham, Isaac, and Jacob. Without frequent prayer, we cannot possibly appreciate the personal side of the theological equation, and we cannot understand what is at stake if we abandon it.

The upshot, then, is that we have a crucial *theological* need—to say nothing of a communal, legal, and emotional one—to develop a vibrant, practicing Jewish community, one which, among other things, prays regularly. Even if logic would seem to require that we settle the philosophical problems with our beliefs before we commit ourselves to Jewish actions,[57] the educational and empirical order is the reverse of the logical order. We must first experience God through deeds and prayer to gain the requisite experiential base to formulate and evaluate theological claims. Consequently, Jewish educators and rabbis are philosophically correct in devoting most of their energies to the tasks of teaching Jewish skills and encouraging Jews to use them. Thinking hard about the issues of Jewish belief is crucial for a strongly held, deep faith, but now, as in times past, Jewish belief will not emerge out of intellectual discussions alone. People must first have the requisite Jewish moral, ritual, and communal experiences to make such thought informed and intelligent. Because prayer speaks to so many levels of our being, it is probably the hardest Jewish practice to acquire, but for that same reason it has the potential to tell us the most about God.

7

OUR IMAGES OF GOD

ANTHROPOMORPHISM AS A FORM OF IDOLATRY

We have explored a number of ways to gain knowledge of God. Reason can and should be used. It cannot produce proofs for the existence of God, as Hume, Kant, and others demonstrated, and it cannot be used in the hypothetical mode made popular by scientific experimentation. If employed in a nonhypothetical way within the context of a community's history and stories, however, it can provide evidence for a theological construction of our experience. That is, it can support a pattern of perceiving the world that includes a vital role for God.

While Jewish tradition used reason to know about God, that was not its primary mode. It rather emphasized divine action in history, divine speech (revelation), human action, especially in observing God's commandments, and human prayer as the principal methods to reach God. In the preceding chapters, we have examined how and what each of these phenomena can tell us about God.

None of those methods, of course, can prove God beyond all reasonable doubt any more than reason can, but each adds evidence to make a theological interpretation of existence ever more plausible. They call attention to aspects of our actions and observations that reveal "footprints" of God. We might wish for more certainty in these matters, but the very nature of God, as depicted in Judaism and the other Western faiths, precludes such confirmation and makes these forms of gaining knowledge of God much more appropriate.

Even if one adopts a theological perspective on experience on the basis of the combined testimony proffered by all of these methods, however, one still is faced with another important problem. How shall we picture God? Indeed, some prominent medieval philosophers held that we can know with certainty of the existence of God, but the limitations of human intelligence and the infinite character of God make it impossible for us to know the nature of God. As we shall discuss at greater length below, Maimonides, for example, claimed that we can only know that God is *not* characterized by any finite attributes such as the ones that humans possess. Almost all of the characteristics we know, however, belong to finite beings, and so it becomes very difficult, if not impossible, to imagine God—assuming that that is legitimate in the first place.

It may not be. According to some interpretations, it is not only philosophically unreasonable to expect to know the character of God; it is also religiously forbidden to depict God in human terms. This prohibition stems from the biblical laws against idolatry.

Moderns usually think of idolatry as an ancient fetish of worshiping statues. It certainly included that, but that was only one of its manifestations. At its core, *idolatry is dedication to a partial view of reality as if it were the whole of it, or to one value as if it were all values.* As such, it is a very modern sin as well as an ancient one. The devotion of the Nazis to Hitler, for example, to the point of overriding all concern for moral values and for non-Aryans, was a flagrant and ruthless instance of idolatry in our own times, but there are many less dramatic, but equally pervasive, examples. Every time people devote themselves unstintingly to money, for example, making that the only goal in life, they are being idolatrous. Similarly, every time people follow the orders of one human being, whoever he or she is, without exercising their own judgment as to the rectitude of those orders, they are making an idol of the person so obeyed. Sometimes people do this because they want to be accepted as the particular person's friend; this is especially common among teenagers. Sometimes, as in the cases of employees vis-à-vis their bosses or soldiers vis-à-vis their superiors, people obey without question because they fear the consequences of not doing so. Many of the followers of the Lubavitcher Rebbe or of cult leaders heed the dictates of such figures because they appear to be all-wise. In all of these cases and in many more, we have modern examples of idolatry, just as surely so as the ancient worship of statues of wood and stone. Judaism began with primary concern about the latter because that was the main way in which this idolatrous impulse expressed itself at the time, but the worship of a supernatural God that is at the religion's core is a powerful denial of the validity of any claim to ultimate value or full reality less than God.[1]

The biblical prohibitions specifically outlaw three related, but distinct, forms of idolatry: the worship of idols, the worship of God with pagan rites, and the making of idols. The first of those, the worship of idols, includes bans against idol worship conforming to pagan rituals; bowing down to an idol; offering a sacrifice to another god, including those represented by an idol; and paying homage to an idol.[2] The second injunction, that against worshiping God with pagan rites,[3] reflects the biblical view that only divinely ordained methods of worship can be assured of according with God's will. And finally, making idols is explicitly prohibited, although only images to be used for worship.[4] This reflects the common practice in the ancient world of requiring a ceremonial consecration before a graven image could become an embodiment of a god.[5]

It is the last of these biblical prohibitions that addresses our issue, in particular the later rabbinic and philosophic expansions of it. The Rabbis proscribed making idols for anyone's worship, not just one's own,[6] but they also went beyond the context of worship in prohibiting the making of any human image:

> Why has it been taught: "All portraits are allowed except the portrait of a human being"? Rav Huna, the son of Rav Idi, replied: "From a discourse of Abaye I learned: 'You shall not make with me' (Exodus 20:20) [implies] you shall not make Me.' "[7]

Since, according to the Torah, human beings were made "in God's image,"[8] making a human image would be tantamount to making a likeness of God. The later codes restrict this prohibition to sculpted images that protrude like idols (excluding those on indented or flat surfaces) and to representations of the full human being and not just the head or a part of the body,[9] but the principle remains: since human beings partake in the likeness of God, to create a graven image of a human being would be, as it were, to create a likeness of God.

Modern Jews may be startled by the prohibitions described here, both because they know that even the most observant Jews take photographs of one another and also because many understand these laws to prohibit only intentional representations of God. The fact that the Rabbis prohibited images of human beings under these laws underscores the importance they ascribed to the biblical verses attributing a divine image to human beings. It also makes it clear that the Rabbis conceived of God, in turn, in human form.

While these injunctions against making images of human beings are perhaps the starkest expression of the tradition's conception of God in human form, they are by no means the only one. In both biblical and rabbinic literature, God is portrayed in human images. In the Bible God has a face, nose, mouth, eyes, ears, hands, fingers, an arm, and feet.[10] The Rabbis continue this use of human imagery to describe God. In rabbinic literature, for example, on the occasion of the wedding of Adam and Eve, God plaits Eve's hair and serves as best man for Adam; He wears phylacteries and wraps Himself in a prayer shawl; He prays to Himself and studies the Torah during three hours of each day; He weeps over the failures of His creatures, visits the sick, comforts the mourner, and buries the dead.[11]

This unbridled use of anthropomorphic imagery stands in sharp contrast to the rationalist tradition in medieval Jewish philosophy. Maimonides, perhaps most of all, cannot tolerate depicting God in human form lest that limit God. Bodies and bodily parts, after all, are finite in extension and ability. Therefore any ascription of a body to God, however strongly one qualifies the comparison, implies a limitation on God's extent and power. Instead, according to Maimonides,[12] one must read the Bible's bodily descriptions of God as negative attributes and, as he summarizes in his Thirteen Principles of the Faith, one must believe in a God who "is no body and . . . who is not affected by bodily accidents."[13]

One does not have to adopt Maimonides' position to appreciate the problematic that motivates it. If we depict God, either physically or mentally, as having human form, are we not simply writing ourselves large? Are we not engaging in an act of human hubris and divine diminution at one and the same time? If we think of God as infinite and omnipotent, as some of the strains of Judaism did, we certainly cannot conceive of the Eternal as having any shape, human or otherwise, for that would set limits to

God, who, by hypothesis, does not have any. Even if we conceive of God as powerful but not all-powerful, as other parts of the Jewish tradition did, to conceive of God in human terms significantly reduces God's stature, depriving God not only of infinity, but of perfection, unity, eternity, and incorporeality as well, as David Hume so acutely and sarcastically demonstrated.[14]

On the other hand, though, the rationales behind the biblical and rabbinic depictions of God in human form are also clear. If we cannot picture God in some form, how are we to conceive of the Eternal at all? Moreover, what is to distinguish a believer from a nonbeliever if both assert that God cannot be conceived? Surely the belief in God must have *some* cognitive content for believers to assert it so strenuously and for nonbelievers to deny it just as vigorously.

For all of the problems that the Rabbis had with idolatry, they thought that it had been conquered. "God created two evil inclinations in the world, that toward idolatry and the other toward incest. The former has already been uprooted, [but] the latter still holds sway."[15] This undoubtedly reflects the historical fact that after the Maccabees, there was little tendency on the part of the Jews to succumb to idolatry in its physical forms. The Rabbis clearly did not mean that psychological forms of idolatry had vanished, for human beings in all ages have made a whole host of objects of finite worth their gods. They may not physically bow down to them or even call them gods, but they surely treat them as such with equally devastating effects.

When viewed from the standpoint of the conceptions that motivate us to act in given ways, this kind of idolatry is at the root of much of the immorality and decadence in modern society, just as it was in ancient society. Confusing the unimportant with the important, the finite with the infinite, leads us mistakenly to devote our time and energy to what are at best only partial or instrumental goals. Only getting a grasp on what is ultimately important in life—in theological terms, learning to discern the difference between idols and God—can save us from such serious mistakes. In practice, we human beings are all too often tempted by the sirens of temporary and improper goals, and it is the ongoing function of religion to remind us of what is really important.

One can readily recognize the practical problems entailed in living lives directed to apt goals; we struggle with that each day. Idolatry, though, is an *intellectual* challenge just as much as it is a practical one. We gain knowledge of God through the various avenues described in the chapters above, and that knowledge presumably suggests that certain understandings of God are more apt reflections of such experiences than others. Because both the Jewish tradition and our own experiences attest to a God who is beyond human conception, however, we can never gain a total understanding of the Divine. Instead, we must formulate images of God based on our own, limited experience of the world and of God. Our epistemological position—our capacity to know and the limitations on that ability—gives us no choice in this; we simply have no other way to assimilate the knowledge our experiences give us of God. The same, of course, was true of the authors of the Bible and rabbinic literature: they too had to translate their experiences into images they could understand, feel, and communicate to others. How, then, do we judge whether we have done this as appropriately as possible? Moreover, once we arrive at a particular idea of God, how do we avoid mistaking our image of God for God? That is, how do we protect against idolatry in our very conception of God?

In this chapter, then, we shall address the cognitive status of images of God. Are they properly understood as literal descriptions of God, as totally metaphoric language, or as something in between? If we choose the last of these alternatives, how is that usage of language to be construed, and into what context of life does it best fit? How does it signify anything in that context? And finally, if God remains beyond human comprehension, can we at all distinguish proper images of God from idolatrous ones, and, if so, how?

IMAGES, CREEDS, AND SYMBOLS

We should first take note of the differences between images, creeds, and symbols and their varying roles in religious life. As I shall show, in levels of abstraction, creeds occupy a middle position between images and symbols, at least as I shall be using the terms,[16] and so it will be helpful first to define the ends of the spectrum, images and symbols.

Some examples of images and symbols will set the stage for a more general description of their differences. As we have seen, the Bible includes anthropomorphic images of God, depicting God in terms of a human body, but it also includes inanimate, naturalistic images of God (e.g., God as a rock, light, fire, and water), animals (e.g., a lion and birds), human artifacts (e.g., a shield, a hammer, a dwelling, and a fortress or tower of refuge), and anthropopathic images of God, based on the mental and psychological faculties of human beings (e.g., God knows, remembers, plans, becomes angry, can be expected to judge morally, forgives, and acts out of loyalty and love).[17] More complicated and controversial instances of images are the description of God coming down on the mountain and, indeed, the very notion of God speaking.[18]

The Bible also refers to some manifestations of God that are more properly classified as symbols. These include the burning bush, the pillars of cloud and fire, the tabernacle, the Urim and Tummim, the Menorah, and the eternal light.[19] The Bible itself classifies the Sabbath and phylacteries as symbols, and the var-

ious words by which God is described, including, most especially, the proper name of God (the Tetragrammaton), are also
symbols.[20] The Torah has taken on increasing layers of meaning
through history; indeed, with the destruction of the Temples, it
arguably has become the central Jewish symbol. The Star of
David is an example of a postbiblical symbol that has become
part of Jewish consciousness.

With these examples of images and symbols in mind, we can
now describe their general character. Images of God are particular, focused, concrete manifestations of the Eternal, while symbols are more universal, imprecise, and suggestive. Images are
direct and present; they engender an immediate, spontaneous
recognition of an aspect of God. Symbols develop power over
time, resonating to history and adding levels of meaning as they
are used and interpreted over time. They make the past and
future impinge upon the present. As a result, they are often
richer in meaning, but also less clear and vivacious, than images.
Images appeal to the imagination and require little thought to
unravel; symbols require extensive reflection and thought. Images sometimes become symbols, but not the reverse, for symbols lack the concrete, immediate character needed to function as
an image, while images can sometimes take on abstract meanings as they get used over time. Moreover, once an image is used
as a symbol for one thing, it can later be used as a symbol for
something else ("polyvocal images").

Michael Goldberg, a Conservative rabbi and theologian,
points out that the status and power of images often depend upon
the underlying narratives in which they occur. When used in
stories, images gain movement and life, and it is the stories that
determine which images are usable at all and which, from among
those, become dominant. He therefore prefers to speak of "master stories" like the Exodus rather than "master images."[21]

I would only note that there are many biblical images unattached to stories that also have had a significant influence on the community's understanding of God. God as rock, light, and fortress come to mind. Goldberg is certainly correct, however, in emphasizing the use of images in stories, for the central narratives of a religious tradition coordinate many of its most frequently used images and, to an extent at least, serve as a criterion for determining which images are usable within the tradition and, among those, which are dominant. Moreover, in the context of stories, images gain added vivaciousness, a stronger claim on communal memory, and a more substantial link to our ongoing actions. All images gain their significance from the concrete world from which they emanate, and images derived from *events* in that world have added power.

Creedal statements enter Judaism only in the Middle Ages, as the result of the systematization that rationalism introduced to all three Western religions at the time as well as the need to defend Judaism against intellectual attacks. While Maimonides' Thirteen Principles of the Faith are by no means the only formulations of Jewish belief, they are probably the most famous, and they will serve as good examples of what we mean by creedal assertions.

1. There is a Creator.
2. He is One.
3. He is incorporeal.
4. He is eternal.
5. He alone must be worshiped.
6. The prophets are true.
7. Moses was the greatest of all prophets.
8. The entire Torah was divinely given to Moses.
9. The Torah is immutable.
10. God knows all the acts and thoughts of man.

11. He rewards and punishes.
12. Messiah will come.
13. There will be resurrection.[22]

Statements such as these remove classical Jewish images further from the concrete world. The Torah, for example, describes God in the *act* of creation; it does not stop to make the general assertion that the Creator exists. Similarly, while the Torah certainly presents God as eternal and incorporeal, it does so in the process of describing God's interactions with the world, not in general statements such as those of Maimonides.

None of the negative images of God in the Bible as wrathful, vindictive, unjust, and brutal survives the move from concrete images to the more abstract principles of Jewish religious belief. God punishes, as Maimonides says, but the reader of his creed expects that that punishment is always justly imposed for violations of the Torah's laws, mentioned in the principles preceding this tenet. The God who angrily wants to destroy the Israelites after the incidents of the Golden Calf and the spies and refrains from doing so only because of Moses' intervention is completely absent from this list.[23]

If creedal tenets thus lose perceptual detail, they gain in breadth of scope and expression. They capture the sense of the beyond and illimitable, the sheer wonder and unspeakable awe which mark significant elements of religious experience. God is "incorporeal" and "eternal," both words stretching beyond the realm of human experience.

But what was clear, precise, and powerful in biblical images becomes indefinite, clouded, and dispassionate in philosophic or theological propositions. What, after all, does it mean to be "incorporeal" or "eternal"? We can define the words, but we cannot imagine what they denote since we have no experience with any other being who has those qualities. And the entire tone of Maimonides' creed is coldly intellectual; it is a far cry from some of the evocative imagery in the Book of Psalms, for example.

Symbols bring us yet further into the world of the abstract. Theological or philosophical statements may be general, but they are meant to be understood as denoting one, hopefully unambiguous, meaning. That univocal message may become clouded as new people and generations interpret it from the standpoint of their own experiences and their differing systems of thought, but the intention of anyone who utters the statement is to describe one belief. Creedal statements also are subject to intersubjective analysis and evaluation of their truth value, adequacy, consistency, and pragmatic implications.

Religious symbols, in contrast, are not intended to have a univocal meaning in the first place. Part of the point of such symbols, in fact, is to capture the undefined, the mysterious in life. The burning bush, for example, is described as mysterious from the very beginning: it burns but is not consumed.[24] As such, it, like religious symbols generally, is open to a variety of interpretations, and it is often difficult to rule out the legitimacy of any particular reading of a symbol. Is the burning bush supposed to catch Moses' attention so that he will turn aside and confront God, as the plain meaning of the Torah there seems to be? Or, given that God speaks out of the burning bush, is its purpose to impress Moses with God's power, to make him believe that God can indeed take the Children of Israel out of Egypt, as God announces from the bush? Or does it signify that God will be with him always, even when other relationships would be spent? Or is it intended to introduce Moses to an incorporeal God, unbounded by the normal rules that apply to physical objects, just as the bush eerily does not pass out of existence despite the fire? Or is the burning bush a symbol for the eternity, warmth, and light of the tradition, as it was used artistically later on? All of these are possible; indeed, it is in the nature of symbols that one applauds every new level of meaning that can be drawn from them and yearns for more.

This feature of symbols means, however, that their truth value—that is, a judgment as to whether they are true or false— is less clear-cut than that of creedal statements. One should expect that result. After all, if the meaning of symbols is open to many interpretations, the truth of any one of the possible meanings would have to be judged independently. At the same time, symbols have the advantage of expressing and communicating that which we human beings cannot fully comprehend or articulate but which is nevertheless part of our experience.

In some cases, a move to greater abstraction undermines the meaning of the original image. One wonders, for example, whether conceiving of God as transcendent and incomparable makes love of God pointless (Spinoza notwithstanding) and prayer fruitless. Similarly, while the Bible surely depicts God as powerful, it never gets entangled in the philosophical problems posed by characterizing God as omnipotent. Furthermore, when the Bible and Rabbis depict God as being eternal, they mean that He is everlasting, extending forward and backward in time without end, not that time does not apply to Him and that He is therefore otherworldly. Philosophers have thought that, and they then have had to determine how a timeless, infinite, perfect being can have anything to do with a finite, imperfect, ever-changing world, especially if God is also immutable and impassible. These serious problems arise when one leaves the world of concrete images and begins to use creeds and symbols.

This should alert us to the varying contexts of images, creeds, and symbols. As Judah Halevi, and Blaise Pascal after him, saw long ago, there is a significant difference between the God of the philosophers and the God of Abraham, Isaac, and Jacob.[25] The God of the philosophers Halevi had in mind was the conception of God in the rationalistic philosophy he knew—universal, abstract, impersonal, unchanging, and detached. That God, Halevi correctly says, is simply not the God of religious experience. It would be hard to pray to such a God, and people would most likely be unwilling to make significant sacrifices in deference to such a God. In contrast, the God of Abraham, Isaac, and Jacob is personal, subject to influence and change, particularly concerned with individuals and with the People Israel as a community, and involved in people's lives. Such a God one can worship in the broadest sense of the term; that is, one can bare one's soul to such a God, pray to Him, seek to learn and follow His will, repent when one does not succeed in doing that, and make sacrifices, including even death if necessary, on behalf of Him and His ways. In short, one can have a variety of relationships with the God of religious experience beyond those derived from the intellect.

Unlike Halevi, however, I would, as I indicated earlier, aver that the God of the philosophers is, and should be, part of our experience of the Eternal. Our minds, after all, are also part of us, and we should learn about God from them, just as we learn about God from our other faculties, actions, and relationships. We should then remember that the knowledge we gain from these various quarters may not immediately fit together well and may indeed seem contradictory; we are not omniscient, and we should expect that varying faculties and viewpoints will yield different pictures. This, however, should not convince us to deny the knowledge we gain from any one part of our experience, but rather to affirm everything we have learned, even if we cannot totally reconcile the various pieces of our knowledge.[26]

In our context, this will mean that we should expect that biblical images are appropriate for the context of worship and should be examined in that context, not expecting them to transfer easily into the realms of creed and symbol. Our task in the remainder of this chapter, then, will be to examine how images function in the context of worship, broadly defined; how their truth may be assessed; and how they gain authority.

The Functions of Images in Worship

To understand the cognitive status of religious images, one must first pay attention to how they function in religious life. Only then can one understand what those who use them intend. Once one knows their meaning, one may then attempt to assess their truth.

Images arrest our attention. Their concrete character enables us to identify with them immediately and to feel their impact. God depicted as a fire at once conveys the warmth, the danger, and the vitality of God. God pictured as a rock conjures up ideas of massive stability, inert resistance to change, dependability, impermeability, durability, and protection—from the elements as well as from human attackers. God imagined as light conveys the mysterious element of God, for light reveals itself and also other objects but is itself difficult to understand, it emanates from some source yet does not seem to diminish the power of that source. At the same time, light, like God, is pleasant and beneficent, and it prevents error and affords a sense of peace. In addition, sources of light like the sun or a fire on earth often provide warmth.

Images like these tap into our emotions and will, reaching deep down into what makes us feel and act as we do. Since life is lived in the concrete world, images drawn from that world influence our feelings and behavior more powerfully and directly than abstract concepts can. Concepts have little or no affect associated with them, and we must exert considerable effort to apply them to our lives in order to understand their meaning and significance. Images, on the other hand, come equipped with all of the emotions of the concrete situations from which they come and are immediately applicable to other, similar circumstances.

Images provide insight and illumination. They do not totally describe their object, but they capture one or more aspects of it so that we can better understand and relate to it. According to the Rabbis, the altar of the Temple weeps in the event of a divorce.[27] This does not explicate all of the feelings of either the couple or the Jewish tradition surrounding divorce, but it does express the sense felt both by the couple and the community of a rent in the order of life and society, a tear that evokes even God's tears. God is depicted as sometimes capricious, unfair, deceitful, and vengeful.[28] Similarly, some of God's punishments are peculiarly repulsive and extreme, and God's hardening the hearts of Pharaoh and the king of Heshbon make their subsequent punishments hard to justify.[29] These descriptions may not appeal to our sense of the just or the good, but they express what the victim of unjustified suffering feels. Never mind that such images do not fit well with other images of a God concerned with law and beneficence; the negative images express and explain part of the world as human beings experience it.

Images convey values through pictures much more effectively than general statements can. It is one thing to state that marriage and study are prized in the Jewish tradition; it is quite another to say, as the Rabbis do, that God Himself matches men and women for marriage and spends part of each day studying His own Torah.[30] Similarly, for the tradition, in seeking peace among human beings, one not only pursues a Jewish goal; one becomes part of the company of Aaron's students.[31] In praying daily one is not only fulfilling one's obligations under Jewish law; one is doing what Abraham, Isaac, and Jacob did.[32] These images make it clear, as no general statement can, that these activities have the full support and encouragement of God and our people from time immemorial. The images also make this endorsement palpable; one not only recognizes their message intellectually, but feels it emotionally.

Does this mean that images are only for the intellectually and emotionally weak or immature, and that people with more developed intellectual and affective faculties should not need them? No, for we all respond immediately and powerfully to concrete imagery, even if we *also* have learned to respond on a variety of levels to the general and abstract.

Images also help one deal with the psychological and social aspects of life. They express our innermost feelings and fantasies, including those which we dare not act out, and they enable us to gain a sense of what constitutes psychological health. They also help us resolve some of our problems. A conflict with a family member, for example, can be given perspective if it is related to one of the stories of such conflicts in the Bible. That process also makes those experiencing the conflict understand that they are not abnormal in having it, that one is not depraved or odd or alone in feeling such feelings. Moreover, one learns from the stories what the community imagines people might do in such situations and what the consequences would be. As Richard Rubenstein has said,

> Before the time of psychotherapy, the Aggadah gave men self-perspective, if not self-knowledge. It did so for all segments of the community in an idiom all could comprehend. No man was compelled to face the maelstrom of his own emotional life alone, unaided, or uninstructed.[33]

While this psychological value of images is most apparent in those arising from human interactions, it also applies to images of God. Indeed, it is our experience of God's love, as depicted by the Jewish tradition, that teaches us how to imagine properly what our love should be toward one another. God's love, loyalty, care, and concern provide positive psychological models of

how we should commit ourselves to one another through thick
and thin. At the same time, God's anger, vengeance, and capri-
ciousness act out some of our negative qualities. Rubenstein
thinks that the Holocaust and modern secularity, self-
consciousness, and psychoanalysis have permanently destroyed
the power of rabbinic images to have psychological value for the
contemporary Jew, but he finds that lamentable:

> Our contemporary gain in critical insight cannot compensate for the loss
> of a medium with which a community was able to express and cope with
> its underlying strivings and preoccupations. The clock cannot be turned
> back. We are children of the secular city. Traditional belief is impossible
> for most men in our generation. Nevertheless, there was more existential
> and psychological truth in the ancient mythic hyperbole of the rabbis than
> in contemporary man's critical precision. We have gained vastly in our
> power to control nature; we have lost much of our ability to deal with our
> unconscious which religion, myth, and legend once afforded. . . . In our
> own times, when the demonic has released itself from its dark and
> brooding cave in men's hearts and stalks about as if possessed of its own
> peculiar dignity, it may yet be possible to see the world of the Aggadah as
> an irreparably lost haven of human truth.[34]

Almost twenty years after Rubenstein wrote that, as Jews in
all branches of Judaism are increasingly seeking meaning by
plumbing Jewish sources and symbols, one wonders whether
the rabbinic view is as "irreparably lost" as he thought. In any
case, this new resurgence of seriousness about religion on the
part of some who exhibited no such interest before makes one
appreciate anew the psychological power of religious images
that he recognized.

In conveying emotions, values, and psychological perspective, images become invaluable means for a community to identify itself, cohere, communicate, and gain a sense of its worth as
a group. Members of the community need only invoke one of its

images to convey meaning and to relate a situation to the larger reality of the community and its worldview. This is especially helpful in the turning points of life (birth, adolescence, marriage, and death), when social imagery bespeaks the feelings and values that nobody can adequately articulate. It is also important, though, in the ongoing happenings of life as ways to express and address our fears, hopes, hostilities, ambivalences, and joys.

Images also warrant and sanction social structure, giving a practical as well as a psychic coherence to the community. You should obey the rabbi acting as judge, for example, because in your generation he stands in place of Moses, even if he or she is not nearly as intelligent, learned, or pious as you imagine Moses to have been.[35]

While reminders of specific members of the Jewish people who did as we now do are effective in accomplishing these social functions of expressing feelings and values and justifying the social structure and its rules, images that refer to God are especially powerful. If God participates in the communal event or chooses the People Israel and commands its members to observe Jewish law, then these aspects of Jewish communal life have not only social, but theological, significance.

The social import of images is not only in the present; it is also in the past and future. Shared images are crucial to the existence and power of communal memory. The central images in Judaism, the Exodus and Sinai, are especially noteworthy here, for they articulate the perspective through which Jews have understood their past, their future, their values, and the relationship of God to all three. Postbiblical images, however, have also shaped communal memory, so much so that a number of them have become symbols denoting realities much broader than the original, specific people or events that they signify. The Maccabees, Yavneh, Masada, Auschwitz, and the Israeli pioneer, for example, have taken on this role, each symbolizing a different facet of Jewish historical experience and Jewish reactions to it. These images are powerful links to the history of the community and, through it, to the community itself.

They also shape the community's vision of its present and future. The extent to which Masada has influenced recent Israeli policy, whether for good or for ill, is a cogent indication of the power of images to evoke memory and fashion the future.

And finally, images have theological import. They move us to shift our attention from ourselves to God. We come to recognize that *God* is the rock, shield, and fire, not we. It is always hard for us to acknowledge our limits, and it is even harder to remove ourselves from our egocentric concerns. Nevertheless, we are, in fact, limited in our abilities, and we must, for both pragmatic and principled reasons, take note of the needs and talents of others. Because images are concrete, they have more power than abstract principles do to impress these lesson upon us.

Images also teach us how to relate to God. We do that by picturing God in all of the concrete ways that the Bible and Rabbis did and by then responding to God in ways appropriate to the particular image we currently have in mind. No human image, of course, will be an adequate reflection of God. We have no full knowledge of the Holy One, and we cannot even satisfactorily express what we do know, despite our attempts to rise above the limitations of descriptive language through the use of images and symbols. Images, creeds, and symbols, though, do enable us to relate to God through the partial truths they afford us—as long as we remember that these are always partial truths.

To put this another way, we need not seek a philosophically adequate conception of God, one that reflects all of the divine reality, in order to relate to God. We cannot achieve such a concept, and intellectually comprehending God is not the prime Jewish way to relate to the Holy One in any case. Such intellectual effort can augment our understanding of God, and, as such, it is valuable, Halevi notwithstanding; our minds are part of us, and we must use them if we are ever to love God with "all our heart, all our soul, and all our might." But the intellect is one feature of life, and it is not the dominant one in *relating* to God. There we call more upon the will, the body, and the emotions, and hence we appropriately use images drawn from those areas of our lives.

How Images Mean

How, then, do we understand the meaning of religious images? Paul Tillich claimed that everything we say about God is symbolic,[36] but, as Wilbur Urban has maintained, without "some literal knowledge of divine things symbolic knowledge is an illusion."[37] Without the ability to translate the meaning of symbols, however inadequately, to more literal language, one has no way of determining whether they refer to anything at all. Under those circumstances, one certainly cannot discriminate between more or less adequate symbols for a given datum of experience. In one critic's words, "Tillich's *via symbolica* becomes a *via negativa.*"[38]

Tillich and many others who speak of the symbolic nature of our discourse also neglect the difference between the meaning of religious symbols when contemplated philosophically and the meaning they have to the religious person using them. Theologians have been worried about limiting God through anthropomorphic images, and some have therefore sought to interpret religious images metaphorically. The classic Jewish instance of this is Maimonides, as we discussed above.

When religious people use images, however, they usually have very concrete things in mind. We have seen that images are distinct from symbols in that the former are more tangible, immediate, and direct than the latter. Here it is important to note that religious people, from the time of the Bible on, have deliberately chosen to use images as well as symbols. They *want* to depict God in concrete language in order to make the experience of God vivid and at least partially intelligible in the terms of their daily lives. They therefore literally picture God as their father—or, perhaps, their grandfather or some other powerful and sagacious-looking man—when they use the father image to refer to God, and they have an ordinary rock in mind (albeit an impressive one) when they talk of God as their rock. For the religious person using these images, the experience of God, however indescribable ultimately, is like that of a father and a rock in some ways.

Moreover, religious people are generally not bothered all that much by conflicts of various degrees in their images of God. Is God like a judge who always demands justice or one who exercises mercy? Is the Holy One hard like a rock or flexible and vibrant like water? Is the Eternal majestically transcendent or affectionately imminent? For the religious Jew, God is all of these things.

The inconsistencies are not disturbing for one or both of two reasons. First, God can be manifest in one characteristic on one occasion and in its opposite on another, just as parents can appear to their children. Moreover, no ascription of a characteristic to God can possibly be adequate in describing the Eternal. Not only is our knowledge limited; our very language, drawn from human experience as it is, is inevitably incapable of capturing that which is beyond it.

As a result, in practice religious people have little difficulty in making a tangible, but not an idolatrous, use of images. Of course, any word or object can be used for idolatrous purposes by those who wish to do so, and most probably have been so employed at one time or another. Strong emphasis on God's transcendence, however, particularly in Judaism and Islam, have meant that historically vast numbers of believers in the West have used concrete images without mistaking them to encompass God. In widespread practice, then, the use of concrete imagery is *not* tantamount to idolatry; it is, instead, a way of making the experience of God immediate and vivid.[39]

The Truth of Images

Even if we can discern what an image means, how shall we determine its truth or falsity? All human statements, whether intended to be taken literally or metaphorically, will, of course, be limited in their truth to what human beings can know, but how can we know whether a given image reflects reality more than it distorts it? That is, how can we decide whether a particular image is helpful or harmful in revealing the truth to us?

Some have thought religious images should be treated as metaphors expressing hypothetical claims awaiting further confirmation. Their truth value would then be assessed according to the usual procedures for testing scientific propositions.[40] So, for example, God pictured as a rock would be construed as a claim, say, that God is strong. That claim would then be confirmed if our experiences of God showed that to be true.

This, however, misconstrues the meaning of the images in the first place. They are not stated in the hypothetical mood, and those who use them apparently want to make declarative statements, not hypothetical ones. Moreover, one wonders how scientific methods would apply to the analysis of religious images. How, for example, can you definitively determine on scientific grounds whether or not God is a rock or water or a fire?

At the other end of the spectrum, other thinkers have asserted that religious language, presumably including religious images, never intends to describe. It instead is used to evoke emotions and/or moral behavior.[41] Picturing God as a rock, for example, is not expected to describe God in any way. The user of the image rather wants to make us feel overawed by God's power and comforted by God's ability to protect and sustain us. For those of these thinkers who take a moral rather than an emotional tack, the purpose of the image is to confirm our assurance that we must be moral because the divinely ordained moral standards which govern the world are as reliable and unchangeable as bedrock and because God, like a rock, will steadfastly enforce them.

As Dorothy Emmett has said, however, religion "loses its nerve when it ceases to believe that it expresses in some way truth about our relation to a reality beyond ourselves which ultimately concerns us."[42] We certainly are moved emotionally by many images of God, and sometimes such images reinforce our desire to act morally. They can do this, though, only if we believe that in some manner they describe the reality of God. Moreover, the people who use them *intend* to describe such a reality. The people of the Bible and the Rabbis who used images certainly wanted thereby to convey the truth about their world—or at least their perception of it—and the same is true for religious people today. If religious people pretend that they do not aim to denote the real world through the images they use, they have both deceived themselves and lost their nerve, for they are then backing away from claims they really want to make.

Denying these extreme positions, though, brings us back to our original questions: how do religious images carry a truth value (that is, make a claim which is either true or false), and how are we to judge that claim? Our previous analysis of the functioning of images will help us to address these issues.

When people say, "God is our Father," they are saying that reality as they perceive it has some characteristics of a father. They may be referring to the fact that their needs are provided for, or that they are protected, or that there are rules to be obeyed, or that they feel personally related to the larger reality they sense—

all aspects of their relationship to their own, human father. When they say that God is a fire, they are saying that ultimate reality enlivens us ("fires us up," as it were) and that it is both warm and dangerous. A similar analysis could be made of all other religious images, for, after all, they all come from human experience.

As an initial description, then, determining whether a given image by which God is described is true would amount to deciding whether ultimate reality is as the image describes. "God is our Father" would then be true if ultimate reality is, indeed, providing, protective, and so on, and false if it is not.

The problem, of course, is that ultimate reality is many things, including some that clash. That is why God is described in conflicting images. God is both as stationary as a rock and as mobile as a pillar of fire. Even the same images can take on opposing meanings. The prophet Nahum, for example, uses those very images to convey the opposite message: "His anger pours out like fire, and rocks are shattered because of Him."[43] Here it is the destruction that fire can wreck that is the point of the image, not the enlightening and guiding role it can have as a pillar of fire that leads the way in the dark. And the rocks have ceased to be as permanent and protective as they usually are, for God, though a Rock Himself, can shatter rocks.

Moreover, while most people acknowledge the fullness of human experience, most also emphasize one or another aspect of reality in their visions of the world. For people like the seventeenth-century British philosopher Thomas Hobbes, for example, the world is generally a nasty place with only a few, transient glimmers of something better, while for people like twentieth-century American philosopher John Dewey, the world is a positive, growing place whose negative characteristics are equally few and transient.

These differences in perspective have an effect even on some aspects of the physical sciences, but they are more muted there.

That is why "scientific proof" carries such an air of certainty for us. Perspectival differences have a much greater effect on the social sciences and humanities. Certainly when people formulate their most encompassing vision of the world, through which they see and evaluate experience and by which they live, differences in viewpoint are crucial.

This has an immediate effect on the truth of images. To return to some of the examples we have been using, Hobbes and anyone who shares his view of life might say that God is not much like a rock and that that image does not ring true, for life is "nasty, brutish, and short," as Hobbes said, and there seems little surety in it, even from God. The image of fire to describe God, on the other hand, might come closer to the truth for such people, but only in fire's destructive aspects and not in its warm and enlivening character.

For Dewey and like-minded people, in contrast, God depicted as a rock would truly convey the confidence that one can have in God and in objective moral standards. The rock image would, however, hide the dynamic character of God and of life in general. It would thus articulate only a partial truth—but so do many, if not most, propositions. It would still be valuable for the truth it communicates, but it must be used with its limitations in mind. God described as a fire would have less shortcomings in the eyes of such people, for fire correctly discloses the warm and enlivening character of life, together with its potential for destruction. It does not, however, reveal life's stationary, dependable aspects, though, as the image of God as a rock does, and so we would need both to transmit a relatively full picture of reality.

Consequently, we must modify our criterion for the truth of an image to read: determining whether a given image by which God is described is true would amount to deciding whether ultimate reality is as the image describes *in the perspective through which it is seen.* We must also recognize that, as with propositions, images often tell the truth, but not the whole truth, and, depending upon how they are understood, they may even mask some truths while revealing others.

This means that we cannot determine whether a given image is true or false in a scientific sense, where the effects of perspective are minimal, but only in a broader sense, where adequate account is taken of viewpoint. One is almost tempted to say, as Clyde Holbrook and John Herman Randall, Jr., have, that one should not talk of truth at all in this context, but rather plausibility or adequacy.[44] I think, however, that one *can* legitimately continue to speak of truth in religion if one keeps the perspectival component in mind. Moreover, one *should* continue to talk of the truth of specific religious images to emphasize that in religion one is still, after all, focusing on reality and that religion's claim to truth is no weaker than that of any of the other areas of the social sciences and humanities where broad perspectives influence what one sees and how one assesses that.

Even recognition of the role of one's viewpoint, however, is not enough. Language, like rituals, laws, and customs, is a *social* phenomenon. A large part of the power of images is a function of how they are understood and used in a community. Human beings can communicate across communal lines, and hence some images are intelligible in multiple communities or even in a general human context. God imagined as a rock, for example, would immediately appeal to Jews, Christians, and Muslims. Since Hindus, Buddhists, Taoists, and Jains believe in the ultimate unreality of physical objects like rocks, that would probably not be the image for God that they would choose, but in some senses it would speak to them as well.

Some images, however, communicate effectively only in the context of one community's vision of the world. God plaiting Eve's hair and serving as Adam's best man provide examples of this. The Eastern religions do not speak of Adam and Eve. For

Christianity, marriage is not the same ideal as that portrayed by this Jewish image. For Islam (except, perhaps, for Sufi Islam), God is too unequivocally transcendent to be involved in this way in the wedding of any couple, even the original one.

Therefore we must say: to determine whether a given image by which God is described is true, one must decide whether ultimate reality is as the image describes it to be in the *communal* perspective through which it is seen. This communicates that judgments of the truth of images are functions of *both* the experiences all human beings have and share *and* the communal, metaphysical glasses through which we see and understand our experience.

There is yet one other important component in the truth of images. It is indicated, in part, by the fact that religious people in the West do not generally speak of "ultimate reality," but rather of "God." There are theoretical reasons for doing this. Religious Jews, for example, name ultimate reality "God" to say, in part, that ultimate reality, as they perceive it and interact with it, is personal. In recognition of this personal quality, they have traditionally called it "He," and they conceive of God as having an intellect, conscience, will, and emotions. God's personhood enables Him to ordain the commandments recorded in the Torah and to act in history. Religious Jews also assert that God is transcendent. Philosophically, they mean that God's being and activity are not limited to the world we know. They do not usually describe God as "Ultimate Reality," however, because they also want to convey that this transcendent God is also immanent, that He interacts with us—something that nothing as cold and unfeeling as "ultimate reality" could do.

The distinction between "ultimate reality" and the term "God" as used in religion, however, is greater than these philosophical points describe. In the practice of religion, "God" signifies that the speaker is not just contemplating ultimate reality, but *relating* to it personally, usually in the context of a *convictional community.*[45] What makes a perspective religious is, as the etymology of the term indicates, the fact that it binds (Latin, *ligare*) the perceiver to God. In theology, one emphasizes the intellectual component of this link, sometimes, unfortunately, to the exclusion of other forms of relationship; but the ongoing practice of religion does not stress any component of our being over any other. On the contrary, one is to love God "with all one's heart, all one's soul, and all one's might."

Thus, to continue our example, religious people encounter God's transcendence most not in the context of theology but rather in worship, where it denotes God's continuing adverse judgment of people's false centers of loyalty, their idolatry. In this setting, God's transcendence is referred to as His holiness, and, as such, it takes on implications for action. The proper responses to God's holiness are not a revised intellectual understanding of God, but humility and repentance, for they are the means by which one regains a proper center of life.[46]

The truth of a religious image, then, will depend not only on its ability to reflect an aspect of our experience, but also on its coherence with a communal framework of belief *and action* to which the particular experience is linked and through which it is understood. As I have explained in previous chapters, experiences and actions are revelatory of God if, and only if, a given community perceives and interprets them to be so.[47] This means that the truth of religious images will depend not only upon their correspondence to reality as all human beings experience it, but also upon the compatibility of such images with the worldview of a particular religious community and with the actions through which it gives expression to its philosophy. Issues of truth in religion are thus ineluctably and indissolubly connected with issues of authority.

The Authority of Images

How does an image become authoritative for a community—
say, the Jewish one? Some of the factors that bestow authority
on an image are the same ones that make laws binding. Although
the Bible acts as an original source for Jewish images and laws, it
is not the final authority. What ultimately matters is *how the
community has interpreted and applied the Bible in their lives.* To
determine that, one must pay attention to all of the following:
what the community has, over time, selectively chosen to ignore
and, in contrast, to emphasize in its educational and liturgical
life; how passages are narrowed or extended in the community's
interpretations of them in the face of new circumstances or new
sensitivities; what new images or practices have been appended
by the legal and literary leaders of the people; and the extent to
which all of this affects the actual thinking and practice of the
masses and, conversely, the extent to which the conceptions and
customs of the masses affect the decisions and creativity of the
leaders. While this process may be strange to fundamentalist
Protestants, it should be familiar to Jews, for it is nothing but the
ongoing work of Midrash.

The authority of images, then, like the authority of law, rests
upon an *interaction* between the constitutive text (in the case of
Judaism, the Bible) and the community that lives by it. On the
one hand, the text gives all subsequent discussion a focus and a
coherence. Interpretations may vary over a wide range, but they
can still be Jewish if they are based on the Bible.

> Lest a person say, "Since some scholars declare a thing impure and others
> declare it pure, some pronounce a thing forbidden and others pronounce it
> permitted, some disqualify the ritual fitness of an object while others
> uphold it, how can I study Torah under such circumstances?" Scripture
> states, "They are given from one shepherd" (Ecclesiastes 12:11): One God

has given them, one leader [Moses] has uttered them at the command of the Lord of all creation, blessed be He, as it says, "And God spoke *all* these words" (Exodus 20:1). . . . Although one scholar offers his view and another offers his, the words of both are all derived from what Moses, the shepherd, received from the One Lord of the Universe.[48]

Conversely, the Bible became the authoritative ground for all subsequent developments of the tradition because, in part, the community made it so. It was the Rabbis, after all, who defined what would constitute the canon for the Jewish people, and that was based, at least in part, on what texts had become accepted as such by the People Israel. This interaction between the text and its community also explains how the Bible has a different list of contents and a different mode of application in each of the three Western religions: in each case, it was the religious leaders of the differing communities who determined the identity and usage of the constitutive text.

An image or a law must also, however, gain *ongoing* social confirmation to remain authoritative for the community. Discerning whether or not it has done so may not be easy to determine, especially in a community lacking a centralized body to make decisions, but it is not impossible. In any community— even highly centralized ones like that of Roman Catholics—it depends ultimately upon the acceptance of the community of the law or image as a factor in their thought and in their lives. Old and new images are subjected to continuing evaluation of their rationality, their truth, their theological coherence and adequacy, their ethical probity and effectiveness, and their practicality. This process may last for a long, indeterminate period of time, but it may also be rapid and final. Imagining Jesus as the Messiah is a clear example of an image that was proposed and quickly rejected in the Jewish community, and discussion in the 1960s of God as dead was also either ignored or roundly rejected in Jewish discussions because of its heavy Christian connotations.[49] On the other hand, the rabbinic image of God as one who studies and the kabbalistic development of the picture of God as the *Shekhinah* are examples of how a new image can become implanted in the consciousness of a community.

Ultimately, though, the communal links of an image are not sufficient to afford it religious authority. That depends upon its ability to evoke experiences of God. A religious image may have impeccable biblical and/or rabbinic pedigree, but it will not influence thought and behavior for long if it fails to link people with God. An image used in religious contexts gains its power from its ability to speak to the devotional needs of the religious individual and community—that is, to perform all the tasks described above in the third section of this chapter. It focuses attention on the mystery of the divine presence. "Awe, wonder, adoration, and the elevation of the human spirit are its milieu, perhaps better confessed in song than trivialized by rote repetition as prose or made the subject of the proddings of an inquisitive reason."[50]

A SAMPLE CASE: FEMININE IMAGES FOR GOD

One contemporary proposal for a new image of God will illustrate the functions, meaning, truth, and authority of images. More than a decade ago Rita M. Gross suggested speaking of God as She in addition to speaking of God as He.

> Let me say immediately that I am quite aware that God is not really either female or male or anything in between. I only wish the people who argue to retain solely male imagery were as aware that God is not really male as I am that God is not really female. I am talking about the only thing we can talk about—*images* of God, not God. And I am talking about female *images* of God. . . . For a poverty of religious imagination, characteristic of the contemporary milieu, makes many people idolaters today. They simply block out of their consciousness the metaphorical nature of religious

language and become addicted to the linguistic conventions, the signs and tools of religious discourse.[51]

Gross specifically, and, I think, correctly rejected speaking of God in gender-neutral forms ("It") because that would no longer be Judaism. As she points out, while theology can be stripped of anthropomorphism, theism and prayer cannot be:

> So much of the Jewish religious enterprise involves talking, not about God, but *to* God. In Jewish God language, forms of address, language in the second person, are more important than language in the third person. That is where an impersonal, abstract God language breaks down in the Jewish context.[52]

Her proposal, then, is to adopt female forms of address in addition to male forms so as to preserve the personal character of the Jewish God and the ability for human beings personally to relate to Her.

There are several reasons why this proposal is sound. A theme running through this chapter and through much of contemporary literary theory is the significant role of the person reading a text in determining its meaning for that person. Therefore, in addition to the religious necessity to avoid idolatry, there is another important reason for using not only masculine, but also feminine imagery for God: it expresses our recognition of the need to take the reader seriously, for, after all, half of the people reading religious texts and using religious language are women.

Gross's proposal also recognizes and speaks to the context of worship in which images of God chiefly play a role. All of the functions of images in worship that were described earlier in this chapter would still apply to a female image of God, but the perception of their divine object would be different, and that would make the quality and tone of such experiences different

too. For example, the communal power of images, when focused on male models, reenforces a sense that the community
should be headed by males, in imitation of God. However, if
God is also depicted as female, then God's image no longer
foreordains a male-centered social organization. One might still
decide for other reasons to differentiate roles by gender,[53] but
the image by which God is worshiped would not predetermine
that, even subconsciously. In a similar way, all of the other
functions of prayer would take on new colorations, sometimes
with significant social impact.

If God were depicted as a woman, new sources of religious
meaning might well be opened for Jewish men as well as for
Jewish women.[54] Women as a group are undoubtedly equal to
men in most areas of life, better in some, and worse in others, but
they are different from men. In recent decades, both men and
women have been softening the distinctions in social roles so
that men are taking a more active part in caring for their children, no longer seeing this as unmanly, and both men and
women have taken jobs previously restricted to the other sex.
Nevertheless, whether for biological or sociological reasons, the
image evoked in the minds of people of both genders when
thinking about men still bears different connotations from that
of women, with men considered more aggressive and rule-
bound and women thought of as more nurturing and more
concerned with individual cases.[55] This association may or may
not be desirable, and it may or may not be subject to change, but
it remains predominant. As a result, attributing "feminine"
characteristics to God amplifies the ways in which we understand and relate to the Eternal, thereby adding new levels of
meaning to our interaction with God.

If God were more commonly, clearly, and directly depicted as
our Nurturer and Comforter, just as God is our Warrior and
Judge, our relationships with God would become broader and

deeper. After all, we react to each of our parents differently. In large measure this is because they are simply different people with different personalities and talents, but part of our reaction, and indeed part of what makes them different, stems from the fact that one is a male and the other is a female. If we were to think of God as female as often as we think of God as male, then we would enhance the variety of expectations and relationships we have with the Eternal. This would enrich our experience with God.

Not only meaning, but truth is better served if one adopts Gross's proposal. Our experience with God manifests both male and female characteristics. Any intellectually adequate image of God, therefore, would have to include both. While male and female human beings share many attributes, they differ on others. Therefore the image of God as one or the other of the genders cannot possibly include all aspects of our experience. At the same time, our experience includes a personal element; we know of conscience, intellect, emotions, and will. Considerations of truth would, then, like concern for a rich experience with God, argue for Gross's proposal of picturing God as personal but alternatively male and female. Each image would tell part of the truth of the totality of our experience with God and would be appreciated as such as long as we keep in mind that no image can be wholly adequate.

Even history is on Gross's side. The attribution of "feminine" qualities to God is not new. Gross's program, in fact, is more a matter of recapturing and reemphasizing traditional meanings than it is an invention of new ones.

Male language for God certainly predominates in the Bible. We hear a great deal of God as King and Warrior. Reign and battle were usually the province of men in the ancient world and continue to be so now, and hence both the writers of these passages and we moderns who read them immediately link these descriptions with males. The pronouns and verbs connected with God in the Bible are masculine. Since Hebrew grammar uses the masculine for gender-neutral sets as well as for specifically male groups, the latter feature may simply be a grammatical convention, but it adds to our imagination of God as male. There are also a few mentions of God as Father where the context indicates that specifically the male parent is intended.

Modern writers, however, have demonstrated that this is only part of the picture. Some passages of the Bible link God with characteristics stereotypically attributed to women. God is, for example, our Healer and Comforter, and God dandles a beloved child. God has mercy *(rahamim)*, a word in Hebrew with at least possible connections to *rehem*, womb. Some verses depict God as Mother.[56] Probably the most definitive biblical proof that God must be conceived in both male and female terms is the opening chapter of Genesis, in which "God created man in His image, in the image of God He created him; male and female He created them" (Genesis 1:27). This declares explicitly that the image of God—the way we picture the Divine—must include both male and female elements.[57]

Why, then, are feminine images of God not enthusiastically sought and adopted by the Jewish community? The reasons underscore the points made in the last several sections. The authority of images is partly a matter of their communal domain and partly a matter of their truth, and feminist images for God suffer on both scores.

The convictional community must validate an image, whether new or old, in its beliefs and practice. While Jewish belief has, on the one hand, claimed that no image can capture all there is to know about God, it has, on the other, used predominantly male images in its theology. Jewish patterns of action have largely followed suit, giving males a more prominent role than females in anything communal. This may be regrettable, but it has become common practice, and it is a habit hard to break—assuming that a person wants to break it in the first place. Whole new forms of liturgy and practice must be developed, and that means changing patterns of action and social organization. People do not like change; it removes the old and familiar.

These communal considerations are not just justifications for being reactionary; one must recognize their significance if one is truthful to the communal context in which images gain their meaning and import. A community, after all, gains much of its value in being stable and reassuring, in establishing norms and patterns of action which everybody knows and likes. Changing this—even for the best of reasons, and even for reasons that emerge from the community's own ideology—carries the price of upsetting the community's stability and familiarity. That would undermine the human, if not the divine, base for the image's authority in the first place.

There is another factor in the contemporary Jewish community's reticence to proceed quickly in this arena, and that is the element of truth. A number of suggestions that feminists have made raise serious theological objections. For example, Marcia Falk previously advocated, as Rita Gross did earlier, the use of feminine images for God, as well as masculine images, in order to counteract the potential for idolatry inherent in using only male imagery—the position that I myself have been proposing. In a recent article, however, Falk goes further. She suggests that the very notion of God's transcendence violates God's unity and is therefore idolatrous. In response to this claim, Lawrence A. Hoffman points out, among other things, that Falk's pantheism undermines the Jewish concern for our having a *relationship* with God.

Similarly, Judith Plaskow struggles mightily to define a sense of Otherness in God while denying God's transcendence. God is to be conceived as our partner and lover, but not as our ruler or as any other image that denotes hierarchical ordering. This, however, simply ignores the truth about our experiences with God. God *is* our covenanted friend, lover, and partner in creation, but God *is also* more powerful than we, more knowing than we, and more moral than we. The biblical images of parenthood and sovereignty are not simply vestiges of ancient social mores; they are part of what it means to come into contact with God. To pretend otherwise is to ignore, ostrichlike, the facts of our experience, for we are *not* on a par with God. God is certainly "more," as Plaskow says, but God is so much "more" that this quantitative difference amounts to a qualitative one. Judaism may not emphasize the awesome transcendence of God as much as colonial Puritans did, but it definitely is part of what it means to experience God in a Jewish way, as the High Holy liturgy and music remind us most poignantly.

This refusal to come to terms with God's transcendence is also at the root of another problem in feminist theology. Plaskow admits that feminists "have not yet fully addressed the theological question of evil as a feminist issue." She maintains, however, that feminists experience evil daily in the form of patriarchy.

In a world of nuclear bombs, homelessness, and poverty, a world in which, according to the World Health Organization, eight thousand children die daily from diseases that could have been prevented by immunization and another eleven thousand die each day for lack of five dollars worth of food, patriarchy is hardly the example of evil I would choose. Indeed, if that is the focus of feminists' concern, it is no accident that they have not formulated an adequate response to evil.

The problem, though, is not only narrowness in social perspective: it is also a narrowness of theological vision. Plaskow's God is simply much too friendly to capture the depth and range of the evil we experience. We surely wish it were otherwise, but God is *not* manifest only in warm, loving relationships—even if they challenge us to be our best, as a good friend or lover would.

God is also manifest in His terrible might, as the Torah and Prophets proclaim. God does judge us, whether we like that hierarchy or not. Worse, sometimes God's judgment is inscrutable and downright mean. The Jewish tradition did not hide from these features of our experience of God. It spoke of God being powerful, demanding, judgmental, and mysterious. It had the wisdom to know that we cannot fit all of our experiences into neat categories and that some of our experiences with God are not to our liking, but that is all the more reason to use images which capture all these facets of our lives. "The seal of the Holy One is truth," the Rabbis proclaimed, and we must tell the truth most especially in our images of the Eternal.[58]

Feminist criticism of the use of exclusively male imagery is astute and correct. We gain more meaning and truth by employing both male and female images, and that is closer to what the tradition, from biblical times on, wanted us to do anyway. The changes that that requires in Jewish thought and practice, however, should come with as little cost as possible to Jewish continuity and identity, and we should certainly not discard the insights and sensitivities of the old images as we adopt more of the new. We should also judge new, feminine images just as we judge the old, masculine ones—that is, on the basis of how accurately the image communicates the experience of God to us within the context of our communal perceptions and practices. The problems and promise of the feminist program for changing Jewish depictions of the Divine illustrate graphically how complex the authority of an image can be—and how much we have invested in our images.

GOOD AND BAD IMAGES

We have probed the workings of images, their meaning, truth, and authority. Ultimately, we have no recourse but to think of

God in images. The only real question is how we choose the images we use. In that process we would reject images that are ineffective because they do not touch us; those which distort or falsify our experience; and those which undermine the community's cohesiveness. On the other hand, we must seek images that have the immediacy of meaning that we seek in images as against creeds and symbols; those that evoke the emotions and actions that powerful images should; those that are true to our experience, even if they cannot be totally so; and those that enjoy the community's validation in thought and action. Above all, we must make sure that our images are not idolatrous, that they do not pretend that the part is the whole, for that would be to deny the truth and to give up our special mandate to be a people true to God.

> For your own sake, therefore, be most careful—since you saw no shape when the Lord your God spoke to you at Horeb out of the fire—not to act wickedly and make for yourselves a sculptured image in any likeness whatever, having the form of a man or a woman, the form of any beast on earth, the form of any winged bird that flies in the sky, the form of anything that creeps on the ground, the form of any fish that is in the waters below the earth. And when you look up to the sky and behold the sun and the moon and the stars, the whole heavenly host, you must not be lured into bowing down to them or serving them. These the Lord your God allotted to the other peoples everywhere under heaven; but you the Lord took and brought out of Egypt, that iron blast furnace, to be His very own people (Deuteronomy 4:15–20).

EPILOGUE

This book has been a concerted attempt to respond to a fundamental question, one that vexed me first at age fifteen at Camp Ramah and that has accompanied me ever since. That question is by no means mine alone; it is the issue that has occupied religious philosophers from time immemorial. Put starkly, it is this: how can I make intellectual sense of a religion that I first find meaningful on other grounds?

This is not exclusively an intellectual question—although it would be significant enough if it were. It is a deeply religious matter as well. We are commanded to "love the Lord your God with all your heart, with all your soul, and with all your might." This verse from Deuteronomy, used in the first paragraph of the *Shema* prayer, has been a veritable leitmotif throughout this entire book. According to the Rabbis, "with all your heart" means with both your impulses, the one for bad as well as the one for good; "with all your soul" means even though God takes your soul (life); and "with all your might" signifies with all your money—or, alternatively, with whatever treatment God metes out to you.[1] This rabbinic interpretation apprises us of some deeply rooted convictions of Judaism, and we have explored some of them in the chapters above.

The plain meaning of the verse, however, is closer to our issue. Since the heart in the ancient world was the seat of thought, "with all your heart" means with your intellect; "with all your soul" means with your affective capacity, your emotions; and "with all your might" means with your physical being, with all the strength of your body.[2] Thus, the Torah demands that our love of God not be based on the shaky foundations of an unexamined, blind faith or a faith that pretends not to see the problems that religious commitment entails. We must rather love and trust God enough to expose our faith to the most thoroughgoing intellectual analysis possible. Only then, after confronting all the problems, solving some, continuing to probe others, and deciding simply to live with yet others, can our faith attain the strength and quality that God desires.

Both the plain meaning of the verse and the rabbinic interpretation of it also point us in the direction we have taken in this book to find and love God. We have seen that reason, when properly used, can be a vehicle for discovering God, but that it is by no means the only one. Our affective side, "our soul," especially as expressed in prayer, can also be a road to God, and so can our physical being when it is used to respond to God's commandments. We have explored just how each of these faculties of ours can be an intellectually and experientially reliable route to God. We have also seen that God can be sensed through continuing divine acts in our lives, through what the traditional prayer book calls "Your miracles which are with us each day"— although only if we learn to acknowledge, bless, and thank God for the bad as well as the good. Deuteronomy 6:5 thus not only set the task for this book, but also sketched much of its strategy for accomplishing its divine goal.

I make no pretensions that the foundations for religious faith that I have delineated here will satisfy everyone, certainly not each day of one's life. Truth to tell, I am not sure myself sometimes whether one or another of the points I have defended above is convincing. Faith is like that: if it is alive and stimulating, it forever raises new questions as it resolves old ones. This, in part, is what it means to be alive, to grow older, to experience totally new things and old things in new ways. Unless we sink into some kind of stupor, we are bound to probe further today what seemed fine yesterday, while we simultaneously wonder what the fuss was all about in last week's problem.

This does not mean, though, that we cannot come to some kind of knowledge, for some things begin to ring true to us for sound reasons over and over again. It is those facets of my faith that I have attempted to capture in the pages above in the hope that they may help others find their own faith as well.

I leave you with my favorite image in the Bible. It is not the simple meaning of the text; it is but an image. Images, though, as we have seen, convey truths at least as much as descriptive words do. The image I like is that of Jacob wrestling with the angel (Genesis 32:15–33). Jews are sometimes called "the Children of Jacob," but the more common name is "Children of Israel." Jacob, though, does not become Israel until he wrestles with God. We, then, deserve our name, "Children of Israel," only when we too wrestle with God. May your own wrestling be vigorous, fully integrating all your faculties, so that it can be a source of meaning to you all your life while it simultaneously expresses your authentic love of God.

ENDNOTES

CHAPTER 1

1. Samuel David Luzzatto, Franz Rosenzweig, and Abraham Isaac Kook, among others, saw in the *Kuzari* the most faithful description of the particular qualities of Judaism; cf. Eliezer Schweid, "Judah Halevi," *Encyclopaedia Judaica* 10:365.

Julius Guttmann is right, however, in warning against interpreting Halevi as arguing for a kind of religious truth independent of reason. Halevi agrees with the rationalists that if it were possible for human beings to attain knowledge of metaphysical matters through reason, we would find that metaphysical truths, like all others, are rational. He even admits that the reduction of the world to a divine principle is required by reason as well as by revelation, and he thinks that philosophy, with its proof of the unity of the divine cause of the world, is superior to all other explanations of the world. He differs from the rationalists only—but significantly—in his assertion that human beings are not capable of learning metaphysical realities through reason. He points to the rampant disagreements among metaphysicians, in contrast to the sublime agreement among logicians and mathematicians, as proof that reason cannot grasp metaphysical truths. Consequently, for Halevi, revelation and history are the only reliable sources through which human beings can learn about God. Cf. Julius Guttmann, *Philosophies of Judaism: The History of Jewish Philosophy from Biblical Times to Franz Rosenzweig*, David W. Silverman, trans. (New York: Holt, Rinehart and Winston, 1964), pp. 122–123, and the references to Halevi's writings there.

Luzzatto, Rosenzweig, and Kook were probably looking for support for their own antirationalist positions in interpreting Halevi as an extreme antirationalist and in praising him as they did. In approvingly citing their description of Halevi as "the most Jewish of Jewish philosophers," however, I am only referring to his emphasis on revelation and history, rather than reason, as the sources of our knowledge of God. In this he imitated the Bible and the Talmud, which depend almost entirely on revelation and its interpretation for their statements about God.

2. See D. M. Dunlap, *History of the Jewish Khazars* (Princeton, NJ: Princeton University Press, 1954, 1967) and the extensive bibliography there. For a brief account, see "Khazars," *Encyclopaedia Judaica* 10:944–953.

3. Judah Halevi, *The Kuzari*, Isaak Heinemann, trans., in *Three Jewish Philosophers* (Philadelphia: Jewish Publication Society, 1960), Book I, pars. 11–15, pp. 33–34, and Book IV, pars. 3, 13, 15–17, pp. 113–114, 116–119. Blaise Pascal wore as a kind of amulet his written memorial of his "second conversion" on November 23, 1654, in which he experienced "the God of Abraham, God of Isaac, God of Jacob, not of philosophers and scientists." See "Biographical Note," in Blaise Pascal, *Pensées* (Chicago: Encyclopaedia Britannica, 1952 [#33 of the *Great Books of the Western World* series]), pp. v–vi. For Pascal, unlike Halevi, the God of Abraham, Isaac, and Jacob was the Christian, and specifically *not* the Jewish God!

> The God of the Christians is not a God who is simply the author of mathematical truths, or of the order of the elements; that is the view of heathens and Epicureans. He is not merely a God who exercises His providence over the life and fortunes of men, to bestow on those who worship Him a long and happy life. That was the portion of the Jews. But the God of Abraham, the God of Isaac, the God of Jacob, the God of Christians, is a God of love and comfort, a God who fills the soul and heart of those whom He possesses, a God who makes them conscious of their inward wretchedness, and His infinite mercy, who unites Himself to their inmost soul, who fills it with humility and joy, with confidence and love, who renders them incapable of any other end than Himself. [Ibid. #556 (p. 271); cf. #430, 601–610, 617–620.]

4. The various theories of revelation are discussed in Chapter 4. There are those who believe in verbal revelation and yet also believe in the Doc-

umentary Hypothesis. These include David Novak and possibly Abraham
Joshua Heschel. See my *Conservative Judaism: Our Ancestors to Our Descendants*
(New York: United Synagogue of America, 1977), pp. 110–155, for a summary of the major positions on revelation. In that book, I interpret Heschel as
believing in verbal revelation. As I demonstrate there, many of his words do
seem to indicate that position. The truth, though, is that he is ambiguous on
this score. Moreover, Lawrence Perlman has since made a yeoman's effort in
explicating Heschel's approach as phenomenological. Since Heschel described
himself that way, Perlman is probably right. See Lawrence Perlman, *Abraham
Heschel's Idea of Revelation* (Atlanta: Scholars Press, 1989), esp. pp. 109–113.
The prophet's words, presumably including the words of the prophet Moses,
are not descriptive, but indicative, that is, they point to a reality that they
cannot adequately describe. Thus Heschel says that the prophet's words "are
not portraits, but *clues,* serving us as guides, suggesting a line of thinking. This
indeed is our situation in regard to a statement such as 'God spoke.' It refers
to an idea that is not at home in the mind, and the only way to understand its
meaning is by *responding* to it. We must adapt our minds to a meaning unheard
of before. The word is but a clue; the real burden of understanding is upon the
mind and soul of the reader" (Heschel, *God in Search of Man* [New York:
Harper and Row, 1955], p. 183). The words of the Torah, then, would emanate out of the prophet, not out of God directly: "Out of the experience of
the prophets came the words, words that try to interpret what they perceived"
(Ibid., p. 265). Heschel, then, would fit into category Conservative III rather
than Conservative I, as described in my book cited above.

5. Half of American Jews polled across the nation by the *Los Angeles
Times* listed a commitment to social equality as the quality most important to
their sense of Jewish identity, whereas only 17 percent cited religious obser-
vance and another 17 percent cited support for Israel. Cf. Robert Scheer,
"Jews in U.S. Committed to Equality," *Los Angeles Times,* April 13, 1988,
Section I, pp. 1, 14–15.

6. The statistics in this paragraph come from the *Los Angeles Times* article,
ibid. On Jews in education, cf. also Steven M. Cohen, *American Modernity and
Jewish Identity* (New York: Tavistock Publications, 1983), Ch. 4; on Jewish
marital patterns, cf. pp. 120–122 of that volume.

7. On the *pro bono* work of Jewish lawyers: Donna Arzt, "The People's
Lawyers," *Judaism* 35:1 (Winter 1986), pp. 47–62; Jerold S. Auerbach and
Donna Arzt, "Profits or Prophets: An Exchange," *Judaism* 36:3 (Summer
1987), pp. 360–367. On Jews and philanthropy: Edward S. Shapiro, "Jews
With Money," *Judaism* 36:1 (Winter 1987), pp. 7–16, esp. pp. 12–13; Gerald

Krefatz, *Jews and Money: The Myths and the Reality* (New Haven: Ticknor and Fields, 1982), Ch. 11.

8. Robert Gordis, *A Faith for Moderns* (New York: Bloch Publishing Company, 1960), Ch. 1; cf. also Ch. 13.

9. James Wm. McClendon, Jr., *Biography as Theology* (New York: Abingdon Press, 1974).

10. I have written at some length about the multiple rationales in the tradition for obeying Jewish law and their relationship to God in my book, *Mitzvah Means Commandment* (New York: United Synagogue of America, 1989).

11. The *Shema* prayer, which Jews recite morning and evening each day, consists of three paragraphs from the Torah—specifically, Deuteronomy 6:4–9, Deuteronomy 11:13–21, and Numbers 15:37–41, in that order. The verse cited here is from the first paragraph, Deuteronomy 6:5.

12. Cf. Van A. Harvey, *The Historian and the Believer* (New York: Macmillan, 1966), pp. 205–230; James Wm. McClendon, Jr., and James M. Smith, *Understanding Religious Convictions* (Notre Dame: University of Notre Dame Press, 1975), pp. 6–7.

13. Cf. Walter Kaufmann, *Critique of Religion and Philosophy* (Garden City, NY: Doubleday, 1958, 1961), pp. 13–16, where he points out how the lack of proper epistemological humility produces philosophers without a sense of humor.

14. Milton Steinberg has taken a similar approach. Cf. his *A Believing Jew* (New York: Harcourt, Brace, 1951), pp. 13–31; and his *Anatomy of Faith*, Arthur A. Cohen, ed. (New York: Harcourt, Brace, 1960), pp. 73–79.

15. I first articulated this in "Two Ways to Approach God," *Conservative Judaism* 30:2 (Winter 1976), pp. 58–67; reprinted in Seymour Siegel and Elliot Gertel, eds., *God in the Teachings of Conservative Judaism* (New York: Rabbinical Assembly, 1985), pp. 30–41.

16. Will Herberg, *Judaism and Modern Man* (Philadelphia: Jewish Publication Society of America, 1951, 1959), Ch. 7, pp. 57–68, has been especially important for me in recognizing the significance and soundness of the tradition's insistence on the personal character of God.

17. Cf. n. 3 above, especially the sections in Book IV.

CHAPTER 2

1. Alfred J. Ayer, *Language, Truth, and Logic* (London: Dover Publications, 1936, 1946), esp. pp. 114–120; reprinted in Ronald E. Santoni, ed., *Religious*

Language and the Problem of Religious Knowledge (Bloomington, IN: Indiana University Press, 1968) [hereinafter "Santoni"], Ch. 6.

2. Karl Popper is probably the first to articulate this position. See his *Logic of Scientific Discovery* (New York: Basic Books, 1959), p. 279 and throughout.

3. A good exposition of this view, in direct response to logical positivism, is Thomas McPherson's article, "Positivism and Religion," *Philosophy and Phenomenological Research* 14:319–330 (1953–1954); reprinted in Santoni (at n. 1), Ch. 2.

4. R. B. Braithwaite, *An Empiricist's View of the Nature of Religious Belief* (Cambridge, England: Cambridge University Press, 1955); sections of that book have often been reprinted, including Santoni (at n. 1), Ch. 20, and Basil Mitchell, ed., *The Philosophy of Religion* (Oxford: Oxford University Press, 1971) [hereinafter "Mitchell"], Ch. IV. Paul Van Buren, *The Secular Meaning of the Gospel* (New York: Macmillan, 1963).

5. In 1950, C. G. Hempel published a thorough, careful survey of the problems associated with the verifiability criterion, ending with the hope that an adequate version would be found; cf. Carl G. Hempel, "The Empiricist Criterion of Meaning," *Revue Internationale de Philosophie*, Vol. 4 (1950); reprinted in A. J. Ayer, ed., *Logical Positivism* (Glencoe, IL: Free Press, 1959), pp. 108–129. Some fifteen years later he indicated that that was still only a hope; cf. C. G. Hempel, *Aspects of Scientific Explanation* (New York: Free Press, 1965), pp. 120 f. Ayer himself, in the introduction to the second edition of *Language, Truth, and Logic* (1946), wrote: "Although I still defend the use of the criterion of verifiability as a methodological principle, I realize that for the effective elimination of metaphysics it needs to be supported by detailed analyses of particular metaphysical arguments" (p. 16). What a plunge from the cocky assurance of the first, 1936 edition!

6. Cf., for example, Ian Ramsey, *Religious Language: An Empirical Placing of Theological Phrases* (London: SCM Press, 1957); D. Z. Phillips, "Religious Beliefs and Language-Games," *Ratio* 12:26–46 (1970); reprinted in Mitchell (at n. 4), Ch. VII.

7. John Wisdom, "Gods," *Proceedings of the Aristotelian Society*, 1944–1945; reprinted many times, including Santoni (at n. 1), Ch. 18, pp. 295–314.

8. Antony Flew in the *University Discussion*, 1950–1951; reprinted in Antony Flew and Alasdair MacIntyre, *New Essays in Philosophical Theology* (New York: Macmillan, 1955), Ch. VI, p. 96, and in Santoni (at note 1), Ch. 19, pp. 315–316. Flew changes the parable to make his point. He tells it this way:

Once upon a time two explorers came upon a clearing in the jungle. In the clearing were growing many flowers and many weeds. One explorer says,

"Some gardener must tend this plot." The other disagrees. "There is no gardener." So they pitch their tents and set a watch. No gardener is ever seen. "But perhaps he is an invisible gardener." So they set up a barbed wire fence. They electrify it. They patrol with bloodhounds. (For they remember how H. G. Wells' *The Invisible Man* could be both smelt and touched though he could not be seen.) But no shrieks ever suggest that some intruder has received a shock. No movement of the wire ever betrays an invisible climber. The bloodhounds never give cry. Yet still the Believer is not convinced. "But there is a gardener, invisible, intangible, insensible to electric shocks, a gardener who has no scent and makes no sound, a gardener who comes secretly to look after the garden which he loves." At last the Skeptic despairs. "But what remains of your original assertion? Just how does what you call an invisible, intangible, eternally elusive gardener differ from an imaginary gardener or even from no gardener at all?"

9. R. M. Hare in the *University Discussion,* 1950–1951; reprinted in Flew and MacIntyre (at n. 8), pp. 101–102, and in Santoni (at n. 1), p. 320.

10. James Kellenberger, *Religious Discovery, Faith, and Knowledge* (Englewood Cliffs, NJ: Prentice-Hall, 1972), p. 17.

11. Thomas Kuhn, Michael Polanyi, and, most recently, Ian Barbour have all carefully and thoroughly demonstrated the use of nonhypothetical reasoning in science. Cf. Thomas Kuhn, *The Structure of Scientific Revolutions* (Chicago: University of Chicago Press, 1962; second edition, 1970) and *The Essential Tension* (Chicago: University of Chicago Press, 1977), Chs. 12 ("Second Thoughts on Paradigms") and 13 ("Objectivity, Value Judgment and Theory Choice"). Michael Polanyi, *Knowing and Being* (London: Routeledge and Kegan Paul, 1969), Chs. 8–12. Michael Polanyi and Harry Prosch, *Meaning* (Chicago: University of Chicago Press, 1975). Ian Barbour, *Religion in an Age of Science* (San Francisco: Harper and Row, 1990), Chs. 2 and 3, pp. 31–92.

12. The quotation is from John Wisdom, "Gods" (at n. 7), in Santoni, p. 303. Wisdom anticipated much of what others have since developed as the paradigmatic structure of science, law, and indeed much of our knowledge. On the element of this process that is the testing of our unconscious predilections, see, in Santoni, pp. 307–308.

13. William James, *The Will to Believe,* first published in 1896 and reprinted many times, e.g., in *Readings in the Philosophy of Religion: An Analytic Approach,* Baruch A. Brody, ed. (Englewood Cliffs, NJ: Prentice-Hall, 1974), pp. 247–264; John Hick, *Classical and Contemporary Readings in the Philosophy of Religion* (Englewood Cliffs, NJ: Prentice-Hall, 1964, 1970), pp. 214–231.

14. This specific issue was addressed before James wrote *The Will to Believe* in a famous essay by W. K. Clifford, "The Ethics of Belief," *Contemporary Review,* January 1877; *Lectures and Essays,* 1879; reprinted, in part, in Brody, ibid., pp. 241–247, and, in full, in *An Anthology of Atheism and Rationalism,* Gordon Stein, ed. (Buffalo, NY: Prometheus Books, 1980), pp. 276–292.

15. John Hick, ed., *The Existence of God* (New York: Macmillan, 1964), pp. 9–12. I raised this point in response to Richard Rubenstein in *Conservative Judaism* 28:4 (Summer 1974), pp. 33–36.

16. McClendon and Smith, *Understanding Religious Convictions* (at n. 12 in Chapter 1), p. 7.

17. Ibid., pp. 167–168. For further, clear and illuminating discussions of the role of stories (narrative) in articulating our philosophy of life, our values, and our faith, cf. McClendon, *Biography as Theology* at n. 9 in Chapter 1, and two books by Michael Goldberg, namely, *Theology and Narrative: A Critical Introduction* (Nashville: Abingdon, 1981), and *Jews and Christians: Getting Our Stories Straight* (Nashville: Abingdon, 1985).

18. Judah Halevi, *The Kuzari,* Hartwig Hirschfeld, trans. (New York, 1964), esp. Part Four, pars. 15–17. Blaise Pascal, *Pensées* #556 *et al.* Cf. Chapter 1 above, n. 3.

19. Halevi, *Kuzari,* Book I, pars. 11–15; Book IV, pars. 3, 13. Franz Rosenzweig, *The Star of Redemption* (New York: Holt, Rinehart and Winston, 1970), Part I, pp. 3–22; Part II, pp. 104–106; "The New Thinking," in *Franz Rosenzweig: His Life and Thought,* Nahum N. Glatzer, ed. (New York: Schocken, 1953, 1961), pp. 179–213. Martin Buber, *I and Thou* (New York: Charles Scribner's Sons, 1958), pp. 81–83; *Eclipse of God* (New York: Harper and Row, 1952), pp. 42–46.

20. It may be the case, however, that Christians would be more sanguine about using philosophy as one way to know God since, from the Fourth Gospel on, philosophy has played a greater role in Christianity than it has in Judaism. Even so, it would not be the primary way.

21. E.g., Richard John Neuhaus, "To See As God Sees," *National Review,* October 28, 1988, p. 24. Cf. also McClendon and Smith (at n. 12 in Chapter 1), and Goldberg (at n. 17) in *Jews and Christians.*

CHAPTER 3

This is the first chapter in which rabbinic sources are cited. In this and all following chapters, M. = Mishnah; T. = Tosefta; J. = Jerusalem (Palestin-

ian) Talmud; B. = Babylonian Talmud; M. T. = Maimonides' *Mishneh Torah*
(= *Hayad Hahazakah*) (1177); and S. A. = Joseph Karo's *Shulhan Arukh* (1565).

1. *Pesikta d'Rav Kahana,* Ch. 15. Although the manuscripts have *se'or,*
"leaven," Prof. Robert Gordis has pointed out that that is probably an error.
"Leaven" is not applicable to Torah, since its metaphoric use refers to
sinfulness. The reading should probably be *ma'or,* "light."

2. Even the Kantian category of "practical reason" is the exercise of our
rational powers in analyzing our practice, not knowledge that arises from our
action.

Educators correctly will point out that school learning is not confined to
formal instruction, that much of what students learn in school comes from
extracurricular activities and from the informal contacts they have with
instructors and with each other. Students, however, generally conceive of
their school learning in terms of what they learn in classes, and it is that
impression to which I am referring here.

3. T. *Sanhedrin* 7:3; cf. B. *Sanhedrin* 36b and M. T. *Laws of Courts
(Sanhedrin)* 2:3.

4. David Hume, *An Enquiry Concerning Human Understanding,* Section X.

5. In many ways this is similar to the Rabbis' assertion that, just as the
Nazarite had to bring a sin offering after a period of abstaining from wine,
those who deny themselves any of the pleasures of life that God has provided
and permitted are outright sinners; cf. Numbers 6:11; B. *Ta'anit* 11a; M. T.
Laws of Ethics (De'ot) 3:1. Saadia, Maimonides, and others in the rationalist
tradition are, of course, especially interested in defending not only the
legitimacy, but the religious necessity of applying reason to religious matters.
Cf. Saadia Gaon, *Book of Doctrines and Beliefs,* Prolegomena, Section 4. Maimonides, *Guide for the Perplexed,* Introduction to Part I; Part I, Chs. 1–2,
31–32; Part III, Chs. 26, 51–54.

6. B. *Yevamot* 109b; M. *Avot* 1:17.

7. B. *Kiddushin* 40b; M. *Pe'ah* 1:1. For an examination of three modern
analyses of this claim—those by Samson Raphael Hirsch, Martin Buber, and
Mordecai M. Kaplan—see my article, "Study Leads to Action," *Religious
Education* 75:2 (March–April 1980), pp. 171–192.

8. Abraham Joshua Heschel, *God in Search of Man* (New York: Harper
and Row, 1955), Ch. 32, and cf. generally Chs. 28–34.

9. B. *Pesahim* 50b; etc.

10. B. *Kiddushin* 31b. Cf. M. T. *Laws of Rebels (Mamrim)* 6:3; S. A. *Yoreh
De'ah* 240:2,4; 228:11.

11. *Tanna d'bei Eliyahu* 26. Cf. M. T. ibid. and S. A. ibid. 240:5 for the law forcing the child to provide food.

12. Philo, *Treatise on the Decalogue,* Loeb Classical Library edition, F. H. Colson, trans., Vol. 7 (1937), pp. 61, 67, 69.

13. *Mekhilta* on Exodus 20:12 *(Yitro,* Section 8); cf. B. *Kiddushin* 30b, where this is in the name of the Rabbis generally.

14. B. *Kiddushin* 31b. Cf. M. T. *Laws of Rebels* 6:3; S. A. *Yoreh De'ah* 240:2,4; 228:11.

15. Both the mother and children, though, are supposed to honor the man of the house. M. *Kiddushin* 1:7; B. *Kiddushin* 29a, 30b, 31a; M. T. *Laws of Rebels* 6:6, 14; S. A. *Yoreh De'ah* 240:14,17. For a general discussion of the tradition's treatment of parent–child relations, cf. Elliot N. Dorff, "Honoring Aged Fathers and Mothers," *The Reconstructionist* 53:2 (October–November 1987), pp. 14–20.

16. B. *Niddah* 31a.

17. J. *Peah* 15d. Honor of God and parents are put on a par in B. *Kiddushin* 30b.

18. Rashi, B. *Kiddushin* 32a, s.v., *podin u-ma'akhilin;* R. Elazar Askari, *Sefer Haredim* (Warsaw, 1879), p. 31; R. Abraham Danzig, *Hayyei Adam* (1810) 67:1. These are all cited in Gerald Blidstein, *Honor Thy Father and Mother* (New York: Ktav, 1975), pp. 56–57.

19. Maimonides, *Responsa,* J. Blau, ed., II, #448, p. 728. Cited in Blidstein, ibid., p. 55.

20. B. *Yevamot* 6a.

21. M. *Haggigah* 1:8.

22. Isaac Arama (c. 1420–1494) in his *Akedat Yitzhak* (55 ed. Bialystok, 1849), pp. 285–289, lists these as the three themes of the day, and Franz Rosenzweig (1886–1929), in his *Star of Redemption* (New York: Holt, Rinehart and Winston, 1970), pp. 308–315, ties them to the evening *(Ma'ariv),* morning *(Shaharit),* and afternoon *(Minhah)* services, respectively. In all three services the blessing and the last paragraph before it are the same, and so Rosenzweig's thesis, which has been adopted here, must be understood to apply to the prose before that. Even then the theory does not work completely because the morning service has several specific references to Creation. There is nothing wrong with that as long as one remembers that Rosenzweig's claim is based on what the primary message of each of the middle sections of the *Amidah* in each service is; the three themes are, after all, not contradictory but complementary.

There is, of course, a fourth service on the Sabbath, that is, *Musaf,* the additional *Amidah* said after the Torah reading. The situation there is somewhat more complicated. The major theme of the middle section is the extra communal sacrifice that was offered in Temple times in honor of the Sabbath, the sacrifice for which the *Amidah* of *Musaf* is a substitution. But the middle section also talks about Creation ("You called it the most desirable of days— a reminder of Creation"), Revelation ("At Sinai they were commanded about it [the Sabbath]"), and Redemption ("Those who keep the Sabbath and call it a delight will rejoice in Your Kingdom"). In a way, that is especially fitting: the *Amidah* is recited every day during the evening, morning, and afternoon, albeit with different middle sections, but the *Musaf* service is said only on special days. The Sabbath *Musaf* service is thus entirely a celebration of the singularity and distinctiveness of the Sabbath, and so it is appropriate that its middle section make mention of all three themes appearing in the other services of the day.

23. Philo, *Decalogue* 96; *Mekhilta of Rabbi Simeon Ben Yohai* to Exodus 20:11. The material in the latter source is tannaitic and hence from the second century C.E., but the redaction of the material probably did not take place until the early fifth century. Cf. Moshe David Herr, "Mekhilta of R. Simeon Ben Yohai" and "Midreshei Halakhah," *Encyclopaedia Judaica* 11:1269–1270 and 11:1521–1523.

24. Moshe Greenberg, *Lessons on Exodus* (New York: Melton Research Center, 1974), pp. 191–193. Actually, since the tenth commandment demands that we not covet objects, the second five commandments concern the relationships of people with each other *and with our environment.* A. J. Heschel, in his book *The Sabbath,* has written eloquently about the need for contemporary people to reorient their concern for things to an appreciation of time. We shall discuss this shortly.

25. Samson Raphael Hirsch, *Horeb* (London: The Soncino Press, 1962), I. Grunfeld, trans., Section 2:21, Vol. 1, pp. 61–78.

26. Judah Halevi, *The Kuzari: An Argument for the Faith of Israel,* Hartwig Hirschfeld, trans. (New York: Schocken, 1964), Part Three, Section 10, pp. 142–143.

27. Abraham Joshua Heschel, *The Sabbath* (Cleveland: The World Publishing Company, and Philadelphia: The Jewish Publication Society of America, 1951, 1963), pp. 5, 6, 8, 16, 10. Cf. p. 73 for some rabbinic sources on the identity of the Sabbath and eternity (the World to Come).

28. Mordecai M. Kaplan, *The Meaning of God in Modern Jewish Religion* (New York: Behrman House, 1937), pp. 60–61 (his italics).

29. *Genesis Rabbah,* Ch. 10, end.

30. Maimonides comes the closest to interpreting Sabbath rest as a preparation for the labors of the week to come. In his *Guide for the Perplexed* (Part
II, Ch. 31), he says:

> God commanded us to abstain from work on the Sabbath, and to rest, for
> two purposes; namely, (1) That we might confirm the true theory, that of
> the Creation, which at once and clearly leads to the theory of the existence
> of God. (2) That we might remember how kind God has been in freeing us
> from the burden of the Egyptians. The Sabbath is therefore a double
> blessing: it gives us correct ideas, and it also promotes the well-being of
> our bodies.

Similarly, in Part III, Ch. 43, he says:

> The object of the Sabbath is obvious and requires no explanation. The rest
> it affords to man is known; one-seventh of the life of every man, whether
> small or great, passes thus in comfort and in rest from trouble and exertion.
> This the Sabbath effects in addition to the perpetuation and confirmation of
> the grand doctrine of the Creation.

But note that even for Maimonides, Sabbath rest is a blessing in its own right,
not a preparation for the week to come. If anything, it is to recuperate from
the labors of the previous week, in line with the rabbinic comment in *Exodus
Rabbah* 1:28. The *result,* of course, is that people are rested for the week to
come, but that is not the *purpose* of the rest. The goal of the rest is to
communicate its specific Sabbath messages, as developed below.

31. Eric Fromm has developed this theme beautifully in *The Forgotten
Language* (New York: Grove Press, 1951), pp. 243–248; reprinted in Elliot N.
Dorff, *Jewish Law and Modern Ideology* (New York: United Synagogue of
America, 1970), pp. 82–87.

32. *Tanhuma Vayetze,* Section 13.

33. *Avot d'Rabbi Natan* 11:1.

34. M. *Ketubbot* 5:5.

35. B. *Nedarim* 49b.

36. The Rabbis specifically recognize the command to work as a separate
command; cf. *Mekhilta of Rabbi Shimon bar Yohai* to Exodus 20:9; *Avot d'Rabbi
Natan* 11:1; and *Genesis Rabbah* 16:8.

37. *Genesis Rabbah* 11:6, which uses mustard, wheat, and even the uncircumcised nature of the penis when a male is born as its examples of the need
for human activity to make the world perfect. Rabbi Pinchas Peli has suggested that this meaning may even be inherent in the biblical text of Genesis
2:3, which, given the apparently superfluous words at its end, can be read as
meaning, "And God blessed the seventh day and made it holy because on it

God ceased all the work which he [God] created [for humans] to do" or "to continue doing"; cf. his column, "Tora Today," in *The Jerusalem Post International Edition,* October 17, 1987, p. 22, and, in a similar vein, cf. the comment of R. Simhah Bunam cited in Louis I. Newman, ed., *The Hasidic Anthology* (New York: Bloch, 1944), p. 61.

The phrase "the partner of God in the act of Creation" does not appear in regard to doing work as such, but rather in connection with judging justly (B. *Shabbat* 10a), acknowledging God's creation by reciting the beginning of Ch. 2 of Genesis on Friday evenings (B. *Shabbat* 119b), and spreading knowledge and recognition of God (*Genesis Rabbah* 43:7).

38. *Avot d'Rabbi Natan* 11:1, based upon Exodus 25:8.

39. *Genesis Rabbah* 17:5 (17:7 in some editions); *Mekhilta* to Exodus 31:13.

40. B. *Sotah* 14a; the biblical proof texts cited there are not included in this abridged translation. Cf. also *Sifre Deuteronomy, Ekev,* on Deuteronomy 11:22.

41. Rashi's comment on Leviticus 19:14. Maimonides even claims that non-Jews fail to fulfill the seven laws, which, by tradition, God commanded all the descendants of Noah if they do not obey them specifically out of a sense of being commanded by God; cf. M. T. *Laws of Kings* 8:11.

42. This is particularly true in the United States, where individualism is perhaps most evident in both ideology and practice. Cf. Elliot N. Dorff, "Training Rabbis in the Land of the Free," in Nina Beth Cardin and David Wolf Silverman, eds. *The Seminary at 100: Reflections on the Jewish Theological Seminary and the Conservative Movement* (New York: Rabbinical Assembly, 1987), pp. 11–28, esp. pp. 11–19.

Roman Catholicism, of course, has developed a sophisticated legal system of its own—i.e., Roman Catholic Canon Law—and Protestant churches have instituted rules of practice in varying degrees of specificity. Canon law is rarely invoked or even studied by diocesan priests, however, and Protestant denominations, whatever the extent of their rules, still stress individual autonomy over law. In any case, Christianity as we know it began with the rejection of Jewish law by Paul in Romans, Chs. 7–11.

43. See, for example, B. *Berakhot* 13a (in regard to saying the *Shema*); B. *Eruvin* 95b–96a (in regard to the use of phylacteries); B. *Pesahim* 114b (in regard to the need for two dippings at the Seder); B. *Rosh Hashanah* 27a–29a (especially, 28b, in regard to blowing the Shofar); and see the discussion in Chapter 6 below on *keva* and *kavvanah* in prayer. See also B. *Shabbat* 72b with regard to the related question of whether one needs to have intention in order to be held liable for violating a law. This latter question had yet a further

development that even those who claimed that unintentional violation did not make one liable nevertheless held that one would be liable if one's violation of the law in doing an act was, though unintentional, an inevitable consequence of acting as one did; cf. B. *Shabbat* 75a, 103a, 111b, 117a, 120b, 133a, 143a; B. *Betzah* 36a; B. *Sukkah* 33b; B. *Ketubbot* 6b; B. *Bekhorot* 25a.

44. B. *Pesahim* 50b, *et al.*

45. From the twelfth century to the twentieth, the community assembled on the Sabbath even acted as a court of last resort. Members who felt that justice had not been done in their cases could interrupt the prayers and have the community sit as a court of the whole. As time went on, restrictions were imposed on this right to insure that it was not used frivolously, but the use of Sabbath services for judicial matters shows clearly the extent to which the Sabbath was and is an occasion for the community. Cf. Louis Finkelstein, *Jewish Self-Government in the Middle Ages* (New York: Jewish Theological Seminary of America, 1924, 1964), pp. 15–18, 33, 125, 138; and, for a description of the practice in Eastern Europe in modern times, cf. Mark Zborowski and Elizabeth Herzog, *Life Is with People* (New York: International Universities Press, 1952), pp. 217–218.

46. Ahad Ha-Am, *Al Parashat Derahim*, Vol. III, 30.

47. For a conspectus of Christian views on this matter, and an argument for the traditional, "Lutheran" interpretation of Paul as making salvation depend not upon deeds but upon faith alone, cf. Stephen Westerholm, *Israel's Law and the Church's Faith: Paul and His Recent Interpreters* (Grand Rapids, MI: Wm. B. Eerdmans, 1988).

48. This, at any rate, is the usual translation, taking the first two words, *"l'david mizmor,"* together. Thus, the new Jewish Publication Society of America translation, for example, is: "Of David. A psalm. The earth is the Lord's and all that it holds, the world and its inhabitants."

Rabbi Richard Levy, however, has pointed out to me that the traditional notes *(trup)* for this psalm suggest a different reading. They divide the first two words, such that the first verse would read: "Of David. A song to the Lord is the earth and all that it holds, the world and its inhabitants." That beautiful translation would make the point I am making here less clear, but there are plenty of other verses to demonstrate it (e.g., Leviticus 25:23, "The land must not be sold beyond reclaim, for the land is Mine; you are but strangers resident with Me"). I have nevertheless used this verse from Psalm 24 to make the point since its usual translation does so beautifully.

49. Cf. the section of Chapter 2 above dealing with McClendon and Smith's book, *Understanding Religious Convictions,* and the other books referred

to in n. 17 there for the crucial role of stories in articulating our philosophy of life, our values, and our faith.

50. Pierre Duhem, *La Theorie Physique: Son Objet, Sa Structure* (2nd edition, Paris, 1914); W. V. O. Quine, "Two Dogmas of Empiricism," *Philosophical Review* 60 (1951), pp. 20–43, reprinted in Quine's *From a Logical Point of View* (Cambridge, MA: Harvard University Press, 1953), pp. 20–46, and elsewhere; Morton White, *Toward Reunion in Philosophy* (Cambridge, MA: Harvard University Press, 1956), pp. 254–258, 263; and especially, Morton White, *What Is and What Ought to Be Done: An Essay on Ethics and Epistemology* (New York: Oxford University Press, 1981).

51. Cf. my paper, "Pluralism," in *Frontiers of Jewish Thought*, Steven Katz, ed. (Washington, DC: B'nai Brith, 1992), pp. 213–234, for a discussion of the theological roots and justifications of pluralism.

52. Cf., for example, A. J. Ayer, *Language, Truth, and Logic* (New York: Dover, 1936, 1946), pp. 49–51; R. B. Braithwaite, *Scientific Explanation* (New York: Harper, 1953, 1960), pp. 255–292; Carl G. Hempel, "Studies in the Logic of Confirmation," *Mind,* New Series, LIV (1945), (I) pp. 1–26; (II) pp. 97–121; Israel Scheffler, *The Anatomy of Inquiry* (New York: Alfred A. Knopf, 1963), pp. 231–314.

53. Deuteronomy 8:17–18.

54. Abraham J. Heschel, *God in Search of Man* (New York: Harper and Row, 1955), Ch. 32, pp. 320–335. Martin Buber, *Eclipse of God* (New York: Harper and Brothers, 1952). Buber himself uses the image of an eclipse of God to underscore that modern people are unreceptive to a God who is always present, not that God has, in the words of the Psalmist, "hidden His face." Emil Fackenheim similarly uses Buber's image to underline our contemporary failure to see or hear God; see Fackenheim's essay, "On the Eclipse of God," *Commentary* (June 1964), pp. 55–60; reprinted in his *Quest for Past and Future* (Boston: Beacon Press, 1968), pp. 229–243, and in Michael L. Morgan, ed., *The Jewish Thought of Emil Fackenheim* (Detroit: Wayne State University Press, 1987), pp. 102–110. Fackenheim disputes the adequacy of this image as a response to the Holocaust, however, since the image assumes that God will not forever and totally be eclipsed, a faith from which the Holocaust removes the ground; see Fackenheim's *God's Presence in History: Jewish Affirmations and Philosophical Reflections* (New York: New York University Press, 1970; reprinted New York: Harper and Row, 1972), Ch. 2.

Be that as it may, apart from the image of the eclipse of God, Buber makes the point that the other party—whether human or divine—must choose to enter into the relationship, if it is to occur, in his *I And Thou* (New York:

Charles Scribner's Sons, 1958), p. 11: "The *Thou* meets me through grace—
it is not found by seeking. . . . Hence the relation means being chosen and
choosing, suffering and action in one . . ." (cf. also p. 76). He thinks,
however, that unlike relationships with human beings, where there is indeed
a risk that the other person will not want to meet you, God is always ready to
enter into relationship with us because God needs us: "You know always in
your heart that you need God more than everything; but do you not know
too that God needs you—in the fullness of His eternity needs you? How
would man be, how would you be, if God did not need him, did not need
you? You need God, in order to be—and God needs you, for the very
meaning of your life" (p. 82; cf. pp. 99, 116).

CHAPTER 4

1. George Felton, "Students of 'The Pitch,' " *Newsweek* 112:13 (September 26, 1988), pp. 10–11.

2. On the cessation of prophecy: B. *Sanhedrin* 11a; *Numbers Rabbah* 14:4.
On the primacy of the revelation to Moses: B. *Megillah* 14a; *Exodus Rabbah*
28:6; 42:8; *Leviticus Rabbah* 1:14.

3. Parallel remarks apply, of course, to Christianity and Islam as well.
That is, Christianity is rooted in how the Church Fathers interpreted the
Bible, and Islam is based upon how Muslim religious leaders interpreted it. In
all three Western religions, the Bible serves as a fundamental, foundational
document, but it is its interpretation and application by each of these separate
communities over time that define each of the religions.

4. *Emet Ve-Emunah: Statement of Principles of Conservative Judaism* (New
York: The Jewish Theological Seminary of America, The Rabbinical Assembly, United Synagogue of America, Women's League for Conservative
Judaism, Federation of Jewish Men's Clubs, 1988), p. 22.

5. For a thorough discussion, with quoted sources and citations for
further reading, of the rabbinic and each of the major contemporary positions
on the nature and authority of revelation, cf. my *Conservative Judaism: Our
Ancestors to Our Descendants* (New York: United Synagogue of America,
1977), pp. 79–157. The three Conservative positions described here are
summarized in Conservative Judaism's official document, *Emet Ve-Emunah,*
ibid., pp. 19–20; cf. also pp. 22–24. See also my *Jewish Law and Modern Ideology*
(New York: United Synagogue Commission on Jewish Education, 1970),

pp. 192–263, for extensive selections from the ideological sources of each of the Orthodox, Reform, and Conservative movements.

6. Probably the most lucid and popular exposition of the evidence for, and forms of, modern critical scholarship is Richard Elliott Friedman's *Who Wrote the Bible?* (New York: Summit Books, 1987). Otto Eissfeldt, *The Old Testament: An Introduction,* P. R. Ackroyd, trans. (New York: Harper and Row, 1965) is the most extensive presentation of scholarship on this topic prior to 1965. Two Israeli scholars have argued against classical biblical criticism, but in different ways and with different conclusions: cf. Umberto Cassuto, *The Documentary Hypothesis and the Composition of the Pentateuch,* Israel Abrahams, trans. (Jerusalem: Magnes [Hebrew University], 1953 [Hebrew], 1961 [English]); and Moses Hirsch Segal, *The Pentateuch: Its Composition and Its Authorship* (Jerusalem: Magnes [Hebrew University], 1967). Other helpful presentations of contemporary scholarly evidence for, and theories of, biblical composition include: James A. Sanders, *Torah and Canon* (Philadelphia: Fortress Press, 1972); Brevard S. Childs, *Introduction to the Old Testament as Scripture* (Philadelphia: Fortress, 1979), esp. pp. 109–135; and William Lasor, David Hubbard, and Frederic Bush, *Old Testament Survey* (Grand Rapids, MI: William B. Eerdmans, 1982), esp. pp. 26–39 and 54–67.

7. William Temple, *Nature, Man, and God* (New York: St. Martin's Press, 1934), Lecture XII, pp. 304–318; reprinted in John Hick, ed., *Classical and Contemporary Readings in the Philosophy of Religion* (Englewood Cliffs, NJ: Prentice-Hall, 1970), pp. 271–281.

8. Stephen T. Davis, in his book, *The Debate about the Bible: Inerrancy versus Infallibility* (Philadelphia: Westminster, 1977), argues for the infallibility of the Bible—that is, that it is "entirely trustworthy in matters of faith and morals" (p. 15), even if one does not always understand its teaching—but against its inerrancy—i.e., "that it makes no false or misleading statements" (p. 16). I find his arguments persuasive. Indeed, in one sense, I adopt a Jewish version of his Christian evangelical position. Like him, I trust the Bible, and especially the Torah, more than any other book to give me instruction (the literal meaning of "Torah") in matters of faith and morals. As a Jew, however, I would restrict the "trustworthy" texts to the Hebrew Bible, and I would put much greater emphasis than he does on the authoritative role of the subsequent, ongoing tradition to interpret and actually to redefine the Bible in applying it to contemporary circumstances, as the following paragraphs will make clear.

9. I delineate it more extensively in "Revelation," *Conservative Judaism* 31:1–2 (Fall-Winter 1976–1977), pp. 58–69, from which the previous para-

graph and the rest of this section are a selection.

10. B. *Shabbat* 31a; B. *Rosh Hashanah* 25a–b; B. *Sotah* 47b; B. *Bava Metzia* 59b. The same is true for practices of the masses, even if embodied in formal legislation; cf. Menahem Elon, "Minhag," *Encyclopaedia Judaica* 12:23–25; "Takkanot Ha-Kahal," ibid. 15:732–735.

11. See Charles S. Liebman, *The Ambivalent American Jew* (Philadelphia: Jewish Publication Society of America, 1973), pp. 42–49, 63–77. Because of this discrepancy between the elite and the folk, Robert Gordis therefore long ago pointed out that the community whose practices should be considered in determining the definition of Jewish law on any issue must be restricted to those who have seriously made it part of their lives; cf. Robert Gordis, "Authority in Jewish Law," *Proceedings of the Rabbinical Assembly 1941–1944* (New York: Rabbinical Assembly, 1944), pp. 64–93; reprinted in Seymour Siegel, ed., *Conservative Judaism and Jewish Law* (New York: Rabbinical Assembly, 1977), pp. 47–78. See n. 4 above with regard to *Emet Ve-Emunah: Statement of Principles of Conservative Judaism.*

12. B. *Yoma* 67b; cf. *Sifra* 86a. These sources concern matters of practice. In the area of thought, the Rabbis had a healthy sense of pluralism within the Jewish community (cf. n. 51 in Chapter 3), but they generally saw the beliefs of other nations not as rationally ambiguous, but as false. Cf. J. *Berakhot* 7d (used as part of the Siyyum ceremony after studying a tractate of Talmud); B. *Berakhot* 7a; B. *Avodah Zarah* 3b; and biblical roots for this view in places like: Exodus 20:3–7, 19–20; Deuteronomy 32:15–21, 27–33. Even so, Gentiles could be righteous, and the righteous of all nations have a share in the World to Come; cf. T. *Sanhedrin* 13:2.

13. *Mekhilta Beshalah,* 5; B. *Shabbat* 87a; B. *Yoma* 75a; B. *Hagigah* 14a.

14. Martin Buber, *Eclipse of God* (New York: Harper and Row, 1952), Chs. 2–5; "Replies to My Critics," in *The Philosophy of Martin Buber,* Paul Schlepp and Maurice Friedman, eds. (La Salle, IL: Open Court, 1967), p. 692. I owe this reference and much of the stimulation for this subsection to Rabbi Neil Gillman.

15. Judah Halevi, *The Kuzari,* Book I, pars. 83, 86, 88; Moses Maimonides, *Guide for the Perplexed,* Part II, Ch. 35. David Hume, *An Enquiry Concerning Human Understanding,* Section X.

16. Everyone present understood Sinai according to his or her own abilities: *Exodus Rabbah* 5:9; 29:1; *Pesikta d'Rav Kahana* on Exodus 20:2 (ed. Buber, pp. 109b–110a; ed. Mandelbaum, pp. 223–224). Differing interpretations were all "the words of the living God": B. *Eruvin* 13b; cf. M. *Avot* 5:20. Rabbinic mediation of revelation is necessary to avoid multiple Torahs:

B. *Shabbat* 31a; B. *Rosh Hashanah* 25a–b; B. *Sotah* 47b. For further discussion on this, cf. pp. 215–219 of my article, "Pluralism," cited in Chapter 3 at n. 51.

17. Compare Exodus 34:11 and Deuteronomy 34:10 with Exodus 34:17–23.

18. Cf. n. 12 above and my article, "The Covenant: How Jews Understand Themselves and Others," *Anglican Theological Review* 64:4 (October 1982), pp. 481–501.

19. Since the Bible assumes continuing revelation, it never records decisions made by communal deliberation. On the contrary, several questions are answered through direct revelations (Leviticus 24:10–23; Numbers 15:32–36; 27:1–11); even the elders were assumed to exercise their leadership and judicial functions through the agency of the divine spirit (Numbers 11:16–29); and tolerance of other opinions was not a common characteristic of biblical kings and prophets.

20. The debate is recorded in B. *Haggigah* 6a; B. *Sotah* 37b; and B. *Zevahim* 115b. Abraham Joshua Heschel has written at length about the two theologies and the two views of revelation underlying these different approaches; see his *Torah Min Hashamayim B'aspakloria shel Hadorot* [*Torah from Heaven in the Perspective of the Generations*—although the title on the English flyleaf is translated *Theology of Ancient Judaism*] (London: Soncino, 1962), esp. pp. xli–23 (Hebrew). The view that God communicated 611 of the 613 commandments of the Torah to Moses and Moses then commanded the people, who only heard the first two of the Ten Commandments directly from God, appears in B. *Makkot* 23b–24a. Cf. also n. 16 above.

21. Rabbi Joseph B. Soloveitchik, *On Repentance,* Pinchas H. Peli, trans. (Jerusalem: Oroth Press, 1980), p. 296, notes that Sephardic liturgy for the High Holy Days does not include the poems of Rabbi Eliezer Hakalir and Rabbi Simeon Hagadol, substituting others by Rabbi Judah Halevi and Rabbi Abraham ibn Ezra. Rabbi Soloveitchik much prefers the Ashkenazic liturgy. As my friend, Mr. Robert Geskin, has pointed out to me, however, this is probably because Soloveitchik's own theology stresses the fearsome transcendence of God. Without Hakalir's compositions, however, the God of the High Holy Day liturgy, while still demanding accountability and repentance, is much warmer and more àccepting toward the penitent. Indeed, Ashkenazic liturgy, influenced heavily by German and Prussian pietism, may reflect a decidedly Christian inflection in portraying God in such austere terms, and Sephardic liturgy, which makes God more loving and caring, may be more authentically Jewish.

22. B. *Bava Batra* 12a.

23. B. *Sanhedrin* 11a; *Numbers Rabbah* 14:4.

24. M. *Avot (Ethics of the Fathers)* 5:25.

25. That all later prophecies were contained in the Torah: *Exodus Rabbah* 28:6; 42:8; 47:1; B. *Megillah* 14a. That all later insights of students and teachers were also contained in the Torah: J. *Peah* 2:6 (2:4 in some editions) (17a); J. *Megillah* 4:1 (74d); J. *Hagigah* 1:8 (76d); *Exodus Rabbah* 47:1; *Leviticus Rabbah* 22:1; *Kohelet Rabbah* 1:9. All classical rabbinic works (Mishnah, Gemara, Midrash, codes) were also contained in the revelation at Sinai: B. *Berakhot* 5a; B. *Megillah* 19b.

26. *Numbers Rabbah* 19:6.

27. B. *Avodah Zarah* 3b; 4b.

28. M. *Avot (Ethics of the Fathers)* 2:6.

29. Cf. Genesis 18:19 for the verse about Abraham. Deuteronomy 4:9; 6:7; and 11:19 are the biblical commands addressed to all Jews to teach children and grandchildren. Cf. also Deuteronomy 5:1. B. *Kiddushin* 29a–30b contains the primary talmudic discussion of the duties to study oneself and teach one's children and grandchildren.

30. Cf. Exodus 12:26–27; 13:8–9; 13:14–16; Deuteronomy 6:20–25.

31. Simeon b. Shetah apparently attempted to create a school system in Jerusalem in the first half of the first century B.C.E., but it was Joshua b. Gamala, working a few years before the destruction of Second Temple in 70 C.E., whom the tradition credits with first establishing a comprehensive school system for all districts in Israel in which Jews resided. Cf. B. *Bava Batra* 21a.

32. On the annual and triennial cycles for Torah reading, see Louis Jacobs, "Torah, Reading of," *Encyclopaedia Judaica* 15:1246–1255, and "Triennial Cycle," *ibid.,* 15:1386–1389. Also see the papers by Rabbis Lionel Moses, Elliot Dorff, and Richard Eisenberg for the Committee on Jewish Law and Standards of the Conservative Movement, to be published soon by the Rabbinical Assembly in the book collecting the papers written between 1985 and 1990. The institution of a translator of the Torah reading into the vernacular is already attested in the Mishnah (M. *Megillah* 4:4, 6, 10), and the justification cited here is in J. *Megillah* 4:1 (74d).

33. On the ambiguity of the biblical passages: Exodus 20:1 and 20:15–18 seem to say that God declared the Decalogue directly to the people, although not the rest of the Torah. Exodus 19:18–25 and Deuteronomy 5:5, on the other hand, reflect another tradition, according to which it was Moses who announced the Decalogue, albeit in God's name. Rabbi Simlai maintained that the people heard the entirety of the Decalogue from Moses, while Rav

Hamnuna claimed that they heard the first two sections directly from God (B. *Makkot* 23b–24a; cf. B. *Horayot* 8a).

34. William A. Graham has made this point well with specific reference to the Vedic, Christian, and Muslim traditions and with passing consideration of others; cf. his *Beyond the Written Word: Oral Aspects of Scripture in the History of Religion* (New York: Cambridge University Press, 1987).

35. The conclusion of the blessing may also be a gerund—i.e., Giver of the Torah. Whether it is a gerund or, as translated here, a verb, though, the implication is the same: God has not only given the Torah in the past, but continues to be the giver of the Torah (i.e., continues to give it to us) each time we read it.

36. Another consequence of this is that nations often portray their beginnings in mythic, "bigger-than-life" terms as a way of saying that their very birth illustrates how special they are. That is certainly behind the Romulus and Remus stories about the founding of Rome, the claims of the Japanese that their emperor is a direct descendant of the gods, and the common depiction of the American Founding Fathers as demigods. The Exodus account is also undoubtedly shaped in part by this natural urge to embellish the story of one's beginnings.

In all of these cases, one approaches the stories incorrectly if one assumes that they were meant to be historical records of what happened and judges them on that basis. One must instead appreciate the role these stories have in their respective cultures, i.e., to celebrate the birth of the people, to relate some of its primary perceptions and values, and to make it feel proud. The proper criterion of judgment, then, is not whether they are literally true, but whether they accomplish their goals—whether, in other words, they are good stories!

37. In postbiblical times Shavuot was understood to be the time of the giving of the Torah. To underscore the fact that the goal of the Exodus was only attained at Sinai, the kabbalists stressed the link between Passover and Shavuot by using the 49 days of the intervening Omer season to denote the ascent out of the 49 "gates" of impurity of the Egyptian bondage to the purity of the revelation at Sinai. The Bible itself links Shavuot to the Exodus as well as to Passover (Deuteronomy 16:1–12).

38. The Bible clearly records Israel's agreement to the Covenant both at Sinai (Exodus 19:8; 24:3,7) and during the reaffirmation in Ezra's time (Nehemiah, Ch. 10), and it asserts that the Covenant was made with the People Israel of all generations (Deuteronomy 5:3; 29:13–14,28), who presumably agreed to it. The Bible also speaks, however, of God "command-

ing" the clauses of the Torah amidst thunder and lightning, it describes the people's fear at the time (e.g., Deuteronomy 5:19ff), it expresses God's wish that the people fear Him enough to obey the commandments (e.g., Deuteronomy 5:26), and it confirms the Covenant in a ceremony designed to inspire awe in the people (Deuteronomy 11:26–32; 27:11–26). All of this certainly does not sound like voluntary acceptance of the Covenant! The Rabbis continue this: one popular Midrash describes God's fruitless search for a people to accept the Torah until He asked the People Israel, who responded with the words, "We shall do and we shall hear" (Exodus 24:7) (*Sifre Deuteronomy* par. 343; *Numbers Rabbah* 14:10), while another equally popular Midrash, as indicated, pictures God overturning Mount Sinai over the people and telling them that they will be buried under it unless they accept the Torah (B. *Shabbat* 88a; B. *Avodah Zarah* 2b; etc.) For more on the similarities and dissimilarities between human contracts and the Covenant between God and Israel, cf. my article, "The Covenant: The Transcendent Thrust in Jewish Law," *The Jewish Law Annual* 7:68–96 (1988).

As the former rabbinic legend attests, the Rabbis understand Exodus 24:7 very honorifically: the Israelites were voicing their trusting faith in God in agreeing to become part of the Covenant without first knowing its terms. The text, however, may simply mean that the Israelites, paralyzed by fear, said, "We shall do [what You have said] and listen [to whatever else You have to say]!"

39. J. *Nedarim* 38b; *Exodus Rabbah* 25:12.

40. M. *Avot (Ethics of the Fathers)* 3:18.

CHAPTER 5

1. B. *Berakhot* 33b.

2. *Genesis Rabbah* 8:4,5.

3. *Genesis Rabbah* 5:1; 78:1; B. *Shabbat* 30a.

4. Two recent, thoughtful expositions of this approach are Irving Greenberg, *The Jewish Way: Living the Holidays* (New York: Summit Books, 1988), pp. 317–326; and David Birnbaum, *God and Evil: A Jewish Perspective* (Hoboken, NJ: Ktav, 1989), Part Two, esp. pp. 54, 61–64, 84–86, 115. The biblical image of God "hiding His face" *(hester panim)* often accompanies this approach as a way of retaining God's presence and ability to intervene but God's refusal to do so lest such intervention undermine our integrity and

identity as human beings with free will. For the image, see, for example, Deuteronomy 31:17,18; Isaiah 1:12; 8:15; 45:14; 54:8; 57:15; 59:1; 64:10; Job 34:29. Another concept commonly used by advocates of this approach is the kabbalistic *tzimtzum,* God's "contraction" of His presence and power to make room for human free will. Birnbaum even lists a number of biblical passages that he reads as evidence of Divine self-limitation (Birnbaum, ibid., pp. 126–127), but he is frankly stretching their meaning. God's presence and power must be limited to afford a place and role for human free will, but that does not excuse God from many manifestations of evil.

5. This, of course, is the theme of Job's "friends," although God in the whirlwind (Chs. 38–42 of the Book of Job) denies this. It is also behind the High Holy Day liturgy's request of God to forgive our sins, "whether we know them or not."

6. This seems unconscionable to contemporary Americans. How is it just to punish children for the sins of parents? Moreover, how can God do this (cf. Exodus 34:6–7; Numbers 14:18–19) while specifically commanding people not to do so (Deuteronomy 24:16)?!

In part, the Bible sees this as an act of mercy on the part of God toward the parents, just as postponing payment on a credit card is understood and felt as a favor. This, of course, leaves unresolved the injustice suffered by the children. Because of this, some sources claim that God only "visits the iniquity of the parents on the children" when the children themselves continue to do the sin. Still others suggest that the unfairness is simply a fact of life, whether or not we understand it. Children, after all, prosper unjustly from the abilities and accomplishments of their parents just as much as they suffer from their parents' deficiencies; it is just that we only complain about the latter! Cf. Jacob Milgrom, "Vertical Retribution," *Conservative Judaism* 34:3 (January/February 1981), pp. 11–16; Robert Gordis, *A Faith for Moderns* (New York: Bloch, 1960), pp. 181–182; and Elliot N. Dorff and Arthur Rosett, *A Living Tree* (Albany, NY: State University of New York Press, 1988), pp. 110–123.

7. A good summary of the rabbinic material on all of the above approaches can be found in A. Cohen, *Everyman's Talmud* (New York: E. P. Dutton and Co., 1949), pp. 110–120 and 364–389.

8. Moses Maimonides, *Guide for the Perplexed,* Part III, Chs. 10–12.

9. Mordecai M. Kaplan, *The Meaning of God in Modern Jewish Religion* (New York: Behrman House, 1937; Reconstructionist Press, 1947), p. 76. The rabbinic source he cites is *Genesis Rabbah* 3:6; cf. 53:4. Milton Steinberg presents this position more convincingly in his *A Believing Jew* (New York:

Harcourt, Brace and Company, 1951), pp. 13–31.

10. Harold Kushner, *When Bad Things Happen To Good People* (New York: Schocken, 1981).

11. Kaplan, *Meaning of God* (at n. 9), p. 76.

12. Ibid., p. 84.

13. This seems to be the message of God out of the whirlwind in Chs. 38–42 of the Book of Job, and it is clearly stated in *Avot (Ethics of the Fathers)* 4:19; B. *Menahot* 29b; and, as R. Meir's position in B. *Berakhot* 7a.

14. On the Holocaust: Richard L. Rubenstein, *After Auschwitz: Radical Theology and Contemporary Judaism* (Indianapolis: Bobbs-Merrill, 1966). On the nuclear threat: Richard L. Rubenstein, "Jewish Theology and the Current World Situation," *Conservative Judaism* 28:4 (Summer 1974), pp. 3–25; cf. also the responses of Arthur Green and Elliot Dorff on pp. 26–36 there. Rubenstein later spelled out the implications of overpopulation, world poverty, and the nuclear threat more fully in his *The Age of Triage* (Boston: Beacon Press, 1983), esp. Chs. 1, 9, and 10.

15. Cf. B. *Sanhedrin* 11a; B. *Bava Batra* 12a.

16. Yehudah Halevi, *Kuzari,* Books IV and V; Mordecai M. Kaplan, *The Meaning of God in Modern Jewish Religion* (New York: The Reconstructionist Press, 1937, 1962), pp. 20–25. Cf. also Martin Buber, *The Eclipse of God* (New York: Harper and Row, 1952), Chs. 2–5. This distinction, introduced first in Chapter 1, and the attempt to integrate its two parts in a coherent form of Jewish belief have been a veritable *leitmotif* throughout the chapters above.

17. T. H. Meek, *Hebrew Origins* (New York: Harper and Row, 1936, 1960), Ch. 3, esp. pp. 84–85, 98–102, 116. Cf. also Norman H. Snaith, *The Distinctive Ideas of the Old Testament* (New York: Schocken Books, 1964), Ch. 2, esp. pp. 21, 29–32.

18. Despite the existence of books like Job, the Bible does not ultimately reconcile God's goodness, which it affirms often (e.g., Deuteronomy 32:4; Jeremiah 9:23; Amos 5:24; Zephaniah 3:5; Psalms 11:7; 97:2; 99:4), with the evil that God inscrutably causes or does not prevent. The Rabbis, however, attempted to construct a coherent view of these phenomena. For them, *"tov"* (good) is God's main attribute (J. *Hagigah* 77c, *Ecclesiastes Rabbah* 7:8, and *Ruth Rabbah* 3:16), and God's mercy will assert itself if a person repents (e.g., *Pesikta* 164a). God requites people according to their own measure (*"middah ke-neged middah,"* T. *Sotah* 3; J. *Sotah* 17a,b; B. *Sanhedrin* 90a,b), but the measure of good always exceeds that of evil and punishment (*"middat tovah merubbah mimiddat puraniyyut,"* *Mekhilta, Beshalah,* ed. Lauterbach, Vol. II, p. 113; ed. Horowitz-Robin, p. 166). One opinion in the tradition (B. *Berakhot*

34b), however, makes messianic times different from our own era only in that the *political* frustration of the Jewish people would be alleviated; otherwise, we would all remain much as we are.

19. Isaiah 45:7; cf. also Lamentations 3:37–38.

20. B. *Berakhot* 11b; cf. Max Arzt, *Justice and Mercy* (New York: Holt, Rinehart and Winston, 1963), p. 49.

21. I Kings 11:14, Psalms 109:6, Job 1:6; for the Rabbis, see, for example, J. *Ta'anit* 65b, B. *Kiddushin* 81a–81b, *Esther Rabbah* 7:13 (on Esther 3:9), etc.

22. *Mekhilta* on Exodus 20:23 (ed. Lauterbach, Vol. II, p. 277).

23. M. *Berakhot* 9:5 (= B. *Berakhot* 54a); cf. *Sifre Deuteronomy* 32. The Mishnah derives this lesson from the phrase, "with all your might." The Malbim suggests another justification for this mishnaic principle. Commenting on Deuteronomy 6:4–5, he notes that the *juxtaposition* of God's unity in verse 4 with the love of God in verse 5 suggests that, when we recognize God as One, we are challenged to love the Eternal as the source of all that happens to us—both good and evil.

24. B. *Menahot* 29b; cf. also the opinion of R. Meir on B. *Berakhot* 7a.

25. See, for example, B. *Ta'anit* 11a; B. *Kiddushin* 40b; and B. *Berakhot* 5b, where the notion appears that the punishment God inflicts is a product of His love.

26. *Sifre Deuteronomy*, "Ha'azinu," par. 329.

27. Cf. A. Cohen, *Everyman's Talmud* (New York: E. P. Dutton, 1949), pp. 110–120. For examples of the incomprehensibility of God's justice, see, for example, B. *Berakhot* 7a and B. *Menahot* 29b, quoted above, and, probably, M. *Avot* 4:19.

28. For Kant, of course, it makes sense only if it is not rewarded!

29. M. *Avot* 4:2. This puts me in direct opposition to the comment in the Tosefta by Rabbi Reuben, about whom the following is told:

It happened once that Rabbi Reuben was in Tiberias on the Sabbath, and a philosopher asked him: "Who is the most hateful man in the world?" He replied, "The man who denies the Creator." "How so?" said the philosopher. Rabbi Reuben answered: " 'Honor your father and mother, you shall not murder, you shall not commit adultery, you shall not steal, you shall not bear false witness against your neighbor, you shall not covet.' No man denies the derivative (i.e., the separate commandments) until he has previously denied the Root (i.e., God), and no man sins unless he has denied Him who commanded him not to commit that sin" (T. *Shevu'ot* 3:6).

I agree that it is *easier* to be motivated to observe the commandments if you think that God will punish you for not observing them and reward you if you do. As the Rabbis recognized elsewhere, however, (1) that is *not* the proper motivation (M. *Avot* 1:3); (2) it does not even work out that way, at least as far as we know (cf. n. 27 above), and it must, therefore, eventually lose force as a motivation; and (3) moreover, it *is* possible to observe Jewish law without a theological whipping stick—indeed, without God at all (cf. *Pesikta*, XV, ed. Buber, 120a–121b, ed. Mandelbaum, p. 254).

30. Cf. B. *Eruvin* 13b for a similar view held by the School of Hillel. In my book, *Mitzvah Means Commandment* (New York: United Synagogue of America, 1989), I discuss at some length the multiplicity of motivations to observe the law that the Bible and Rabbis delineated. They certainly did not restrict the motivations to observe the law to divine reward and punishment—although that certainly was included.

31. Psalm 146 is a good example of this, but it is only one of many.

CHAPTER 6

1. For example, a prayer that accompanied a sacrifice is recorded in Deuteronomy 26:1–11; one said while setting aside the tithe for the poor appears in Deuteronomy 26:12–15; and an example of a personal prayer is that of Hannah in I Samuel 2:1–10. Cf. Moshe Greenberg, *Biblical Prose Prayer as a Window to the Popular Religion of Israel* (Berkeley: University of California, 1983).

2. B. *Berakhot* 32b; B. *Ta'anit* 2b, 27b; *Pesikta* 165b.

3. M. *Berakhot* 9:3; T. *Berakhot* 6:7, ed. Lieberman, p. 35. Cf. B. *Berakhot* 54a, 60a; M. T. *Laws of Blessings* 10:22, 26; S. A. *Orah Hayyim* 230:1.

4. *Genesis Rabbah* 72:6; *Tanhuma*, "*Vayetze*," Section 8; J. *Berakhot* 9:3. Gerald Blidstein describes these two disparate, rabbinic approaches in his article, "The Limits of Prayer," *Judaism* 15:2 (Spring 1966), pp. 164–170; reprinted in Jakob Petuchowski, ed., *Understanding Jewish Prayer* (New York: Ktav, 1972), pp. 112–120. He also points out that just as the Rabbis disagreed with regard to the efficacy of petitionary prayer to change a natural fact or law, they also differed on its effects on God's Rosh Hashanah judgments and decrees.

5. The story of Elijah's sacrifice is in I Kings 18:20–46. Joshua's prayer is specifically followed by a verse that claims that "neither before nor since has there ever been such a day, when the Lord acted on words spoken by a man" (Joshua 10:14; the story begins with 10:1). The Rabbis' position against

relying on miracles: B. *Kiddushin* 39b; cf. B. *Pesahim* 64b, where this is Rava's position in opposition to Abayae's. Cf. also B. *Shabbat* 32a and B. *Ta'anit* 20b, according to which "a person should never stand in a place of danger and say that a miracle will be done for me lest a miracle not be done for him, and if a miracle is done for him, he suffers a reduction in his merits" [in the accounting of the World to Come]. The world follows its own course: B. *Avodah Zarah* 54b.

6. Cf. Kenneth H. Norwich, "The Physics of Prayer and the Origin of the Universe," *Conservative Judaism* 40:2 (Winter 1987/1988), pp. 14–15.

7. Petuchowski, *Understanding Jewish Prayer* (at n. 4), p. 66.

8. Abraham Joshua Heschel, "On Prayer," *Conservative Judaism* 25:1 (Fall 1970), p. 3; reprinted in Petuchowski, *Understanding Jewish Prayer* (at n. 4), p. 71.

9. Martin Buber, *I And Thou*, Ronald Gregor Smith, trans., second ed. (New York: Charles Scribner's Sons, 1958), p. 83.

10. Heschel, "On Prayer," at n. 8, p. 2; in Petuchowski, *Understanding Jewish Prayer* (at n. 4), p. 70.

11. Dudley Weinberg, "The Efficacy of Prayer," Jewish Chautauqua Society, Pamphlet #2; reprinted in Petuchowski, *Understanding Jewish Prayer* (at n. 4), p. 135.

12. Petuchowski, *Understanding Jewish Prayer* (at n. 4), pp. 41–42. The talmudic passage he cites is at B. *Yevamot* 64a.

13. *Sifra*, Behar 5:3 (on Leviticus 25:36); B. *Bava Metzia* 62a. Cf. Jakob J. Petuchowski, "The Limits of Self-Sacrifice," in *Modern Jewish Ethics: Theory and Practice*, Marvin Fox, ed. (Columbus, OH: Ohio State University Press, 1975), pp. 103–118.

14. The obligation for each person to say, "For me the world was created," appears in M. *Sanhedrin* 4:5. "Though I am but dust and ashes" are Abraham's words to God in Genesis 18:27. This hasidic saying is quoted in the name of Rabbi Bunam in Martin Buber, *Tales of the Hasidim: Later Masters* (New York: Schocken, 1948, 1961), Vol. 2, pp. 249–250.

15. Two twentieth-century Jewish thinkers have stressed this point, drawing different implications. Cf. Franz Rosenzweig, *Star of Redemption* (New York: Holt, Rinehart, and Winston, 1970), pp. 3–5, 9–12; Rosenzweig, "The New Thinking," in *Franz Rosenzweig: His Life and Thought*, Nahum N. Glatzer, ed. (New York: Schocken, 1953), pp. 190–208, esp. pp. 205–207; and cf. Dov Baer Soloveitchik, "The Lonely Man of Faith," *Tradition* 7:2 (Summer 1965), pp. 5–67.

16. So, for example, the command to "serve" God (Deuteronomy 11:13)

was understood to mean study of the Torah; cf. *Sifre Deuteronomy,* par. 41, 80a.

17. Eliezer Berkovits, "From Temple to Synagogue and Back," *Judaism* 8:4 (Fall 1959), pp. 303–311; reprinted in Petuchowski, *Understanding Jewish Prayer* (at n. 4), pp. 138–151.

18. *Mekhilta d'Rabbi Ishmael, Massekheta d'Shirah,* Ch. III, ed. Horovitz-Rabin, p. 127.

19. *Pesikta d'Rav Kahana,* Ch. 10 (on Deuteronomy 14:22), ed. Mandelbaum, p. 164; ed. Buber, p. 97a. Cf. also *Pesikta Rabbati,* Ch. 25, ed. Friedmann, p. 127a.

20. Romano Guardini, *Vom Geist der Liturgie,* 19th ed. (Frieburg: Herder, 1957), pp. 53f, 57f. Translated by, and quoted from, Petuchowski, *Understanding Jewish Prayer* (at n. 4), p. 31.

21. The commandments to appear before God on the pilgrimage festivals and not to come empty-handed but rather with whatever gifts one can afford: Exodus 23:14–17; Deuteronomy 16:16–17. The commandment to rejoice before God on those days: Deuteronomy 16:11,14. That the Second Tithe must be consumed in Jerusalem: Deuteronomy 14:22–27.

22. Buber, *I And Thou* (at n. 9).

23. Abraham Joshua Heschel, *Man's Quest for God* (New York: Scribner's, 1954), pp. 27–46. Selections of that are reprinted in his *Between God and Man* (New York: Harper and Brothers, 1959), Fritz A. Rothschild, ed., Ch. 35.

24. Numbers 15:39–40.

25. Abraham Joshua Heschel, *Man's Quest for God* (New York: Scribner's, 1954), pp. 27–46. Selections of that are reprinted in his *Between God and Man,* Fritz A. Rothschild, ed. (New York: Harper and Brothers, 1959), Ch. 35.

26. Maimonides, *Guide for the Perplexed,* Part III, Ch. 51; cf. Ch. 54.

27. M. *Sotah* 7:1; B. *Berakhot* 13a, 40b; B. *Sotah* 32b–33a; B. *Shevuot* 39a; M. T., *Laws of Shema* 2:10; S. A., *Orah Hayyim* 62:2; 101:4.

28. Louis Jacobs, *Principles of the Jewish Faith* (New York: Basic Books, 1964), pp. 95–117.

29. Hayyim Nahman Bialik, *Essays,* cited in Reuven Alcalay, *Words of the Wise* (Jerusalem, 1970), p. 495, #4757.

30. Elie Wiesel has written movingly of such an experience on Yom Kippur evening in Moscow in his *Jews of Silence* (New York: Holt, Rinehart, and Winston, 1966), pp. 19–22. When he tried to talk with the Russian Jews surrounding him in the synagogue in Yiddish, they pretended not to understand Yiddish. "It was only when I began to pray aloud, in witless desperation, that the barriers fell. The Prince of Prayer had come to my aid. They

listened closely, then drew nearer; their hearts opened."

31. Rosenzweig, *Star of Redemption* (at n. 15), pp. 300–302; reprinted in *Franz Rosenzweig: His Life and Thought* (at n. 15), pp. 296–299.

32. See my article, "Training Rabbis in the Land of the Free," cited in Chapter 3, n. 42. Compare our voluntaristic ideas with the Rabbis' declaration, "Greater is the person who is commanded and acts accordingly than the one who is not commanded and nevertheless does the same act" (B. *Kiddushin* 31a).

33. B. *Ta'anit* 2a.

34. M. T. *Laws of Prayer* 1:6.

35. Jakob J. Petuchowski, *Understanding Jewish Prayer* (at n. 4), pp. 22–23.

36. See my book, *Mitzvah Means Commandment* (New York: United Synagogue of America, 1989) for an extensive discussion of this. A shorter treatment was included in Elliot N. Dorff and Arthur Rosett, *A Living Tree: The Roots and Growth of Jewish Law* (Albany, NY: State University of New York Press, and New York: The Jewish Theological Seminary of America, 1988), pp. 82–123, 246–257. For a more historical discussion of this theme, readers of Hebrew may find a thorough discussion in Yitzhak Heinemann, *Ta'amei Ha'mitzvot B'sifrut Yisrael (Rationales for the Commandments in Jewish Literature)* (Jerusalem: Jewish Agency, 1942, 1966), 2 vols.

37. Abraham Joshua Heschel, *Man's Quest for God* (New York: Scribner's, 1954; recently reprinted under the title *Quest for God*), p. 97.

38. Eliezer Berkovits, "Prayer," in Leon D. Stitskin, ed., *Studies in Torah Judaism* (New York: Yeshiva University Press and Ktav, 1969), pp. 119–120.

39. M. T. *Laws of Reading the Shema* 2:1; *Laws of Prayer* 10:1; cf. also 4:15–16.

40. B. *Berakhot* 8a.

41. Deuteronomy 8:14, 17–18.

42. B. *Shabbat* 115b. The context, however, may restrict this condemnation to those who write blessings in amulets.

43. Not to make one's prayer a fixed routine: M. *Berakhot* 4:4; M. *Avot* 2:13. Rava's definition of *keva:* B. *Berakhot* 29b.

44. Heschel, "On Prayer" (at n. 10), pp. 2, 7; in Petuchowski, *Understanding Jewish Prayer* (at n. 4), pp. 70, 77.

45. See, for example, Louis Finkelstein, *The Pharisees* (Philadelphia: Jewish Publication Society of America, 1966), Vol. I, pp. 145–159 (esp. pp. 158–159) and Vol. II, pp. 742–751 (esp. pp. 750–751) in regard to the second blessing of the *Amidah*. (I am indebted to Mr. Robert Geskin for suggesting the example of *"V'khol Ma'aminim"* to me for the point in the previous

paragraph.)

46. Awareness of these features of our knowledge of God is also the foundation for pluralism, both among Jews and between Jews and non-Jews. Cf. my articles, "Pluralism" (cited at Chapter 3, n. 51) and "The Covenant: How Jews Understand Themselves and Others" (cited at Chapter 4, n. 18). Cf. also Chapter 4, n. 11. (I am indebted to my friend and colleague, Dr. David Gordis, for this point on the indeterminacy of Jewish belief.)

47. Abraham Joshua Heschel, *Man Is Not Alone: A Philosophy of Religion* (New York: Farrar, Straus, and Young, 1951), Chs. 14 and 15. See also his book, *The Prophets* (Philadelphia: Jewish Publication Society of America, 1962), Chs. 12, 14, and 15.

48. B. *Sanhedrin* 11a; B. *Bava Metzia* 59b; B. *Bava Batra* 12a.

49. The Torah is ambiguous even about whether Moses could see God. On the one hand, it says, "The Lord spoke to Moses face to face, as a person speaks to his friend" (Exodus 33:11), but in that same chapter God also tells Moses, "You may not see My face, for a person cannot see My face and live" (Exodus 33:20). Deuteronomy's final description of Moses, though, is, "Never again did there arise in Israel a prophet like Moses, whom the Lord singled out (knew) face to face" (Deuteronomy 34:10). Whether Moses saw God's face or only His back side (Exodus 33:23), the only other biblical prophets who report a vision of God were Isaiah (6:1 says that "I beheld *my Lord* seated on a high and lofty throne," but the rest of the chapter does not describe Him) and Ezekiel (1:26–28 reports his vision of God). All the other biblical prophets confidently report what God told them orally, though. The Rabbis say that Moses experienced ("saw") God through one clear lens while the other biblical prophets had to look through nine cloudy lenses (*Leviticus Rabbah* 1:14) and that everything in the later prophets' prophecies was already included in that of Moses (*Exodus Rabbah* 28:6; 42:8) except the Book of Esther and the Feast of Purim (B. *Megillah* 14a). Thus the authenticity of what the biblical prophets heard was not in doubt, but that was only because it was a recasting of what had already been heard at Sinai—and then with less visual (and, presumably, auditory) fidelity!

50. See Deuteronomy 8:5, according to which we are to "bear in mind that the Lord your God disciplines you just as a man disciplines his son." Deuteronomy 11:13–17, 26–28, and Ch. 28 are two of many passages that articulate the expectation of a *quid pro quo* relationship between Israel's actions and God's punishment or reward.

51. See, for example, Leviticus 19:2 and the *Sifra* on that verse; *Mekhilta, Shirah,* 3; *Sifre, Ekev,* 85a; B. *Sotah* 14; etc.

52. Martin Buber has stressed this point, especially in his *I and Thou* (at n. 9). See also Will Herberg, *Judaism for Modern Man* (Cleveland: World Publishing Company, 1951), Ch. 7.

53. From the *Yigdal* prayer, which is based on Maimonides' "Thirteen Principles of the Faith." Cf. Philip Birnbaum, trans., *Daily Prayer Book* (New York: Hebrew Publishing Company, 1949), pp. 11 and 153 (the third of Maimonides' principles).

54. Maimonides, *Guide of the Perplexed,* Part I, Ch. 46.

55. Cf., for example, Ian Ramsey, *Religious Language* (London: Student Christian Movement Press, 1957); Frederick Ferre, *Language, Logic, and God* (New York: Harper and Row, 1961); James A. Martin, *The New Dialogue between Philosophy and Theology* (New York: The Seabury Press, 1966).

56. John Herman Randall, Jr., *The Role of Knowledge in Western Religion* (Boston: Starr King Press, 1958), Ch. 4, pp. 103–134; the citations are from pp. 117, 122, 132–133, 111, and 112.

57. So Rabbi Reuben in the second century said: "Nobody proceeds to commit a transgression without first having denied Him who prohibited it" (T. *Shevuot* 3:6).

CHAPTER 7

1. Will Herberg has written a powerful statement identifying modern versions of idolatry. See his *Judaism and Modern Man* (Philadelphia: Jewish Publication Society of America, 1951), Part I, pp. 3–43.

2. Prohibitions against idol worship conforming to pagan rituals: Exodus 34:14; Deuteronomy 12:30; cf. B. *Sanhedrin* 61b. Prohibitions against bowing down to an idol and against paying homage to an idol in other forms: Exodus 20:5. Prohibition against offering a sacrifice to another god, including those represented by an idol: Exodus 22:19.

3. Deuteronomy 12:31.

4. That making idols is prohibited: Exodus 20:4,20. That this applies only to objects used for worship: cf., for example, Leviticus 26:1.

5. I have used here the categorization found in Jose Faur, "Idolatry," *Encyclopaedia Judaica* 8:1231.

6. *Sifra* 7:1, end.

7. B. *Rosh Hashanah* 24b; B. *Avodah Zarah* 43b.

8. Genesis 1:26,27; 5:1; 9:6.

9. M. T. *Laws of Idolatry* 3:10,11; S. A. *Yoreh De'ah* 141:4–7. They follow the Talmud (B. *Avodah Zarah* 43b), although *Mekhilta*, Yitro, Ch. 6 on Exodus 20:4, seems to prohibit indented representations, too. Cf. *Hagahot Maimoniyot* on M. T. *Laws of Idolatry* 3:10.

10. A *face:* e.g., Exodus 33:20,23; Numbers 6:25,26. A *nose:* e.g., Exodus 15:8; II Samuel 22:9,16 (repeated verbatim in Psalm 18:9,16). A *mouth:* e.g., Numbers 12:8; 14:41; 22:18; 24:13; Deuteronomy 8:3; Isaiah 1:20; 40:5; 45:23; Jeremiah 9:11; Psalm 33:6. *Eyes:* e.g., Genesis 6:8; Deuteronomy 11:12; 32:10; Isaiah 43:4; 49:5; Psalms 17:8; 33:18. *Ears:* e.g., Numbers 11:1; 14:28; I Samuel 8:21; Ezekiel 8:18. *Hands:* e.g., Exodus 3:20; 15:6; I Samuel 5:6; Psalms 8:7; Job 12:9. *Fingers:* e.g., Exodus 8:15; 31:18; Deuteronomy 9:10. An *arm:* e.g., Exodus 6:6; Deuteronomy 4:34; 5:15; 26:8; 33:27; Isaiah 40:11; 51:9; 52:10; Jeremiah 21:5; 27:5; Psalms 77:16; 79:11; 89:22. *Feet:* e.g., Exodus 24:10; II Samuel 22:10; Psalm 18:10; Nahum 1:3; Habakkuk 3:5; Isaiah 60:13; 66:1; Psalms 99:5; 132:7.

11. God plaits Eve's hair and serves as best man for Adam: B. *Berakhot* 61a. God wears phylacteries and wraps Himself in a prayer shawl: B. *Berakhot* 6a; B. *Rosh Hashanah* 17b. He prays to Himself and studies the Torah during three hours of each day: B. *Avodah Zarah* 3b. He weeps over the failures of His creatures, visits the sick, comforts the mourner, and buries the dead: B. *Haggigah* 5b; *Genesis Rabbah* 8:13.

12. *Guide for the Perplexed,* Part One, esp. Chs. 1, 26, 28, 31, 35, 46, 50–60.

13. Maimonides, *Commentary on the Mishnah,* Introduction to Sanhedrin, Ch. 10 *(Ha-Helek),* Section 5, Fundamental Belief 3.

14. David Hume, *Dialogues Concerning Natural Religion* (1779), Part V.

15. *Song of Songs Rabbah* 7:8; cf. B. *Yoma* 69b.

16. I am here following the usage of Clyde A. Holbrook, *The Iconoclastic Deity: Biblical Images of God* (Lewisburg, PA: Bucknell University Press, 1984). I have been greatly influenced by Chs. 4 and 14 of his book, especially pp. 61 and 192–198, in writing this section of this chapter.

17. The image of a *rock* to depict God is especially frequent in the Book of Psalms (e.g., Psalms 18:2,32; 28:1; 31:3,4; 42:10; 62:3,7,8; 71:3; 92:16; 94:22; 144:1) and in Isaiah (e.g., 17:10; 30:29; 44:8), but it occurs elsewhere as well, e.g., Deuteronomy 32:4,15,18; II Samuel 22:47. *Light:* e.g., II Samuel 22:29; Isaiah 60:1,19,20; Micah 7:8; Psalms 4:6; 27:1; 44:3; 89:16. *Fire:* God's presence is marked by fire (e.g., Exodus 3:2–5; 13:21; 14:24; 19:18; Numbers 14:14; Deuteronomy 4:12,33,36; 5:4,21,23), and sometimes God is depicted as fire, e.g., Deuteronomy 4:24; 9:3; Isaiah 10:17. *Water:* e.g., Jeremiah 2:13; 17:13. *Animals:* e.g., the lion (e.g., Isaiah 31:4; Jeremiah 4:7; 25:30; Hosea

13:7-8; Amos 1:2) and birds (e.g., Deuteronomy 32:11; Isaiah 31:5.) *Human artifacts:* e.g., a shield (e.g., Genesis 15:1; II Samuel 22:3 = Psalm 18:3; Psalm 84:10,12), a hammer (Jeremiah 51:20), a dwelling (Psalm 90:1), and a fortress or tower of refuge (e.g., II Samuel 22:2; Nahum 1:7; Psalm 71:3; 91:2). *Anthropopathic images of God, based on the mental and psychological faculties of human beings:* e.g., God knows (e.g., Genesis 3:5; Joshua 22:22; I Samuel 2:3; Isaiah 10:13; 40:28; Ezekiel 37:3; Psalm 44:22; 94:11; Job 12:13; 21:22), remembers (e.g., Genesis 9:15,16; Exodus 2:24; 6:5; Leviticus 26:42; Jeremiah 31:19; Ezekiel 16:60), plans (e.g., Genesis 41:32; Exodus 3:19-20; Isaiah 37:26-32; Jeremiah 1:5; 29:11), becomes angry (e.g., Numbers 11:1; Deuteronomy 7:4; 11:17; 13:18; 29:27; Jeremiah 7:18; 8:19; 25:6; Nahum 1:6; Zechariah 8:14; Psalms 2:12; 6:2; 38:2; 90:11), can be expected to judge morally (e.g., Genesis 18:25; 31:53; Deuteronomy 32:4; Isaiah 45:19; Psalm 11:5-7), forgives (e.g., Exodus 33:19; 34:6; Numbers 14:18-20; Deuteronomy 4:31; Psalm 111:4; II Chronicles 30:9), and acts out of loyalty and love (e.g., Genesis 24:12,27; 39:21; Exodus 20:6; 34:6,7; Numbers 14:18,19; Deuteronomy 5:10; 7:9; Psalm 25:8-10; and often in Chronicles, Ezra, and Nehemiah).

18. God coming down on the mountain: Exodus 19:18,20; 34:5.

19. *The burning bush:* Exodus 3:1-5. *The pillars of cloud and fire:* Exodus 13:21,22; 14:24; 33:9; Numbers 12:5,10; 14:14. *The tabernacle:* Exodus 25:8 and Chs. 25-27 and 35-38 of Exodus, generally. *The Urim and Tummim:* Numbers 27:21; I Samuel 28:6. *The Menorah:* although the seven-branched menorah in the Temple (Exodus 25:31ff, esp. v. 37) is usually used symbolically, its meanings are probably mixed in most people's minds with the eight-branched, Hanukkah menorah. Cf. its usage as the emblem of the State of Israel. *The eternal light:* Exodus 27:20-21.

20. Biblical symbols: *The Sabbath:* Exodus 31:17. *Phylacteries:* Exodus 13:9,16; Deuteronomy 6:8; 11:18. *The Tetragrammaton:* Exodus 3:13-15.

21. Michael Goldberg, *Jews and Christians: Getting Our Stories Straight* (Nashville: Abingdon, 1985), p. 20, n. 2; and his *Theology and Narrative: A Critical Introduction* (Nashville: Abingdon, 1981), pp. 66-70, 91-95.

22. Maimonides, *Perush Ha-Mishnah (Explanation of the Mishnah),* Introduction to *Sanhedrin,* Ch. 10 *("Perek Ha-Helek"),* end; translated in Isadore Twersky, *A Maimonides Reader* (New York: Behrman House, 1972), pp. 401-423, esp. pp. 417-423. This short statement of these principles appears in Philip Birnbaum, *Daily Prayer Book* (New York: Hebrew Publishing Company, 1949), p. 154, note.

23. Exodus 32; Numbers 14.

24. Exodus 3:2.

25. Judah Halevi, *Kuzari,* Book IV, pars. 3, 13, 15–17; Book V, pars. 16, 21; Blaise Pascal, *Pensées,* #555; cf. #430.

26. I first articulated this in "Two Ways to Approach God," *Conservative Judaism* 30:2 (Winter 1976), pp. 58–67; reprinted in Seymour Siegel and Elliot Gertel, eds., *God in the Teachings of Conservative Judaism* (New York: Rabbinical Assembly, 1985), pp. 30–41. See the discussion in Chapter 1 above.

27. B. *Gittin* 90b.

28. For example, Exodus 33:19; Numbers 11:33; 15:32–36; 17:6–15; 21:4–9; II Samuel 24:1–15; Isaiah 6:9–10; 63:17; Jeremiah 4:10; 15:18; 20:7.

29. Repulsive and extreme divine punishments: e.g., Leviticus 26:28; Deuteronomy 28:56,57. God's hardening of Pharaoh's heart: Exodus 7:3ff. God's hardening of the heart of the King of Heshbon: Deuteronomy 2:30ff.

30. *Genesis Rabbah* 68:4; B. *Avodah Zarah* 3b.

31. *Avot (Ethics of the Fathers)* 1:12.

32. B. *Berakhot* 26b.

33. Richard Rubenstein, *The Religious Imagination* (Boston: Beacon Press, 1968), p. 183.

34. Ibid., pp. 182–183.

35. B. *Rosh Hashanah* 25a–b. Cf. Charles Y. Glock, "Images of 'God,' Images of Man and the Organization of Social Life," *Journal of the Scientific Study of Religion* 1:1 (March 1972), pp. 3–5.

36. Paul Tillich, *Systematic Theology* (Chicago: University of Chicago Press, 1957), Vol. 2, p. 9. Cf. Vol. 1, pp. 237–86 passim.

37. Wilbur M. Urban, *Humanity and Deity* (London: George Allen and Unwin, 1951), p. 238.

38. Lewis S. Ford, "Tillich and Thomas: The Analogy of Being," *The Journal of Religion* 46:2 (April 1966), p. 244. Cf. John Y. Fenton, "Being-Itself and Religious Symbolism," *The Journal of Religion* 55:2 (April 1965), p. 79; Paul Edwards in Norbert O. Shedler, ed., *Philosophy of Religion, Contemporary Perspectives* (New York: Macmillan, 1974), pp. 186–205.

39. Cf. Ian G. Barbour, *Myths, Models, and Paradigms: A Comparative Study in Science and Religion* (New York: Harper and Row, 1974), Ch. 4, for a discussion of how religious language is analogical in its meaning, and cf. Ch. 5 for a discussion of how conflicting images can complement each other without negating the quest for a unified, coherent, integrated model.

40. For example, Earl R. MacCormac, *Metaphor and Myth in Science and Religion* (Durham, NC: Duke University Press, 1976), p. 93; Lyman T. Lundeen, *Risk and Rhetoric in Religion* (Philadelphia: Fortress Press, 1972), pp. 192–193.

41. *Emotive:* A. J. Ayer, *Language, Truth, and Logic* (London: Dover, 1936), Ch. 6. *Ethical:* R. B. Braithwaite, "An Empiricist's View of the Nature of Religious Belief" (Cambridge, England: Cambridge University Press, 1955); reprinted in many anthologies of articles in contemporary philosophy of religion such as *The Philosophy of Religion,* Basil Mitchell, ed. (Oxford: Oxford University Press, 1971), pp. 72–91; *Religious Language and the Problem of Religious Knowledge,* Ronald E. Santoni, ed. (Bloomington, IN: Indiana University Press, 1968), pp. 333–347; *Classical and Contemporary Readings in the Philosophy of Religion,* John Hick, ed., 2nd ed. (Englewood Cliffs, NJ: Prentice-Hall, 1970), pp. 394–405.

42. Dorothy M. Emmett, *The Nature of Metaphysical Thinking* (New York: MacMillan, 1957), p. 4.

43. Nahum 1:6.

44. Holbrook, *The Iconoclastic Deity* (at n. 16), pp. 75ff. John Herman Randall, Jr., *The Role of Knowledge in Western Religion* (in Chapter 6, at n. 56), p. 133.

45. Cf. James Wm. McClendon, Jr., and James M. Smith, *Understanding Religious Convictions* (Notre Dame, IN: University of Notre Dame Press, 1975), esp. Ch. 1.

46. Cf. Holbrook, *The Iconoclastic Deity* (at n. 16), pp. 202–212.

47. I make this point most explicitly with regard to God's words in Chapter 4, but it carries over also to human actions (Chapter 3), divine actions (Chapter 5), and human words (Chapter 6). Cf. also an earlier expression of this thesis in my article, "Revelation," *Conservative Judaism* 31:1–2 (Fall-Winter 1976–1977), pp. 58–68, although there I restricted my attention to words and did not acknowledge that *actions* in accordance with communal laws and customs can also be revelatory.

48. *Numbers Rabbah* 14:4.

49. Even Richard Rubenstein, who denies a God who acts in history, has trouble with the imagery of God as dead because it is, in his eyes and those of all other Jewish writers, much too Christian; see *After Auschwitz* (Indianapolis: Bobbs-Merrill, 1966), Ch. 14, and cf. Ch. 13.

50. Holbrook, *The Iconoclastic Deity* (at n. 16), p. 223. Cf. p. 218.

51. Rita M. Gross, "Female God Language in a Jewish Context," *Davka Magazine* 17 (1976); reprinted in *Womanspirit Rising,* Carol P. Christ and Judith Plaskow, eds. (San Francisco: Harper and Row, 1979), pp. 168–169.

52. Ibid., p. 172.

53. I argue for some such differentiation, while yet preserving equality, in my paper, " 'Male and Female God Created Them': Equality with Distinc-

tion," *University Papers* (Los Angeles: University of Judaism, March 1984), pp. 13–23.

54. Ian Barbour has made a similar point with regard to an atheist. Contrary to Ronald Hepburn, who claims that an atheist and a theist can have identical experiences and yet interpret them differently, Barbour wonders whether the atheist would be open to having the theist's experiences in the first place. Cf. Ian G. Barbour, *Myths, Models, and Paradigms* (at n. 34), p. 123. Similarly, each gender needs to be trained to see the world through the eyes of the other, and symbols of the opposite gender help one to do that—just as symbols of one's own gender help one to understand the meaning of being male or female.

55. This was the thesis, for example, of Carol Gilligan's seminal work, *In a Different Voice* (Cambridge, MA: Harvard University Press, 1982). Recent psychological and physiological studies have attempted to identify more accurately which gender characteristics are biologically determined and which are the results of social expectations during one's upbringing.

56. *God as our Healer:* Exodus 15:26. *God as Comforter:* Isaiah 49:13. *God as handling a beloved child:* Jeremiah 31:20. For a thorough exploration of these feminine themes in biblical images of God, see P. Trible, *God and the Rhetoric of Sexuality* (Philadelphia: Fortress, 1978), esp. pp. 31–71. In rabbinic literature, God continues functioning in such "feminine" roles. According to B. *Sotah* 14a, for example, God consoles mourners, clothes the naked, and visits the sick.

The few times God is depicted in the Bible as Father: Deuteronomy 32:6; Isaiah 63:16; 64:7; Jeremiah 3:4,19; 31:9; Malachi 1:6; 2:10; cf. Exodus 4:22; Hosea 11:1. Note, however, that according to Psalm 27:10, God assumes the role of both the absent father and mother. Second Isaiah, who uses much Divine Warrior imagery (cf. esp. Isaiah 51:9–52:12), also employs female language for God: "Can a woman forget her sucking child, that she should have no compassion on the son of her womb? Even these may forget, yet I will not forget you" (Isaiah 49:15); and just after one of the Divine Warrior passages, God says, "Now I will cry out like a woman in travail" (Isaiah 42:14). And the Song of Moses in Deuteronomy 32 depicts God in a number of androcentric metaphors ("Father" in v. 6; "King" in vv. 8–9; Divine Warrior in vv. 22–23, 40–42), also includes the following verse (v. 18), albeit with masculine verbs: "You were unmindful of the Rock that bore you, and you forgot the God who suffered travail to bring you forth."

Two contemporary biblical scholars have pointed out that the biblical image of God incorporates elements of both the male Canaanite god El and

Notes for pages 244 to 250

the female Canaanite god Asherah, even though the features of the former predominate in the biblical God's description. They also note that other ancient Near Eastern deities were specifically depicted as both father and mother. Thus a correct reading of biblical theology is that God was already seen then as having both male and female characteristics, not because He was androgynous, but because He had both "male" and "female" characteristics—and simultaneously transcended them. As Mettinger says, "God is above and beyond; the images and symbols should remain what they are: not solid prison walls, but the fragile stained-glass windows of transcendence." See Tryggve N. D. Mettinger, *In Search of God*, Frederick H. Cryer, trans. (Philadelphia: Fortress, 1988), pp. 204–207 (the citation is on p. 207); and Mark S. Smith, *The Early History of God: Yahweh and Other Deities in Ancient Israel* (San Francisco: Harper and Row, 1990), pp. 97–103.

57. Tryggve (ibid., pp. 204–205) makes the point that even Ezekiel, who among the biblical writers comes closest to describing God, emphasizes that his vision of God only captures the divine reflection *(demut)*, not God's essence (Ezekiel 1:5,10,16,22,26,28; see also Psalms 58:4; Isaiah 13:4; Daniel 10:16). We must thus distinguish the *mental concept* of God *(Gottesvorstellung)* from the *express form (Gottesbild)* in which this concept is communicated in texts, iconographic representations, rituals, etc. The latter will always be partial and will always need to be complemented by other images, including conflicting ones.

58. To my knowledge, the first person sympathetic to the feminist agenda to begin to raise such issues was Arthur Green. See his "Keeping Feminist Creativity Jewish," *Sh'ma* 16/305 (January 10, 1986), pp. 33–35, and the discussion that followed it in that issue of *Sh'ma* (pp. 35–40) by Ronnie Levin, Drorah Setel, and Arlene Agus. The article cited by Marcia Falk is, "Toward a Feminist Jewish Reconstruction of Monotheism." Both that and Lawrence A. Hoffman's response to it are in *Tikkun* 4:4 (July/August 1989), pp. 53–57. The work cited by Judith Plaskow is her "Divine Conversations," *Tikkun* 4:6 (November/December 1989), pp. 18–20, 85 (the quotation on evil is on p. 20), reprinted as part of her book, *Standing Again at Sinai* (San Francisco: Harper and Row, 1990). "The seal of the Holy One is truth" appears in J. *Sanhedrin* 1:1 (18a); B. *Shabbat* 55a; B. *Yoma* 69b; B. *Sanhedrin* 64a; *Genesis Rabbah* 81:2; and *Deuteronomy Rabbah* 1:10.

EPILOGUE

1. M. *Berakhot* 9:5 (B. *Berakhot* 54a); cf. *Sifre Deuteronomy* 32.

2. So, for example, W. Gunther Plaut, *The Torah: A Modern Commentary* (New York: Union of American Hebrew Congregations, 1981), p. 1366.

INDEX

About the Author

Elliot N. Dorff was ordained a rabbi by the Jewish Theological Seminary of America in 1970 and earned his Ph.D. in philosophy from Columbia University in 1971. Since then he has directed the rabbinical and masters programs at the University of Judaism, where he currently is Provost and Professor of Philosophy. He is a member of the Conservative movement's Committee on Jewish Law and Standards, its Commission on the Philosophy of the Conservative Movement, and its commission to write a new Torah commentary for Conservative synagogues. In Los Angeles, he serves as a member of the Board of Directors of Jewish Family Service and chairs its Jewish Hospice Commission. He is also a member of the ethics committees at the Jewish Homes for the Aging and UCLA Medical Center.

Rabbi Dorff's publications include some forty articles on Jewish thought, law, and ethics, together with four books: *Jewish Law and Modern Ideology, Conservative Judaism: Our Ancestors to Our Descendants, A Living Tree: The Roots and Growth of Jewish Law,* and *Mitzvah Means Commandment.*

He is married and has four children.